Linguistics for the Teacher

Linguistics for the Teacher

Dr. Joseph C. Mukalel
M.A., L.Ph., M.A. (U.K.), Ph.D.

School of Gandhian Thought and Development Studies
Mahatma Gandhi University
Kottayam (Kerala)

DISCOVERY PUBLISHING HOUSE
NEW DELHI—110 002

Published by :

Discovery Publishing House
4831/24, Ansari Road, Prahlad Street
Darya Ganj, New Delhi—110 002 (INDIA)
Phone : 327 92 45
Fax : 91-11-3253475

First Published—1998
Reprint : 2012

ISBN 81-7141-411-7

Laser Typeset by :

Allied Computers,
Karnal (Haryana)

Printed at
: Dynamic Printers

Introduction

English is spoken in different countries at different levels. In countries like England or the United States English is spoken as L_1 or the first language. In countries like India or Pakistan English has come to be used as L_2 or the second language in a technical sense. While in countries like China or Russia English is equally learned in several educational institutions like universities and institutes of English. Here we have English is learned as L_3 or foreign language. English in India is therefore not a foreign language at all, like France or Germany, Russia or China. English in India is the associate official language of the country as formulated in our three language formula system. English is read, written and spoken in India and has become part and parcel of the educational and socio-cultural life of the country.

All these attitude to English in India somehow or other determine the approach to English Language Teaching and the way we organise our training procedures. Teaching itself is a complex phenomenon when analysed adequately. When it comes to the teaching of a language in general and English in particular the problem becomes a matter of clarity in objectives. Recognising the importance of teaching English in this country English Institutes were established here with a view to providing adequate and specialized training to teachers of English and ELT specialists as well as teacher educators. This has been going on for the past several decades. This consistent attempts at evolving a system of English language Teaching both in theory and practice has been successful.

All the same the teacher at the individual level is certainly lagging behind in utilising the question of information provided to him at various levels and by means of a variety of information mechanisms. The teacher of English today needs to be aware of the large area that lies awaiting to his disposal for equipping him for excellence. English language teaching today has become a very highly specialised field with advanced research and information facility awaiting his attention. It is here that serval levels of knowledge that he is called upon to help for his own and his students benefit.

As said above ELT is indeed a complex phenomenon. It is to be developed into such a highly unified experience that the classroom experience of language learning becomes unique. The teaching techniques that the teacher resorts to in the classroom are to be developed out of a spectrum of approaches both proximate and remote. Linguisties, psycho-linguistics, socio-linguistics, theoretical phonetics etc. constitute part of this large spectrum of theoretical bases for the teaching of English. Of these the most important indeed is linguistics. Linguistics as outlined in the present work is a vast area of knowledge, a science in its own right and field of enquiry fast progressing.

The book intends to acquaint the teacher of languages in general and English in particular with what we shall call descriptive linguistics as contrasted to, say, historical linguistics, and structural linguistics as contrasted to, say, psycho-linguistics which pertains to language as behaviour. Linguistics as envisaged in the present work is thus a structured system of presenting the phenomenon of human language as a given object. Just as the human body is described in terms of its anatomical specifications, language is thus observed and brought to description in terms of what the structure of human language is. Such a structural description made linguistics scientific and unique in the early twentieth century, where such a structural description of language become the only acceptable pattern of language study for a group of linguistics after 1920s that school of linguistic study came to be known as structuralism.

The present work aims at introducing the teacher to the field of linguistics that should form the basis of his own understanding of what language is. The book begins with a treatment of the Nature of language. An understanding of the Nature of English as a language as such becomes essential for the teacher as he begins evolving adequate classroom methodology and teaching techniques for providing learning experiences in English as a language whose basic skills the learners have not yet mastered. His own treatment of the classroom situations largely depends on these linguistic specifications which are provided to him by the linguist. The following chapter undertakes a treatment of the structure of English language in an expository manner. The chapter provides an outline of the details on which the book is based. Language a here is looked at in terms of its fundamental structural components of phonology, morphology etc. The teacher here is led to a compository understanding of the basic structural components which are elaborated in the following chapters. He has the view of these linguistic elements as if in a nutshell.

Chapter 3 of the book deals with language, individual and society. It is important for the teacher to know the determining role language plays on the individual and society. As we know the mental development and the language acquisition process are highly correlated. Language development ultimately becomes a socially based cognitive process. The teacher is therefore required to know the sociological bases of language from a structural viewpoint. The dialect diversity of language helps the teacher to know the significance of variations especially in the spoken form of the language. In the chapters on linguistics and detailed disciplines it is intended to acquaint the teacher with the large number of sub-disciplines that have been developed under linguistics as a field of study. Among these are literature, philosophy, physics and Biology which have helped linguistics to develop very specialised areas of language study and investigate into perspectives that are fascinating. Psycholinguistics, sociolinguistics, Biolinguistics and Metalinguistics are instances of areas of investigation that would provide the classroom teacher ample scope for creative understanding of perspectives related to language.

The chapter on the Grammar, Usage and Use of language provides a touch of considerable novelty and analytic freshness with regards to the intricacies of vertical and horizontal dimensions of language. The tremendous formal variation within every language can effectively by organised under the three terms employed in this chapter. A clear orderliness is provided to the stream of formal elements starting with the core grammar to the surface use of language. An explanation is sought for the universality that is fundamental to all the languages in the world, in terms of universals and differentials.

The teacher of English is necessarily introduced to the phonological component of human languages in general and English in particular. The phonological component has certain behavioural features as well as structural features. When English is taught in the classroom the teacher turns out to be scientist who handles things systematically. A deeper understanding of the phonology and phonetics of English and the specifications of this level of English helps him perform with much greater efficiency.

The chapter on the Morphology of language introduces the teacher to the morphological, lexical structure of language. Ordinarily the teacher has confusions between aspects of morphology and aspects of syntax. In fact what has traditionally been treated under syntax or grammar was aspects of morphology. The chapter enables the teacher to obtain a picture of the morphological structure of language. The nature of the syntactic component of language is presented in the chapter on syntax. Ordinarily the teacher has peculiar notions of the aspects of syntax. An understanding of the meaning of syntax based on the contributions of transformational generative grammar is essential today to further obtain later developments in the contemporary theories on grammar. The surface structure deep structure notions and the generative mechanism of language will never lose its flavor inspite of later developments.

The chapter on semantics is characteristic in several ways. The novel approach to the semantic component of language would pave way to a comprehensive understanding of the meaning level of language. The significance of meaning units and conceptual organisation enables the teacher to have a clear idea of the deeper role of meaning in the structure of language.

The book exposes for the teacher a comprehensive perspective of the linguistic components that have been gradually brought to our attention by the linguist as a result of his researches into the nature of language. The teacher of English attempting to handle his classroom situation on the one hand and to have a deeper understanding of the nature of language for the purpose of personal professional satisfaction and development will depend on such an accounting of the linguistic aspects of human language as presented in the work.

1
The Nature of Language

1. Language as a Structured System

Man confronts all kinds of reality around him, and the puzzling questions that hang over him like the impending sword of Damocles are the 'why? and what' ? of things. The myriad of stars above him has become the object of his observation just as his own physical body, the many in one, a *unity* in a sort of *multiplicity*. Down the ages man has discovered that stars in their infinitude are not so scattered and orderless as they seem to be, and the human body, though apparently one, consists of microsegments of material units. The order and super-organisation found in the stellar and the solar realms we call a *system*; and the unity of many in the one human body we call a *structure*.

But there is phenomenon that has aroused in us more curiosity and interest than any other down the ages: Language. Language is concrete and abstract; language is one and many; and it reveals all the characteristics of both a structure and a system. A close observation of a set of utterances produced by man reveals the fact that it is not an unanalysable, indivisible thing. An *utterance*, a spoken sentence or what may be called a unit of discourse, e.g. *The boy is ill*, affects the auditory organs of the listener in terms of certain units of *sounds*. e.g. /b/, ɔi/, /i/. This most extrinsic layer or component of language is called the *phonological component*. A systematic study of the structure of this component is the *phonology* of the Language.

Going further deep into the language in terms of the utterances under consideration, the linguistics scientist discovers that the sound set of units which are themselves further analyzable, are combined into patterns of sequences based on some specifications of meanings which the sequences of sounds are intended to reveal. The linguist calls these minimum meaningful units morphemes e.g. boy, -s, fall, -ing. The branch of linguistics which takes care of these meaningful components and their structure in the language is *Morphology*.

The structural organization of the language does not end with that. On observing the sentences of the language we find that the *words* and the *morphemes* are ordered in a definite manner, and that each utterance has a structure to reveal exactly as each word of the language has a definite *structure*. This ordering of the words into phrases, phrases into clauses and further into sentences is the *syntactic component* of the language. e.g. *The boy is ill* by contrast to *Is the boy ill*?. A study of this component forms the *syntax* part of *linguistics*.

The entire range of language is not susceptible to the senses. The auditory organs are able to sense or receive only the most extrinsic component of language. As we have examined to some extent there is the much more to language than this extrinsic aspect. Ferdinand De Saussure, the initiator of modern linguistics speaks of the *expression* and the *content* aspects of language. That language also consists of something not susceptible to the pure senses is a fact known from time immemorial. This aspect of language which in fact makes up its core is the *semantic component* of the language. The specialised area in linguistics which studies this semantic component is semantics. In the sentence *'Ill is boy the'* though the syntax is damaged, it makes sense to a native speaker because of its semantic integrity. The structure of language consists of all the above mentioned components. Each has a definite place in the system *i.e. language*. One is not the other, although the demarcations are not easy to define. Language is a *structured* system: one composed of several elements organized with a view to functioning for a definite purpose. This chief purpose of language is communication. All the elements are organized to achieve this target.

2. Language is for Communication

Eventhough the role of language for purposes of communication was always emphasized, present-day linguistics has become all the more aware of this *teleological* role of language. Although modern linguistics studies all aspects of language and all kinds of language including the language of literature, the most adequate data for purposes of linguistic investigation and description are the spoken utterances of language used for the purpose of communication among the individuals of a given linguistic community.

It happens that a man comes home all wet from the rain outside, and his wife after having seen the heavy rain outside and the way the man has come home asks him, *Oh ! You are all wet' aren't you?*. Linguistically speaking, this is no question at all. She expects no answer in the true sense of the term. The facts that it was raining and that the man was wet all over were obvious enough to the speaker and the listener. The environment of the particular utterance did not call for any *information* to be conveyed, or as what we may say, any *intention* to be fulfilled. The utterance did not achieve either an informational or an international target. It was just a way of speaking and reacting to a given situation, without expecting an informative answer. As we shall examine later in the section on communication, no communication in the proper sense of the term took place in the above context.

Communicability is the essence of human language. Any utterance any discourse, as we may call it, takes place in a context where at least two individuals must be present. The teleological nature of language is not present in a context where some one is merely soliloquizing. Soliloqui is sheer thinking aloud. All of us have experiences of having heard someone or other speaking to himself at some situations, especially of excessive joy or sorrow. Communication proper is teleological. It begins from an individual and terminates in another. Linguistics concerns itself not with soliloquies primarily but language as employed for purposes of communication in sociocultural contexts.

3. Language is Symbolic

If communication takes place between human individuals, how exactly does language pass from one to another? An answer to this calls for technical support from biology, acoustic physics and communication engineering. But linguistics tackles this problem to a certain extent. Language Functions in terms of *signs* and *symbols*. A sign is a representative mode, it represents a unit of meaning. From the commonsense viewpoint a sign stand for something else. A sign doesn't function on its own right. It is always *representative*. A symbol is a much more complex notion than a sign. A sign conveys a unit of meaning; a symbol, in the true sense of the term, represents a complex reality, or a set of values.

Both these notions are equally applicable to the reality of language at various levels. Language has sign functions and symbolic functions. In other words language has sign values and symbolic values. The speaker, a physical entity has no way of penetrating the mind of the listener who is another physical entity, except through a medium that makes such a thing possible. The expression features of the language which themselves are set of physical entities (because they are susceptible to the sense of audition) function as bearers of the content features of language. This is how it becomes physically possible for man to communicate. The language elements produced by the articulatory organs of the speaker are conveyed through a medium (*e.g.* air) in terms of the acoustic principles, and received by the auditory organs of the listener in their audio-modality. The listener receives the element of information contained in the content specifications of the language.

In otherwords what the articulatory organs produce and the organs of audition receive are "meaning carriers" or words and utterances that function as a symbol. The symbolic value, at the extrinsic level, is thus attached to the words and their combinations is meaningful order. At one level this is what we understand by language functioning as *symbolic*. There is another aspect to the same at a still deeper level. The relation that exists in a linguistic context in terms of the elements involved may be represented schematically as follows:

Language	3	Verbal symbols	1
		↑ ↓	
	2	Conceptual elements	2
		↑ ↓	
	1	Features of experience	3

There are three layers that require consideration. We have seen that the verbal features (elements of the utterance) function as symbolic bearers of the specifications of meanings or the concepts. But are concepts or meanings end in themselves? This is where the second and deeper functions of symbolism come in. The meaning specifications, as we may call them, represent deeper levels of reality or what we may call the actual experience of individuals. Therefore human language functions at a two-level representation: at the level of concepts and at the level of experience or reality.

It is the symbolic features of language, in fact, that make it an effective medium for communication as well as for all characteristic uses for which human language is employed. Language is structured in such a way that several physical and meta-physical elements go into the making of it. This ***unity*** makes language all that it is.

4. The Vocal Characteristics of Language

There are over three thousand languages in the world. This overwhelming number of human languages are all attached to a particular community which we may call a linguistic community. All these languages have had their natural growth along with the progress and formation of the community. In otherwords we seldom, if ever, find a language which is not used in the speech-habits of a community. All natural languages (opposed to those that have been constructed by linguists) have had their origin in speech. It all began with some community trying to communicate among the individuals. The initial growth and development of any such language sprang up from the individuals who communicated for purposes of social interaction.

In otherwords, language, above all, is *speech*. The written forms are all mere frozen representations of what the individual speakes, or supposed to be speaking. Not that there is less nobility in reading or in writing, but that speech takes predominance over wrighting so far as language priorities are concerned. Language is thus, vocal. This vocal language forms the 'primary data' of linguistics. In this context we may say that language is the product of the vocal or articulatory faculties of man. Language is characterized by these vocal features of man. It is very much restricted and determined by these vocal features. However intelligent a man may be, he will be handicapped so far as the spoken language is concerned if his vocal organs do not function properly.

There are several reasons for us to believe that language is basically speech. Some of the chief reasons are the following: (1) The origin of all natural languages is in speech; (2) Communication in a linguistic community can be had only through speech; (3) speaking and listening are skills which naturally develop; (4) speech requires no other external tools to function; (5) speech achieves the quickest communication; (6) the individual's specifications and characteristics reflect much more in speech than in writing; (7) speech habits reflect the changes in a language more than writing does; (8) speech is as though living and evolving; it is the most dynamic element of society.

For all these reasons modern linguistics has been emphasizing the spoken form of language. As we shall examine later, the reasons mentioned above have made speech the centre of attention in all modern foreign language teaching methods. Today speech is considered this primary form of language and speech forms the primary data for linguistic research. But some of the latest approaches to language have attempted to revive the emphasis on this written form of language on an equal footing.

5. The Arbitrariness of Language

In several senses language is ***arbitrary***. It is a property of human language that has several deeper implications than it would seem to us. Take for instance the word '***man***'. To the native English speaker or to any one very much conversant with the English language the word '***man***' is something taken for granted. One seldom asks the question if the word means anything. But at the same time, to a foreign language speaker who is not conversant with English, '*man*' is a non-sense unit. It may even sound ridiculous to a native speaker of another language, because a similar word may mean something quite funny.

What happens here? What makes the word '*man*' an absolute stranger to a non-English speaker? It can be explained only through the arbitrariness of language.

The meaning element '*man*' (in the specific sense of the term) is expressed in very different ways in different languages. The meaning element here is a fact of human experience, and therefore forms a part of any language man speaks. But on examining various languages we find that each language has some distinct unit of language to express this concept. It means that there exists no one to one correspondence, or any basic, essential corresponding between the *form* chosen to express the sense, and the *sense* or signification itself. This is the essence of linguistic arbitrariness.

There are several other levels of arbitrariness in language. There is practically no rationale behind the way the sound clusters, the word forms, the phrases or the idioms are structured. All this developed due to the force of convention which played most significant role in language development. Again, the usage, the structural forms, the sentence patterns are all proofs of the arbitrary nature of language. Almost the entire component of the *expression* part of language developed arbitrarily. But each of these aspects became a norm in language once the usage was accepted by the majority of those who had the last say in the affairs of the community. This property of the language shows that no part of the *expression* aspect of language can be an absolutely permanent feature.

6. Language is Changing

Changeability as a major property of language came to be emphasized only in modern linguistics. This goes very much against the notions held by the philosophical grammars of the Middle and early Modern Ages. The changeability of language was not a characteristic feature in the context of 'Universal Grammar'. 'Universal Grammar' held the belief that the grammars of all language in the world were the same and consequently the structure of Greek or Latin could be a basis for describing any language. In other words more or less language was looked upon as a phenomenon of unchanging characteristics, and the changing aspects such as those features of the spoken language were not considered significant.

But with the onset of Modern Linguistics, especially structuralism, emphasis was placed on the spoken form of language. With this some new insights into the structure of language came to develop. Language is no longer studied as an unchanging, wholly absolute phenomenon. Today stress is put on the changing characteristics as well. As the spoken form of language came to be emphasized, and insights are developed with regards to the changing nature of the spoken language, the role of *change* in language came to receive considerable attention.

In fact almost all aspects of language in one way or other undergo change. Although extreme, it could be said that language is in a state of flux, meaning that *change* pervades every component of language. Examining the *phonology* of language, one finds that it undergoes change in long periods of time. The set of sounds, the vowels, the consonants, the diphthongs, the triphthongs and the sound clusters of Old English period were not very much the same used in the middle English. *Cu*: *monne, sunne* and *childe* etc. are not understood today. In otherwords there is a large scale give and take in the phonology of the language, as languages have come into more and more intimate contact.

The *morphology* of the language changes from time to time. The Old English was a highly inflected language; the inflectional suffixes *i.e.* chiefly the declensions and conjugation were reduced to the minimum in the Middle English. As English language developed in tune with the requirements of the times, the present day English retains exceptionally few inflectional endings. All that today English language has one the following : (1) the plural suffix $\{-Z_1\}$ (2) The genitive suffix

{$-Z_2$}, the third singular suffix {$-Z_3$}, the past time suffix {$-D_1$} the past participle suffix {$-D_2$} and the gerund as well as present participle suffix {-ing}. Added to these we have the adjective suffixes {-ex} and {-est}. This shows a constant change in the forms of language.

The ***syntax*** of language is another component that affects change. There are several very basic structural aspects that remain more or less the same throughout, such as the basic ordering of a sentence. We do not know of any period in English when the subject as a rule was placed at the end of a sentence. But the surface ordering of the language, the structuring of phrases, the use of the pronouns, prepositions, articles, and the way the auxiliaries are employed have undergone changes from time to time. Similarly the ***semantic structure*** of language keeps on changing along with communal, social and cultural changes that affect the speech community. New experiences and new meanings supplement and substitute old ones.

There are several forces that affect change in languages. Owing to several circumstances languages come into mutual contact. Wars, travels, business and commercial relations between communities, new inventions and discoveries, social revolutions migration and a number of other factors play powerful roles in bringing languages together as well as in having new additions to the language. No language at any phase reveals any observable change. What we experience is only the cumulative affect of a continual change. A decade or two can hardly reveal any observable change in a language.

7. Language is Culture-based

The fact that any language is culture-based hardly needs any comment. It may require a full Volume to show the relation between language and culture. In the broadest sense ***culture*** is all that a people are: their ways of doing, thinking and believing as well as all the characteristics and things they possess. In the narrowest sense culture stands for the products of a society as society: the habits, beliefs and things handed down from generation to generation. Language in any sense of the term is a major component as well as the most complex element of culture. The language of a community contains the verbal replica of all aspects of its culture. At the same time language is a part of the culture of a community. Culture includes all aspects of the community's behaviour; language is socio-individual behaviour in the fullest sense of the term. Verbal behaviour *i.e.* language, is representative of all aspirations and beliefs of the society as well as it perpetuates those elements in a striking manner. One could not imagine a society without the ability to maintain communication among the individuals. Language is the embodiment of culture so far as all cultural elements somehow or other get embedded as a part of the verbal behaviour.

8. The Creative Nature of Language

One of the properties of language that has come to be emphasized only during the late twentieth century is the creative aspect of language. Noam Chomsky's writings have placed the creative aspect of language in the right perspective. Language functions in a stimulous→reinforcement→response context, all right. But this is not the whole of language. Nothing else but ***linguistic creativity*** can explain the fact that a human child with his relative mastery of a language is in a position to produce sentences that are fully original, sentences that perhaps no one has ever uttered before or those that the child has never heard any one uttering before. This unique capacity to organise and produce new sentences of a language is called linguistic creativity. B.F. Skinner's dictum of language being purely a ***stimulus-response*** product is counteracted in Chomsky's notion of linguistic creativity. This is very relevant to our context here because this concept provides several new insights into the language teaching-learning process. Language in the classroom should be taught keeping in mind the creative potential of the child. The child is not a machine, nor is it like any other infra-human organism. The human child is a person with a lot of creative potency and intelligence functioning in a social set up.

9. The Uniqueness of Language

Languages are unique in themselves. Based on this principle Modern Linguistics has ventured out to investigate into the structures of languages. The belief was held earlier, as we saw in the section on the changeability of language, that the structures of all languages boil down to one and the same thing in the last analysis. Against this belief came the view that there is some level of specificity with regards to the components of each and every language, that no two things are exactly the same with two languages. The *phonology* of language is unique as different languages share in the 'total human sound resource' in different manner. No two languages have exactly the same set of consonants, vowels and their clusters. Similarly, the *morphological* aspects, the suffixes, the prefixes, the inflections and the component-formations differ from language to language. On the level of *syntax* too, languages are very different. Different languages have different structural ordering the rules of patterning words in sentences. Lastly and perhaps most important of all languages are different at the level of meanings. The foregoing discussion on the cultural implications of language helps us to understand how far the meaning component of languages differ among one another. No two languages are the same from all viewpoints.

10. A Few Other Characteristics

There are several other predominant features which languages reveal. One may examine a few important ones among those. It is some times said that only man is capable of telling a lie, that animals are not. It is true so far as language is concerned. Language is a means for man to express himself, but it is interesting to see that the same language helps him to hide things. It is a dual property of language, along with other dual properties as expression and content. For the famous philosopher Wittgenstein, the main function of language was to obscure and hide things. Perhaps he was right in the sense that language as expression has no one to one correspondence with meaning or content. All natural languages are so full of homophonous, homonymous, synonymous and ambiguous expressions that we do not always understand the language of others the way we think we do. This is where what we call 'misunderstanding' and 'misinterpretations' arise. Languages have their natural metaphoric way of putting things. Also there are several levels and layers at which languages function. The poet's language is not the philosopher's language, the mystic's language is different from the politician's language. Language places before the human mind problems that are puzzling and the interesting the thing is that all these problems regarding language can be dealt with using only the same human language.

2
The Structure of English Language

1. The Phonology of English

An introduction to English language teaching may seem incomplete without a word on the phonology and phonetics of English. At the outset we have to be clear regarding the distinction between phonology and phonetics, two interrelated aspects of the study of language. The sounds of a language can be looked at from two different viewpoints. On the one hand each sound, whether a consonant, monophthong diphthong or triphthong, is not an indivisible entity. It is a sum total of several distinctive features. In other words a sound consists of several structural elements or as we may call them, characteristics. These structural features of a sound are not relative to the environment in which it occurs except in cases of morphonological instances when the distinctive features of a particular sound are somehow affected and in place of one sound another structural or distinctive features such as: the plosive, voiceless, bilabial features of | p |, or the plosive, voiced, bilabial features of | b | or the front, close, neutral-lipped, and sonorous features of | i: | are characteristics which do not in any way change by the positionally varied occurrence of these sounds. A study of these structural features of sounds irrespective of their occurrence in or relation to a particular language is phonetics. It studies the speech sounds as objective entities irrespective of this organization in a language.

Phonology, on the other hand, concerns with the identification and description of the minimal sounds units of any particular language, and on the other it includes the study of the ordering of these minimal sounds units to higher classes of sounds, morphemes and words. A full-fledged study of the formation and forms of morphemes is reserved for Morphology. Phonology uses several devices for the identification of phonemes. A phoneme | p | is a kind of an abstraction, in the sense that the actual occurrence of | p | takes place in the form of the allophanes of | p | i.e. [p^h– –], [–p–], [– –p] and as [p] occurring in several environments before and after various consonants and vowels, with aspiration and without aspiration. Therefore the minimum sound units realized in a language are the allophanes. But since allophones of the same or similar distinctive features can be grouped together we have the concept of phonemes. For the sake of analysis and description the phonemes are takes as sound units for study in phonology.

In other words we can say that phonology is the study of the phonemes of language. The distribution of these phonemes in a language takes place in a characteristic manner. There are, what we call, complementary distribution and contrastive distribution. These are pre-eminent features to be considered in the identification and description of the phonemes of a language. By complementary distribution we mean the occurrence of the allomorph of a phoneme in place of which no other allomorph can occur. The voiceless alveolar stop, | t | occurs initially with aspiration [t^h – –], the medically without aspiration or release [–t–], and in the final position with release, but not aspiration [– –t].

i. | tɔp |, | stɔp |, | spɔt |

ii. | tæp |, | stræp |, | pæt |.

Consequently we say that the allomorph aspirated [t^h] the occurring initially is in complementary distribution with the allomorph [–t–] occurring medically or with that occurring in the final position. In other words the aspirated [t^h] is set for the fixed initial position.

In contrast to this we have sounds occurring in contrastive

distribution. | hauz | and | mauz | are two words in which | h | and | m | occur in what we call contrastive distribution in a similar or identical environment. The environment being identical there occurs a difference in the meaning of the word due to a contrast in one sound or what we may call a minimal sound contrast. This technique of identifying distinctive sounds on the basis of their contrastive occurrence in words has been very much in use in the study of modern languages. A such minimally contrasting words are known as minimal pairs.

1. pit, bit, chit, sit, tit, hit, knit.

2. read, heed, need, seed, feed, lead.

3. sad, mad, lad, had, fad, bad.

4. pin, chin, bin, din, in, sin.

All these are minimal pairs in which there is a contrast in meaning because of a contrast in sounds.

Phonology has been the chief preoccupation of linguistics during the early half of twentieth century. The study of sounds as the last building bricks of a language has certainly highlighted the phonological component of language. Each language shares in the total stock of possible human sounds which is indefinite. The phonemic organization of language has been considered almost the starting point of linguistic analysis as this phonemic organization and structure of phonetic units are the first to be susceptible to the human senses in terms of stimulus-response features. The sounds are the building-bricks of language, and the combination of the sound of a language determine what kind of a formal unit is employed in symbolizing a particular meaning.

2. An outline of English Phonetics

The difference between phonology and phonetics has already been discussed at length. Phonetics can be said to be the most advanced field of study in the linguistic science due to the kind of technological and it has been receiving from various co-related fields. Physics, concerned with the structure and behaviour of the acoustic properties of sound transmission properties of sound transmission enabled phonetics to get better insights into the acoustic aspect of language transmission. Communication engineering, for that matter, deeply concerned with the functioning of the element it communication in all aspects, has been of great help to the advancement of the science of phonetics. Biology, investigating into the biological substratum of language has helped phonetics in its study of the articulatory features of language production and in the study of the auditory aspects of language reception.

In other word, there are specialized fields of enquiry within phonetics too. The natural divisions in the speech-function leads to a natural divisions in phonetics. Speech is a product proximately of the functioning of the organs of speech starting with the air-stream from the lungs and ending with the exterior speech-organs. We say that speech is secondary activity of these organs as these are more basically biological activities such as breathing and consumption of food attached to these organs as their primary work. The study of the structure and function of these organs of speech in terms of speech is called Articulatory phonetics. Once the speech sounds are produced in their necessary sequence, they are transmitted into the medium (e.g. air). The study of the characteristics of the transmission of speech sounds in a medium is the concern of Acoustic phonetics. This same physical properties of sound transmission is also studied by physics and communication engineering. The organs of audition receive the speech sounds and feed them into the nerves. The mechanism involved in this process of the speech-reception is studied under Auditory phonetics. These are the three major fields of enquiry in phonetics: Articulatory, Acoustic and Auditory phonetics.

Among the three above mentioned fields of investigation, the most elaborate are articulatory and acoustic phonetics. Owning to investigational restrictions auditory phonetics has not advanced to any significant level. The advanced among the three and the most elaborately studied is articulatory phonetics. It is concerned with the organs of speech, the manner of producing various speech sounds, the place where the speech sounds are articulated an the structure i.e. the distinctive physical features of the sounds.

The lungs are the source of the breath which is the raw material for all sorts of sounds. The breath passes through a pair of elastic foldings which have the capacity to be in various positions and thus control the flow of air. These elastic foldings are the vocal cords. When the vocal cords are fully open we have the normal breathing. Voice is produced as these foldings lie close to each other causing vibrations, of various intensity when the breath passes through. In other words voice is the result of the vocal cords vibrating at various intensities.

The trachea in the windpipe contains the vocal cords. The breath passing through the vocal cords enters the oral cavity. The month contains the chief articulatory organs. If the voice produced at the trachea is sent through without constrictions in the mouth but modified by the positions of the tongue and the lips we have the vowels. The vowels are sonorous and have long carrying power. Consonants, on the other hand are produced by various constrictions at the mouth by the organs of articulation, chief the tongue and the lips. The consonant sounds can be studied from two distinct points of view : (1) The manner in which each sound is articulated, (2) and the points where the sounds are produced. These are known as : manner of articulation and points of articulation. The vowels are classified on the basis of the various positions at which the tongue lies as the sounds are produced i.e. with regards to the height of the tongue in the mouth, and the part of the tongue raised.

The classification of the English vowels

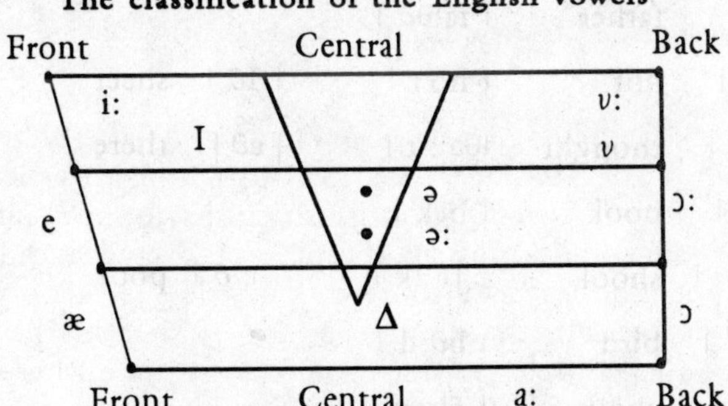

The Classification of English Consonants

	Bilabial	Labio Dental	Den- tal	Alveo- lar	Palato Alveolar	Palatal	Velar	Glottal
Plosive	pb	--	--	td	--	--	kg	--
Affricate	--	--	--	--	tʃ dʒ	--	--	--
Fricative	--	fv	θð	sz	ʃ ʒ	--	--	h
Nasal	m	--	--	n	--	--	ŋ	--
Lateral	--	--	--	l	--	--	--	--
Semi-vcwel	w	--	--	r (post-Alveo)	--	j	--	--

The vowels include monophthongs, diphthongs and triphthongs. The monophthongs are single, carrying vowels; the diphthongs are vowel sequences consisting of the vowel sounds, while the triphthongs one sequences of three vowels.

English Monophthongs			English Diphthongs		
| i: |	these	|ði:z|	| eI |	gate	| geit |
| I |	kit	| kIt |	| əI |	fight	| fəIt |
| e |	bed	| bed|	| ɔI |	soil	| sɔil |
| æ |	sad	| sæd |	| əʊ |	home	| həʊm |
| ʌ |	bus	| b ʌs |	| əʊ |	mouse	| məʊs |
| a: |	father	| fa:θə |			
| ɔ |	hot	| hɔ t |	| Iə |	sheer	| ʃi ə |
| ɔ : |	thought	|θɔ : t |	| ɛə |	there	| ð ɛ ə |
| ʊ |	book	| bʊk |			
| ʊ : |	shook	| ʃʊ :k |	| ʊ ə |	poor	| ρʊə |
| ə: |	bird	| bə:d |			
| ə |	above	| əbʌv |			

3. The Morphology of English

The phoneme is a unit of distinctive sound features. But as such the phoneme is representative of no meaning. When one or more of these phonemes of a language as a single unit (eg. | ai | I) or in a sequence (| mi | me) represent. Some meaning we have what is called a morpheme. A morpheme is a representative unit of meaning. In other words a morpheme is 'a minimal meaningful unit.' It is the minimum unit of sound or sequences of sounds which stands for some meaning.

The concept of morpheme is employed in linguistics in order to avoid the manifold ambiguities attached to the concept of a word. It has been found impossible to define a word because it crossed all boundaries of a definition. A minimum unit such as | ai | as well as a polysyllabic unit such as | inəksprisibiliti | inexpressibility or a compound are labelled as a word. The concept of morpheme as the basic unit of morphology has become very convenient in linguistic analysis. Leonard Bloomfield (1933) was the first to furnish a comprehensive description of a morpheme. Since then the morpheme has become the object of concentrated study by later linguists.

In the traditional sense of the term inexpressibility is a word. Still we consider it a word but composed of several 'minimum meaningful units'. The linguist divides their word down to further smaller units all its further indivisible (in terms of meaning) parts are discovered. Minimum units that recur alone or in combination with other morphemes can be conveniently isolated through contrast as momernic units. An analysis of the above word would yield the following minimal units:-

1.	in–	in, inactive.
2.	–ex–	explicit.
3.	press	Free morpheme (base).
4.	–able–	countable
5.	–ly–	fully.
6.	–ty	ability.

Each of the six parts above is thought of as a morpheme in an abstract sense which is actually realized as allomorphic variations in different environments. As in the case of phonemes, the morpheme is an abstraction or an average of allomorphic occurrences which have identical meaning. Functionally the morpheme can be compared to the phoneme, the morph to the phone and the allomporphs to the allophanes.

The relation between the morpheme and the allomorph can be illustrated by examining the structure of the inflectional suffixes in English. An examination of English morphology shows that there are two basic types of morphemes : bound and free morphemes. In the example above (inexpressibility) only two components of the word ***in*** and, ***press***, and ***able*** occur as independent morphemes. All other units have no independent occurrence in English. Therefore those units which occur independently (eg. I, me, able, press) are free morphemes and those which have no independent occurrence in the language (e.g. ex-, un-, -able, -tion, -ly, -ty) are bound morphemes. The bound morphemes are usually classified into prefixes and suffixes. Ex- and un- are prefixes and -able, -tion, -ly and -ty are suffixes.

Suffixes in English vary with regard to their function. These are derivational suffixes and inflectional suffixes. The presence of a derivational suffix in a word makes the word category grammatical different from the one without it. ***Count*** is a free morpheme which belongs to the class verb (used also noun). The presence of *-able* in countable makes the word an objective. On the other hand the presence of inflectional suffixes in a word does not render it a different grammatical class.

This leads us to the notion of paradigms in English morphology. The set of inflectional suffixation determining the varied forms of any grammatical class (e.g.. Noun, Verb, Adjective) makes up a paradigmatic class. Walk, -s, -ed, -ing forms a paradigmatic class. The predominant classes in English are: Noun paradigms, pronoun paradigms, verb paradigms and adjective paradigms. Inflectional suffixes are endings while paradigms classify the word on the basis of these endings, and other formal specifications that determine the function of a grammatical class. The inflectional suffixes of English may be grouped as follows:-

1. The plural suffix : $\{-Z_1\}$

$$\{-Z_1\}\begin{cases} |\text{-s}| \\ |\text{-z}| \\ |\text{-iz}| \end{cases}$$

2. The Genitive Suffix : $\{-Z_2\}$

$$\{-Z_2\}\begin{cases} |\text{-s}| \\ |\text{-z}| \\ |\text{-iz}| \end{cases}$$

3. The Third Singular Suffix : $\{-Z_2\}$

$$\{-Z_3\}\begin{cases} |\text{-s}| \\ |\text{-z}| \\ |\text{-iz}| \end{cases}$$

4. The preterit suffix : $\{-D_1\}$

$$\{-D_1\}\begin{cases} |\text{-t}| \\ |\text{-d}| \\ |\text{-id}| \end{cases}$$

5. The past participle suffix : $\{-D_2\}$

$$\{-D_2\}\begin{cases} |\text{-t}| \\ |\text{-d}| \\ |\text{-id}| \end{cases}$$

6. The genitive suffix : $\{-D\}$

$$\{-D\}\begin{cases} |\text{-t}| \\ |\text{-d}| \\ |\text{-id}| \end{cases}$$

7. The present participle/Gerund Suffix $\{\text{-i}\eta\}$

8. Comparative suffix $\{\text{-}\partial\text{r}\}$

9. Superlative suffix {-ist}

But all the inflectional morphemes are not so regular as shown above. There are what is traditionally known as irregular morphemes. Nos. 1, 3, 4 and 5 above occur as irregular forms. the characteristic things in morphology is that all the regular (s, z, iz) as well as irregular (men, sheep, oxen) of the English plural (for instance) are the allomorphs of the same plural morpheme $\{-Z_1\}$. The same is true of all other morphemes in varying degrees.

4. English Syntax

For quite a long time in the history of linguistics the chief preoccupation in the name of syntactic studies was the analysis, classification and description of the word-structure. Syntactic studies never went beyond certain description of the English phrases. Departing from the traditional parts of speech classification and definitions, the structuralist linguists made attempts to highlight the phrase-structure. The structuralists never committed themselves to any theoretical explication of the syntactic phenomenon. Assuming a taxonomic approach, the structuralist linguists attempted a supposed to be comprehensive listing of the immediate constituent structures of sentences. In this context syntax is defined as 'the principles of arrangement of the constructions formed by the process of derivation and inflection into larger constructions of various types.' the whole word-order is seen in a hierarchical perspective. All the English sentence types may be broken down to smaller units of binary constructions until at last the indivisible morphemes are isolated and described. The need for a comprehensive theory of syntax to function as the basis for such a description was not so much felt by the structuralists. This is a major difference between the structuralist approach and later approaches to syntax.

With the onset of a new school of linguistics, the transformational generative approach the understanding of language and thereby the study of syntax has taken a new turn. It is almost impossible to summarize the description of English syntax without close reference to these theoretical stands in linguistics. A syntactic description of a particular language may be said to be adequate if it fully accounts for the sentences produced by the fluent native speakers of the language. The syntactic description in other words should account for the competence of the native speakers of the language, competence being the native speaker's subconscious knowledge of the full syntactic descriptions of the language. Competence and performance are the two fundamental notions of Noam Chomksy's transformational generative grammar on the basis of which all later transformational grammars are developed. This competence is the capacity that is actuated in speaking, listening, reading and writing. Performance is the actual exercise of the language with a view to communicating or comprehending.

The linguist explicates this competence when he attempts a formal description of the manner in which the grammatical sentences are produced by the native speaker. There are different levels at which the linguist in expected to work in order to achieve such an explication of the native speakers competence. Noam Chomsky further developed the traditionally recognized view that language functions at different structural levels. On examination of the following sentences:

1. All these men standing here are hard working farmers.
2. You, gentlemen, walk awfully fast.
3. It is very good to go to that place for rest.
4. Those who are sitting there are all tall.

reveal that the given sentences can brought down to certain very basic, deeper and necessary structures the transformation of which yield the sentences given above. In other words there are what Noam Chomsky called deep structures to the surface sentences of a language. The very essential structures from which the sentences above are drawn can be stated as follows:-

1. These men are farmers.
2. You walk fast.
3. Going to that place for rest is good.
4. They are tall.

Another proof Chomsky produced for the justification of deep structures was ambiguous sentences. A surface sentence like 'flying plane can be dangerous' have two deep structure sentences in the form of i) It is dangerous to fly planes; and ii) planes that are flying are dangerous. Another surface utterance ' The boy's photograph is stollen' has a similar ambiguity which too may be resolved by explicitating the deep structures that will reveals two distinct ideals : i) Some one's photograph the boy had in possession is stolen; and ii) The boy's own photograph he had in possession is stolen. Such ambiguous sentences can be made explicit only by obtaining two distinct true diagrams representing the distinct deep structure sentences embedded in the surface sentence.

In the same manner sentences which are approximately identical in meaning but differ in surface structures have the same deep structure.

i. It is true that the Minister has resigned.

ii. That the minister has resigned is true. the two sentences above have the same deep structure underlying them:

The Minister has resigned. It is true.

The syntax of a language is, thus, the description or the theory of the principles underlying the formation of all the grammatical sentences of the language. When the linguist attempts to write the grammar of the language, he is expected to provide explicit form to this description or theory internalized by the fluent native speaker of the language. Acquiring mastery over the English language is the internalization of this formal syntactic system, which will function like a generator in enabling the individual to produce the sentences of the language. The trend in present day linguistics is to acquire greater insights into the interaction within the syntactic and semantic components of language, and thus to develop a theory comprehensive enough to describe the nature of language, not of a handful of sentences.

5. The Semantics of English

The fundamentals underlying all linguistic endeavour is

to establish the essential correspondence between the expression of language and the meanings underlying. To put it more technically, the basic objective of linguistic research is to establish or describe the correspondence between the phonological and the semantic components of language. The present day linguistics is coming more and more to the realization that the phenomenon of language cannot be described satisfactorily unless the syntax and the semantics of language are studied simultaneously and that insights into the one alone can help insights into the other. An exclusive preoccupation of any one field will only handicap linguistics research.

The structuralist linguistics, having been very much tied down to the stimulus-Response basis of language data failed to recognize the fact mentioned above. Instead, holding on to a set of mechanical principles and procedures the structuralists, beginning with bloomfield, advocated anti-mentalism in linguistics. This resulted in an exclusively ***heuristic*** study of the semantic aspects of human language. Any full-fledged enquiry into the semantics of language with a view to explicating the complexity and structure of meanings came to be out of question.

The principal reasons for this neglect of semantic studies were the following:

i) Questions on meanings invariably led to philosophical and psychological problems. It was though that a scientific enquiry into language could not affort to take such risks.

2). Traditional enquiries into language were philosophy-oriented, and mostly led to the notions of universality in grammar. Universal grammar was unconditionally rejected by the structuralists.

3) Lastly, to maintain the scientific nature of linguistics and to preserve the reliability and validity of the procedures, linguistics had to neglect a field which called for mentalistic and intuitive procedures. Thus it was thought that the study of semantics was not feasible in the context of a scientific linguistics.

But the importance of a thorough enquiry into the structure of semantics is not only recommended in present-day linguistics, in some quarters the study of semantics has been fully identified with linguistic investigations as a whole. It has been understood that no questions on language can be fully resolved without studying the semantics of language. The semantics of a natural language such as English is full of complexities: the same form expressing several meanings, (Homonyms) the same meaning expressed by several forms (synonyms) the same oral form represented in different spellings (homophones) and contrary as well as contradictory meanings expressed in a variety of forms (antonyms). Words possess layers of meaning specifications; words differ in their meaning extensions. Utterance contain words which are essential, and words which are redundant with regards to the basic information conveyed. All these are semantic features of a natural language.

But the most characteristic thing in this context one what we may call the semantic features. On the basis of semantic features it has been possible to explain the semantic structure of words in a variety of situations. The first major attempt to account for the interrelations of these semantic features or meaning specifications was that of Katz and Fodor, and later by Kotz, and Postal who did a pioneering work in establishing and giving shape to the properties of the semantic features of language. Considerable amount of innovative as well as critical material has been produced in this regard by later linguists.

Semantic features have their basis on the fact that meanings of words can be brought down to more specific elements. A combination these specifications build what we may call the 'meaning of a word'. In the words the meaning of each word is not a homogeneous or indivisible unit but a heterogeneous and divisible unit. The specific (***man*** in contrast to ***cat***) as well as the generic (***man*** in contrast to ***tree***) properties of words are determined by the semantic features that go into the making of the meaning of a word.

Take for instance, the words, *occulist* and *eye-doctor*. These two words are considered synonyms because the combinations of semantic features in the two words are at least approximately the same, if not identical. The movement from synonyms to antonyms is in degrees of semantic feature combinations. Symmyms have approximately similar combinations and antonyms possess approximately opposite combinations of semantic features. In between these two extremes it is possible to arrange words in terms of varying degrees of semantic feature combinations. These semantic features are represented through + or – specifications. Man [+Human, + Masculine], woman [+ Human, – Masculine], boy [Masculine, + human, + young one] girl [+Human, +young one, –Masculine]. Making use of such a set of semantic feature representations it is possible to describe the semantic structure of English words. When meanings are brought down to such feature specifications we find that meanings differ only in degrees of such specifications.

With greater insights into the semantic structure of language and with the application of formal logic and mathematics to achieve accuracy in description, present-day linguistics hopes to make head-way in the study of language.

3
Language, Individual and Society

1. Language and the Individual

Language is a form of behaviour that is most proper to man as man. No one would deny the fact that it is man's most complex behaviour. Animals are said to have certain level of sign function at the sensitive domain. A dog sees a bone and knows it at some level; but to turn back to its own relation to the bone in the context and make further reflections is beyond the ability of the dog, in the sense that we have no evidence of any such reflection behaviour in animals. But man is capable of all these; he exercises levels of reflection. The human language is an embodiment of all that goes on in human mind. In an era of transformational generative grammar one may confidently speak of the human intellect. But this is not in the purview of this paper.

There is an apparent conflict between the facts that language is individual on the one hand, and social on the other. Just as the individual is the basic building block of society, and no society can be visualized except in and through individuals, language is essentially attached to the individuals in society. The apparent conflict ceases to be the moment we compare language and society and see the relation between society and the individual. Language as a phenomenon is realized and it functions in and through individuals who form society.

But there are several aspects to this problem. The fundamental point is that the individuals come and go while the language of the community lives on. It does not get annihilated until and unless the community ceases to be. As long as the community gets in some way perpetuated, the language too lives on. Therefore it becomes a problem to decide as to what the exact role of the individual is. The most interesting eve to the solution of this puzzle is the fact that in a vertical, historical, perspective language is introduced to the individual to society; while in a horizonal, ontogenic, perspective the individual is introduced to the language which is a heritage of society. In the former case the individual internalizes the linguistic system of the community the way it is feasible and convenient to him constrained by the psychophysical environment. The individual has an upperhand here; he learns a language the way he is capable of, with his own unique contributions to make towards its performance. In the latter case the role of the language is seen in a brighter perspective. The individual is a new addition to the community; the language has the weight of a few hundred centuries, perhaps. Weight of a few hundred centuries is balanced against that of a few years in the case of the individual. From this latter view point the individual is almost wholly subservient to the modality of the language with very few options left to him. This is why schools of philosophy like the language Analysts believe that all problems of philosophy regarding reality are problems of language. If language is properly understood, these problems would be solved and there would be unanimity among philosophers. Language has such a tremendous infact on man that his very thinking operates on the basis of language. Whether language or thought comes first has been a very interesting question and the answer is extremely complex. Many believe that the individual cannot think except through linguistic symbols to which the corresponding symbols are the concepts. One reason attributed for its justification is the fact that we articulate audibly or inaudibly (technically known as vocalization or sub-vocalization) when we think. Some people have to speak aloud to think systematically. At any rate, one thing is sure that the human individual is in several ways determined by his language, although he learned the language as an external system which he internalized in the learning process. The principal reason for this determination is the fact that this language which is the only door for any communication with his community is the embodiment, already, of the entire cultural system.

2. Sociological Basis of Language

The preceding discussion on the relation between the individual and language has already highlighted several points on the role of language in society. Society is defined as a union of individuals with a view to achieving certain ends. Language is the most complex form of human behaviour, a symbolic system that links together the individual members of a community. Only such a symbolic or sign system as language can perform this function. Society is an abstraction; the moment the individuals cease to be the society or the community ceases to be. The potency called society is actuated by individuals. But these individuals are not external; they come and go. In the continuity of generations the community is perpetuated. If it is so, there should exist something that is alive and dynamic, and at the same time will not degenerate as the individuals do. The generations that come and go need an agency, a link that is representative of the experiences and the total culture. Language does all these functions. It is the perpetuating and linking agency; and it possesses the capacity to preserve the cultural components in symbolic manner.

It is such a language that the individual learns and employs for communicative purposes. The communication and the personal interaction among the members of the community is possible only because the language is such a perpetuating agent, and contains all the experiences of the past generations. The language of community is, thus, well equipped to meet the communicative requirements of the community. The essence of the word 'convention' consists in this. It is not that the earliest members of the community set down and 'created' a language by mutual understanding. This would render itself to sheer nonsense. From the earliest members or members downward there began the development of symbolic system for purposes of interaction and communication, which preserved all the necessary components of this system in the historical process of change that affected the system. The system perhaps began with mere rudimentary physical signs that consisted of gestures etc. which in course of time became more and more complex and significant along with rudimentary utterances. These utterances received symbolic signification and abstract quality.

Therefore the language of a community has had a slow and lingering growth, depending on the social need and keeping in time with the manifold demands of the community. That is why it can well be said that the language of a community, however primitive it may be, is well equipped to meet the requirements of that community and therefore perfect. There is no sense in branding any language as backward from the viewpoint of its primary requirements. Also it is true that all language develop according to the needs of the community either borrowing components or symbols from other languages or by inventing symbols for itself. New communal experiences call for new and changed symbolic units for representation. A new discovery or invention, a new mode of thinking, a set of new social attitudes call for new language units to give expression to these. Language thus render itself to change to keep up to the changing needs of the community.

The view that the language of community it once for all fixed is no longer acceptable because of the importance given to the changing nature of language. There is no community in the world that is not in some way changing. It has new experiences of several kinds: progress or regression. Interactions with other communities complete to adapt to features that need be a part of the community. Whatever be these features they have deep-seated impact on the language. Wherever individuals have to come together and communicate themselves, the language will include ways and means of achieving this communication. The constant increase in the lexicon of any language is due to this factor. Language possesses the basis dynamism to develop all its components to meet the requirements of the community.

The language of a community reflects the culture of the community. The specific social experiences get embodied in the language in a symbolic manner. However antiquated a language may be, if we may have access to it, it tells us about the kind of society which used the language as a symbolic system. Language in relation to society is like an exposed film which receives all the impressions that fall in its focus. Once received the impressions cannot get easily erazed. That is why language is a perpetuating agent. It perpetuates all the socio-cultural experiences and makes them readily available to generations to come. The only way to get some insights into the socio-cultural life of the people of Mohan-jo-daro and Harrappa was to decode the remnants of the language of that society. Language is the vehicle of the culture of a community.

Language and society exercise mutually influence. It is surprising that the language of a community can determine its behaviour in several ways. A close reading its behaviour in several ways. A close reading of the preceding discussion will leave no doubts about it. Language is the embodiment of a community total cultural heritage and it is bout to exercise determining influences on the thinking system and consequently on the behaviour of the community, just as the community due to the force of convention does influence changes in the language.

3. Dialect Diversity in Language

A characteristic feature about language is that it is almost impossible to speak of a given language without being aware of the striking varieties which it exhibits. The true language lies with the individual just as the essence of society lies with the individuals. Owing this unique characteristics there is no language on earth wherein some level of varieties will not be present. The language that is exercised and used by the individuals is technically known as the *idiolect* (for detailed examination, see the section following). The idiolect retains all the specificities that are characteristic to an individual in a community. It needs no elaboration that it is only the individual who ultimately 'performs' language.

It happens, then, that the persons belonging to a particular geographical region i.e. the part of the community which belongs to that region retains several sets of regional linguistic features that one not part of the speech habits of the rest of that linguistic community. Such features of the language which are exclusive to a section of the society give rise to a ***dialect***. It is bout to be a fairly extensive region in relation to the bulk of the society. These features of the language may consist in pronunciation, vocabulary, constructions, idiomatic usage, slang forms, and differences in denotations and connotations of words.

The sum total of the idiolectic peculiarities of a given region may said to form a dialect. The sum total of such peculiarities of another region forms another dialect. This is how what we call a language comes to be the sum total of all the dialectic variations peculiar to different regions as parts of the community. But what are the demarcating borderlines ? How can we distinguish the dialect of one language from that of another ? Although the dialects of a language which differ from each other on the basis of regional differences are said to form a unit by itself definable in terms of a given set of features characteristic to each, these dialects present no difficulty in comprehension. The relative difficulty of using a different terms or a sound is overcome through the familiarity achieved through close contact. In other words there is not communication-bar between the dialects of the same language. The less the obstacles to keep each dialect separate, and the more the chances of mutual contact, the dialects are bound to merge into each other forming what we today call, the ***standard language***.

If a person travels from the central regions of a community, he meets various dialects of same language on the way, finds no problem in recognizing the differences. But as he moves on the language becomes more and more difficult to understand; and language elements become more and more strange and he feels that he is moving away from his own community and is entering the realm of another linguistic community. On his way there comes a region where the language is absolutely unknown to him. No communication is possible and no comprehension is achieved. Here he is in the midst of another language which he has not learned. It becomes no longer the problem of dialect differences; but of an unfamiliar language itself. He is in the midst of a different linguistic community. So far the differences lay in a few strange words, sets of vowels or consonants, or few idioms. But not it becomes a question of all aspects of comprehension.

In fact what we meet in this strange community is another dialect; but it is not a part of the community 1. It is a dialect wholly different and new; it is a part of the community 2. A comparison of a dialect in community (Language) 1 and of a dialect in community (Language) 2 would tell us that there are few features common to both. Our journey was a movement from the fully familiar → partly familiar → fully unfamiliar. The region with partly familiar language consisted of a mixture of members from both the communities and of a mixture of features belonging to both the languages.

In such a situation, the communicability of the language (or dialects) would vary. A person belonging to language (A) will find another language (which he has not learned) comprehensible in varying degrees. This comprehensibility depends on the affinities both the languages have towards each other. It may be that the language belong to the same stock; or there has been close borrowing between the two. In such cases the level of comprehension or the density of communication between the members of both the communities will be high. Depending on the similarities of language items i.e. lexicon and structure, a person belonging to language (A) will understand language (B) without formally learning it.

The opposite is also true. The greater becomes the dissimilarities in terms of the sounds, lexicon and structure, if the two language have no affinities and are in no way related. To illustrate the above mentioned factors: one may contrast English and German or Danish or Finnish. Or it may be contrast of Hindi, Gujarati or Bengali. An Englishman would understand a German much better than he would understand a Chinese, due to the close affinity of the language as both belong to the same 'germanic' group of the 'Indo-European' language family. Hindi would much better be understood by a Bengali (leaving out the formal transactions) than by a Tamilian as Hindi and Bengali, again, have closer relation than between Hindi and Tamil. Tamil belongs to the Dravidian language stock while Hindi and Bengali are modern progenies of the same India group of the Indo-European family of languages.

In short, the level of communication between dialects depends on a number of factors : (1) The dialects may belong to the same language and have the maximum level of communication between the two dialectical groups. (2) The dialects may belong to two different languages but belonging to the same language family or have borrowing affinities between the two. In this case the level of communication can be considerably high. (3) The dialects may belong to two language which have no borrowing affinities and are in no way related. In such cases the level of communication is expected to be the minimum. Between category (1) and (3) there can be any degrees of variation depending on the relation between the languages.

Dialectic studies alone truly give us insights into the pulse of the language. The actual informal or general language spring from the dialectic variations. But formal education and growing interaction among the members of a community as well as between communities themselves is more and more doing away with dialectic difference and permit the growth of a standard language.

4. Idiolect, Registers and Language

The foregoing pages have highlighted the structure of language from the geographical and sociological points of view. We have seen that the actual occurrence or performance of the language his exclusively with the individual. This forms the starting point of our understanding of idiolects in language. The members of the community speak, listen to, and write the language. The actual performance of the language is coloured by several individual characteristics. There are several factors which determine the individuals use of the language as we shall examine below. The *idiolects* of the language, thus consists in the individual's use of the language with all the physical, physiological, psychological and social factors determining his use of the language. In contrast to the specificities that are peculiar to a group of people or a region forming a dialect, within those specificities again there are bound to be further individual variations. These individual specificities of the language makes up an idiolect. In other words, the sum total of a person's language is an idiolect.

There are several physical factors affecting the language of an individual person. These consist of the physical environment. Geographical features (mountains, plains), climatic conditions (deserts, tropical regions) etc. to great extent determine the development and the use of a language. Several physiological factors affect the development and the use of a person's language. Perhaps, this is a major source of individual variations in language. Although every normal human being is equipped with the organs necessary for language production and reception, as a biological factor, these organs may be structured in a variety of ways differing only in details. Each element of different in the biological structure of these organs of speech affect the production of speech. The tongue, the teeth and the lips, together known as the articulators, control the nature of the individual's speech-function. Any inadequacy, handicap or malformation is bound to show out in speech. Depending on the features of the vocal cords, even the voice of people differ vastly in its frequency (tone) and amplitude (volume).

Then there are sociological difference affecting the speech of the individual. Man in society is highly susceptible to social characteristics. It is said that children who under parents who are unduly strict begin developing language handicaps. Stuttering and stammering are attributed to similar treatments received from others. Whatever be the objectivity of these factors, one thing with which everyone would agree, is that the social environment does play the major role in the formation of language in the individual. The individual's language acquisition process itself is determined by the aid he receives from his social environment.

A person intensely excited finds it difficult to express himself. Emotional (psychological) factors affect the acquisition, formation, and production of language. The person's state of mind is very much reflected in the language he produces. Psychological factors have a lot to do with the way the human person uses his language. All these factors we have discussed above determine the individual's language in such a way that the variations we find among idiolects become a reality. No two persons speaking the same language, at the same time or at different times, in fact, produce it in a perfectly identical way. One is reminded of Noam Chomsky's concept of Creativity at this instance. The native child who is in the process of acquiring his language, or the grown up native individual or any one who has achieved mastery over the language in question is said to produce sentences that he or she has never heard others use or the individual himself has never produced before. In other words the speaker of a language, on the basis of his linguistic generative capacity can produce an infinite variety of sentences using the basic material of his language.

Idiolects are not just limited to these individual variations mentioned above. Its scope is vast and varied. The linguistic community, it must be remembered, is a complex unit with varying occupations, professions, socio-economic strata and so forth. A consideration of these adds to our understanding of the idiolect. It is from this that we shall derive our understanding of ***registers*** later. A farmer or a blacksmith with their occupational specificities has access to a kind of language which a merchant or a nurse will not have. Each occupation calls for a set number of words specific to the occupation and expressions common among those who are in the occupation. There may be several features of the farmer's language which, though will be understood, are not useful to the Carpenter or the merchant. Again, the same is much more true of other professions. A doctor's terminology, words specific to his profession, technical as well as non-technical do not make sense to a lawyer. There is no common basis for the use of the language peculiar to each profession unless the interest overlaps. All these specificities, again, fall under the category of idiolects. Language is all that. We may speak of the teacher's idiolect, the doctor's idiolect and so on until we cover all aspects of social involvements.

Again, there are socio-economic strata: the upper class, the middle class and lower class. It may not be found surprising that each level in society employs a language which is not common to other levels in society. The richman's language, especially of social etiquette which may not be part of the language of the poor. The language used by the educated can be described as the formal and informal standard language; but the language of the uneducated or the illiterate mostly ranges from the non-standard, dialectical forms of the same language. All these specificities, again, fall under idiolectic variations. The study of these variations and their peculiarities is important for the language teacher and these we shall be examining later.

What are registers ? The discussion on the idiolect suffices to meet the understanding of registers in a language. A community may be examined from a variety of view points: occupations, professions, interests of various types, and involvement and aspects of recreation like games. The things, factors and events with which the members of the community come into contact are varied. It is possible for us to enlist sets of words on the basis of each of the categories mentioned above. This would yield for us an array of ***registers*** relevant to the experiences of the community, symbolized in the language. It can be called an organization of the 'lexicon' of the language on the basis of features that are part of that community. Registers have, again, an important role to play in the teaching of foreign languages.

Idiolects form the ultimate basis of any language; the combination of idiolects belonging to the same geographic region, originally, forms a dialect; the combination of the dialects of a linguistic community forms the language of the people.

4
Linguistics and Related Disciplines

1. Linguistics and Literature

Twentieth century is highly characterized by a cross-breeding of disciplines so much so that specialization in any one area without sufficient background in disciplines which are correlated is almost impossible. This is especially is almost impossible. This is especially true of those basic fields of knowledge which feed other discipline with the basic and general principles necessary. There are several fields of knowledge with which linguistic comes essentially in contact. Some of these are : literature, Psychology, philosophy, physics, sociology, biology and anthropology. More than any other field of knowledge such an interaction is true of linguistics because linguistics' concern is language as such which somehow or other falls in the scope of other fields of knowledge. Having language as the object of study is both an advantage and a disadvantage for linguistics due to various reasons. While all other disciplines employ language as the medium for investigations into various other phenomena, linguistics has to employ the same language which is the object of study as its medium of investigation. This is perhaps a great handicap which linguistics experiences in its research. In the same token it is indeed a prestigious thing that linguistic deals with the very subject matter which functions as the medium for research for all other disciplines. Consequently the findings of linguistics are of great value and assistance to other fields of knowledge.

Literature consists in the artistic use of language. A novel, a play or a literary essay is a piece of art, just as a drawing is a piece of art. The difference here lies in the medium employed. While painting makes use of the visual media of colour, literature employs language as its medium of expression. Language is employed for purposes of literary expression. The novelist, the poet and the essayist are, in fact, literary artists, if I am allowed to say so. On the other hand the entire object of linguistics is different. Linguistics is a science in the sense we understand the empirical sciences. The linguist approaches languages not as an artist, but as a scientist with a set of objectives much different from that of a literary artist. The linguistic scientist attempts to study the language as an objective phenomenon amenable to observation and scientific analysis. The tools of scientific analysis are equally applicable to linguistics as the study of language can begin from some empirical data.

But literature is merely aesthetics and the novelist is not merely an artist of language. The literary artist, in other words literature has a higher and nobler function to perform. Literature imprints life itself in the medium of language. Varied facts of human life with a universal implication find expression in literature. A poem or a novel is not merely a piece of art: It is life painted on the canvas of language. It is a depiction of life in the medium of language. But the literacy artist invariably uses language and nothing else. This is an important point to consider. This is where literature and linguistics meet on an interdisciplinary ground.

An understanding into the proper function of language as such and the manner in which the sounds correlate with the meanings in the language has become a necessity for the study of literature. The role of creative language in creative literature is immense. It is in the manipulation of linguistic forms that literary forms are given birth to. Literary symbolism is rooted in and springs from linguistic symbolism. The former cannot be thought of apart from the latter, so to say they are the two sides of the same coin. Stylistic analysis has received much emphasis in recent years as part of research in linguistics. This is a field where the tools and methods of research in linguistics are employed for the purpose insight into literature large-scale statistical counts highlight the stylistic bend of an author and a lot of insight is achieved into the structure of the language employed by the author in producing his genre.

The unique achievement of literature is its append both to the intellect and emotions. All forms of art of some level or other achieve these ends; but unlike a painting, literature, characterized by its expression in language, assumes a special symbolic feature. This quality arising out of its linguistic structure makes literature the most effective medium for expressing human emotional and intellectual experiences. Acquaintance with this is an added advantage of a student of literature in contrast to a student of any science. Linguistics helps literature in its investigations into the deeper realms of human experiences with universal implications. It takes a whole life-time to perceive the reality of life that literature, e.g. a novel, depicts in a few hundred pages. In this depiction of the reality of life, again, the determining factor is language, and the intricacies involved in human language are exploited in the literary genre to increase the stylistic complexities and the formal apparatus which function as the medium. Thus linguistics and literature converge at several points on interdisciplinary grounds and further strengthen the tools and methods that go into investigation in both the fields. The final achievement can be in terms of greater and fuller insights into human language and human life.

2. Linguistics and Philosophy

From time immemorial inquisitive minds asked questions on the reality of the world i.e. on the ultimate causes and explanations of things. Thus came to existence philosophy, the field of knowledge which enquires into the ultimate meanings and reasons of reality. The beginnings of the recorded history of philosophy shows a marked interest in the phenomenon of language. Why is it that philosophers of so early a period got interested in language? The answer may be found in the fact that of all the aspects of reality around which caught the attention of the philosopher, language was found a very immediate and complex problem to solve. Some of the questions that puzzled the early philosophers regarding language are the following: (1) What is the nature of language? (2) What is the relation between language and ideas ? (3) What are ideas? (4) How do ideas represent reality? (5) How does language represent reality?

It has always been felt that there is some intricate relation between the world outside and the language we speak. These two aspects, matters of the common man's experience, could not be denied by most. The central problem lay in the factors that related these two aspects of reality: whether ideas existed or not. Even today the whole world of philosophy may be separated on the basis of this: materialism and mentalism, the former denying and the latter asserting the existence of the mind and of ideas.

Consciousness is a very significant aspect on which both philosophy and linguistics coverage. Philosophy attempts to understand the role of consciousness in reality and the levels of consciousness in existence. It is the root of and the key to the understanding of the nature of man. Man is conscious; animals are conscious and it is held by philosophers that not only infrahuman beings but inanimate things too share some level of consciousness which is too indistinct to be susceptible to human perception. Language cannot be studied and understood except against the background of human consciousness. All forms of human behaviour is rooted in human consciousness; language is the most complex form of human behaviour. Consequently consciousness is the very substratum of the language. This is why the confused utterances of a mad man, the utterances we produce in our sleep or in any other unconscious stage may not rightly be considered language. Although the native language speaker produce the sentences of the language not always with a conscious awareness of the very production and of the structural intricacies involved, the entire act takes place in a state of consciousness. Thus philosophy and language study meet chiefly at the level of consciousness.

Philosophy in all aspects of its investigations has to depend on language. Just as the painter expresses himself in paint, and the literary artist organizes his language and creates a genre of literature, the philosopher employs language to express his thoughts on reality. Here comes a major and age-old question: to what extent does human language express human thoughts. To a common man his language expresses all that he thinks, mirroring the reality outside the mind. But for philosophers like Wittgenstein what human language does is to hide the thoughts ! In other words here we have two extreme views: one upholding a sort of one to one correspondence between thought, language and reality and the second maintaining little relation between human thought and human language. Wittgenstain's, view is a reaction against what the language Analysts' held that a right understanding of language can solve all problems of philosophy. For the language. Analysts all philosophical differences are rooted in linguistic expression of ideas. A right analysis of language, therefore, will solve all problems of philosophy. All these views certainty are the results of carrying to the extreme the complex features of language which have been a puzzle to philosophers of all the ages.

Although several of the views such as mentioned above are simple linguistic facts carried to the extreme, these have high lighted various aspects on language. Problems of philosophy, for instance, have a lot to do with problems of language. A proper understanding of the structure and functions of language will certainly clear several metaphysical questions. Language is in fact man's door to reality. Linguistics today is not interested in any kind of partial and one-sided understanding of language such as some aspects of grammar. The primary aim of linguistics today is defined as an investigation into the universal properties of human language with a view to discovering its fundamental nature. This is where philosophy and linguistics can work together and establish a kind of liaison that will effect a resonance on ultimate explanations of reality as such. As the very human thinking itself cannot easily to distinguish from the language a man speaks, the right understanding of reality is closely linked with the right understanding of language.

3. Linguistics and Sociology

The scope of behavioural sciences is vast. Behaviour viewed from a broad perspective includes the properties of even physical entities. As we shall be examining in the following section, physics is concerned with behaviour in the broad sense of the term, i.e. the behavioural properties of physical things. Psychology too is a science of behaviour; as such it is concerned with the behaviour of human beings. The relation of psychology and linguistics will be treated in Part II : Psycholinguistics.

Behaviour can be considered the generic definition of the disciplines mentioned above; but each has to be narrowed down in terms of its specific definitions: psychology as the behaviour of human beings as individuals, physics as the behaviour of physical entities and properties. Now it is possible for us to contrast psychology and sociology. Both concern themselves with human behaviour. But one needs to make specific distinctions: psychology deals with the behaviour of the individual and consequently the structure of the individual's psychic personality; on the other hand sociology studies the behaviour of the human individual in society and the structure of the individual personality in relation to society.

The sociological aspects of language are so significant that there is a specialized field in present-day linguistics known as 'Sociolinguistics'. As it has been discussed, language is both social as well as individual. The individual human being functions in social setting and as such makes use of language to communicate himself and maintain social interaction. Sociology as a science concerned with the individual's behaviour in society is highly dependent on the functions of language in society, by the use of which alone proper social interactions are possible.

Language is the chief Functional medium in society. All sorts of social operations are characterized by the individual's ability to make use of this resource called language. There are several questions that the linguist and the sociologist have to answer on an interdisciplinary plain : (1) Is language primarily social or individual ? (2) To what extent does language reflect its sociological substratum? (3) How far is individual language, the idiolect, determined by sociological factors ? (4) How far is the behaviour of the human individual determined by the language he uses? (5) To what extent does the structure of a society influence the change and development of the language used? (6) How far does the language spoken in a society influence and change or determine the structure of the society? These are some of the most fundamental questions that may be raised so far as the relation between sociology and linguistics is concerned.

Then there is the phenomenon of bilingualism. Bilingualism is a thoroughly sociolinguistic phenomenon. By bilingualism we understand the ability to speak and understand more than one language. As such this feature is intimately bound up with our country where most states have more than one language to use. Bilingualism has been a matter of serious study in present day linguistics. The major problems involved in bilingualism are the following: (1) How does the bilingual child develop the competence necessary for the variety of language? (2) How does the bilingual child avoid a full-fledged interference of the syntactic structures more than one language? (3) In what manner does the bilingual adjust himself to different linguistic communities ? (4) What problems are involved in the bilingual's adjustment to different communities. (5) Is it possible for the bilingual to satisfactorily belong and feel one with the different linguistic communities ? There are several such questions which the linguist and the sociologist have to answer with bearing on factors that involve the fundamental principles of both the disciplines. Bilingualism is a sociological phenomenon, but in equal intensity it is a linguistic phenomenon. It is the use of a variety of languages that primarily enable a man identify with different communities; at the same time the fact that is able in principle to identify with different communities creates a variety of sociological problems of adjustment.

Bilingualism is just an instance where the linguist and the sociologist have to come together to make investigations. Since language is primarily a product of society and as language fully represents the socio-cultural elements of a given community, language has been in a kind of historical conflict with the individual. On the one hand society calls for orthodoxy in language while individuals in whom language subsists are ever prone to introduce new elements into language. But the conflict is only apparent since the social forces cannot in any way be segregated and realized without a realization of the aspirations of the individual. The final outcome is a balancing between orthodoxy in language and inconsistent change. The shape of the language is determined by these balancing forces.

4. Linguistics and Physics

Linguistics as a science has been able to achieve a break through in modern period mainly because other sciences like physics and biology directly or indirectly have helped its progress. The chief concern of physics so far as language is concerned is its acoustic aspects. The articulatory and the auditory phenomena have not been of any interest to physicists. Sounds being the stimulus-response aspect of human language are said to travel through a medium in the form of sound waves. Since sound as such in terms of its properties and characteristics is the concern of physics, it includes any form of sound. But language or speech sounds being the most characteristics phenomena employed by man, physics has been concerned with the acoustic aspects of language. The area which studies sounds is labelled 'acoustic physics'.

Linguistics from very early periods had to clear many questions in regard to the vehicle of language, the sounds. Unless proper insight into the phenomenon of sounds is obtained no much could be said of language the spoken form of which consisted of sounds. Consequently the earliest interest in scientific linguistics was vested in the study of the speech sounds and their structure and production. The area of linguistics which thus enquired into sounds, as we have seen already, was known as phonetics. Within phonetics the area that specialized in the acoustic aspects came to be known as acoustic phonetics. In other words the interests of acoustic physics and that of acoustic phonetics are broadly the same. Physics gets interested in the acoustic of language for better understanding of the phenomena of sounds and the behaviour of the laws of sound. On the other hand, linguistics is interested in the behaviour of the physical entity called sounds for purposes of understanding the nature and properties of language. Thus both the disciplines study the same phenomenon for different ends.

Today the acoustic understanding of language has reached its peak and it may be called experimentally the most advanced field of study in linguistics. This advancement is mainly due to the co-ordinated work of phoneticious and acoustic physicists in the area of sound transmission. Sound is transmitted in the form of waves. The study of the sound waves and the pattern and design of there waves according to the distinctive features of sound units became thoroughly experimental and objective with the development of two devices: the spectrograph and the pattern playback. Spectrograph enables phoneticians to convert sound patterns into visual designs and thus study the structural components of individual sounds and sound sequences. On the other hand pattern playback or oscillograph enabled phoneticians to transform the visual designs back into sounds and thus further study the structural relationships. These two instruments now widely used in research laboratories for phonetics, were mainly the products of research by physicists working in the area of speech sounds.

Using the instruments mentioned above it was possible to define the features of sound waves (see. section on Acoustic phonetics for details). The most characteristic features of the sound waves are : amplitude, frequency and wave quality. Amplitude is defined as the distance of a wave from its apex to the base: 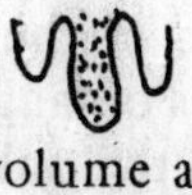 The amplitude of the sound waves determines the volume and consequently the loudness of a sound. Frequency, on the other hand, is determined by the number of waves produced at a given second, Frequency is measured in terms of CPS i.e. cycles per second. The wave frequency specifies the tone of the sound. The greater the frequency the higher the pitch level. It is held that as a rule male voice has higher volume and female voice has higher pitch level.

Such a meta-linguistic or suprasegmental understanding

of language has a lot of do with the way we tend to correlate the sounds with meaning and thus define the nature of langauge. A full-fledged and highly advanced empirical science such as physics will be able to throw light on the physical features of language. Linguistics on the other hand in its specialized treatment of communication in psycholinguistics contributes significantly to the understanding of aspects related to linguistic acoustics. It is in this context that communication engineering becomes relevant. Communication engineering has been enquiring into the structure of communication via any medium. The object of such a study is to increase communication efficiency at all levels. Transmission of maximum information without redundancy at the maximum speech is the target of investigations into the structure of communication. The hand-to-handwork of linguists and communication engineers has proved most useful in understanding the structure of communication and thus in increasing communications efficiency.

5. Linguistics and Biology

Biology is a life-science, concerned with the structure and function of living beings, plants and animals. As a life-science biology studies man as a biological organism: man's anatomical and physiological properties. As such the human brain as the substratum of all human activities falls under the scope biology. In other words biology as a life-science studies the structure and functions of the human brain. Brain, thus is the meeting ground for both the sciences: linguistics and biology. Linguistics, on the one hand, aiming at highlighting the nature o: language interacts with biology in the study of the structure and function of the brain. The properties of the brain, it is believed, has a lot to do with the properties of language as the physical brain undoubtedly functions as the substratum of language. A damaged brain results in a damaged language; no brain means no language. The biologist, on the other hand, aiming at highlighting the structure and function of the human brain and of the nervous system as a whole studies language which is the external manifestation of the internal workings of the brain and the nervous system. An insight into the nature of language, it is believed, will certainly yield insights into the nature of the brain.

The specialized field in linguistics which studies the nature of language on the basis of the biological substratum of the brain and the nervous system is known as Biolinguistics. This field has created much controversy regarding the nature of language. Biolinguists hold the view that human language in all its variety of manifestations is the product of the nervous system. The brain is not merely the substratum of language, as a biological basis for an immaterial function, but the brain answers all questions in regard to language. [see the section on biolinguistics for details].

Whether the brain is a mere biological basis for an immaterial function or it is the entire operating principle of language is not a question to be answered in this context. The interdisciplinary research into the brain and the nervous system has certainly yielded some very essential information on the relation between langauge and the brain. Some of the problems that have received attention from both the linguist and the biologist one the following : (1) The development of the brain in relation to the development of language. What is the contribution of the brain in the acquisition of language by the human child? (2) Is language a biologically localized phenomenon? If so, to what extent is the brain the localized signal-station of language? (3) How is language affected when the brain is damaged? (4) How far do brain-disorders result in diseases like 'aphasia'?.

Apart from endeavoring to find answers to questions such as above biology has helped linguistics in trying to understand the articulatory as well as auditory functions of language. The articulatory and the auditory functions are closely linked with the nature of language so far as its production and reception is concerned. As organs of the human body the structure and functions of the human organs of speech and audition come directly under the purview of biology and much insight has been achieved in this regard with the help of biology.

Language is primarily a biological function. But it does not mean that language is only a biological function. It is more than all that biology can explain. It rises above the biological substratum of the brain and the nervous system as a whole. It reaches a level which is beyond the grasp of biology. Yet biology has been doing great service in the understanding of the nature of language.

5
Applied Linguistics

1. Psycholinguistics

Taken in the narrow sense of the term, applied linguistics may not include specialized fields such as psycholinguistics or sociolinguistics as these too contribute considerably to the basic set of principles on language that make up general linguistics. Psycholinguistics is still put under applied linguistics here only for advantages of grouping and to avoid unnecessary duplication. General linguistics deals with the set of basic principles in language analysis and description yielding the very fundamentals regarding the nature of language. Applied linguistics, on the other hand, employes these fundamental principles for purposes of understanding and working out solutions to several practical questions such as the teaching of a foreign language, stylistic analysis, computational problems and application of mathematics to problems of linguistics known as mathematical linguistics : This area also includes research on dialectical linguistics, and lexicography. As vast and highly specialized fields of knowledge aspects of applied linguistics draws from the resources of general linguistics on the one hand, and contribute significantly to the understanding of the general nature of language.

Psycholinguistics is a highly interdisciplinary area of knowledge on language in which the basic principles of psychology as well as linguistics are brought together to bear upon each other. [See Part II for details]. Psychology fundamentally is concerned about the behaviour of the human individual i.e. the psychological structure of the human individual. The most significant and complex of human behaviour and one that is essentially a characteristic of the species as such is language. Language as behaviour, thus, is the meeting ground for psychology and linguistics. Today psycholinguistics is not merely the meeting ground for linguistics and psychology, but it has emerged as a discipline in its own right with its own set of general principles. In other words it is possible to define the role of psycholinguistics in contrast to that of linguists in contrast to that of general linguistics. Linguistics studies the structure of an objective reality called language without in any way considering the functional aspects involved in the production. This has been the way the structuralist linguistics viewed linguistics. On the other hand, psycholinguistics concentrates on the functional aspects of language production and the processes involved therein relating language production to the speaker (in source) and the listener (the target). The transformationalists do not consider this distinction fundamental and Noam Chomsky's distinction between competence and performance include aspects of language production. Psycholinguistics studies several functional, dynamic aspects of what human speech is. Acquisition of the native language, acquisition of a foreign language, the psychological factors involved in the learning of the L_1 and L_2, the functional characteristics of language, the creative choices involved in the production of language etc. are some of the major problems discussed in psycholinguistics. Since it draws upon the general principles and findings of psychology, the insights psycholinguistics yields are of great value in the understanding of the functional nature of language.

2. Sociolinguistics

Sociolinguistics is a specialized off-shoot of linguistics of recent origin. Sociological problems involved in the use of language and problems of language arising from the complex social structure of communities have been the concern of sociolinguistics. Language and society are so highly interrelated that one cannot be explained without the other as one cannot be understood without the other. The complex, varied structure of society determine the structure of language. Our discussion on language and the individual, society, dialect, idiolect and registers (ch.3) has highlighted several aspects of the relationship between language and sociological factors. The child as a native language speaker grows up in the social setting and the given social environment plays great roles in shaping the language of the individual. The role-play of the individual in society and the social demands placed on him by the community have a lot to do with the shaping of the individual's language. Slangs take us to the very root of sociological problems at times. Slangs are expressions very peculiar to social groups. A very positive view of slangs usage will justify the fact that every sociological group has levels of slangs. The adolescent peer groups, cliches, and to a great extent sports associations of formal kinds entertain sets of slangs which are characteristic to the group.

3. Biolinguistics

Biolinguistics is, again, another specialized off-shoot of very recent origin, and it has been a very controversial field of enquiry into the nature of language. The most fundamental question that biolinguistics tries to answer is how far language is determined by the neural process of man i.e. what is the role the brain and the nervous system as a whole plays in the origin, development and process of language both in individual human begins and in so far as the linguistic history of humanity is concerned. [ontogeny and phylogeny, the technical terms employed for these perspectives are avoided here for reasons of simplicity].

Biolinguistics has mostly developed as a result of the linguistic interests of neurologists and biologists. Recent developments in the understanding of cerebral process and neurological functions in man have turned the attention of a considerable number of neurosurgeons to the nature of language. One of the most outstanding among them in K.H. Krishnamurti who has undertaken some significant research into the linguistic functions of the human brain. Accordingly, from a purely behaviouristic viewpoint, it has been claimed that the entire spectrum of language starting from its acquisition by the child and ending with the very nature of language is explainable in terms of the cerebral functions in man. It is not required to bring in any immaterial principle like the mind to explain the phenomenon of language.

The brain is most merely the seat of language, but the total functioning principle of language. Human language in its genesis and operation in the individual is considered essentially a biological process : the former the result of organic evolution and the latter are of neuromuscular physiology. It is thought that human language is a product of man's organic evolution like several other aspects of the evolution such as man's bipedal motion, erect posture, opposable thumb and the like. Therefore an explanation of all language phenomena are sought in the 'functional integration of tissue and environment. A sentence of a language is considered an operative way of dealing with an information.

Human speech and language are considered the product of three distinct processes: phonation, audition and cerebration. The whole thing is a process of manufacturing components. The sense of the language used is manufactured in the brain and its information proper is generated. This process is the cerebration. Then the sense is phonated; the listener experiences audition and finally the cerebration of the listener does the function of decoding the sense of the language. Biolinguistics has endeavoured to picture a fine mosaic of a theory of language but leaves untouched what is said to be the higher aesthetic, artistic, poetic and mystical flights of language. But the insights that have been acquired through experimental investigations on the physiological aspects of the human brain are of tremendous value in the ultimate understanding of the structure, function and nature of language.

4. Stylistics

The interrelations of linguistics and literature has already been examined (Ch. 4:1) and we found that the aesthetic bend of literature and the scientific bend of linguistics almost complement each other. This interrelation manifests itself sharply in what is known as stylistics. In recent years there has grown great interest in stylistics among linguistics who are trained in literature. This interest has given rise to greater investigations into what literary style is and how exactly the style of an author can be scientifically explicated and described by means of statistical analysis.

Style is defined in several ways and from serval viewpoints. Essentially literary style consists in the manner in which a writer chooses from a multiplicity of available language items and in the way he chooses to organize his language against the background of several possible ways of organization. Ultimately whether consciously or habitually the essence of style consists, thus, in the linguistic choices an author makes. As a speaker of the language, the author exercises his basic linguistic creativity with a set of linguistic choices already involved to structure his sentences. But as a writer his linguistic dimensions become manifold: over and above the ordinary basic creativity the writer exercises a hovering literary creativity which in fact makes him a literary author. His literary style is determined by the nature and extent of the choices involved in this latter creative experience. This is also what makes style very personal, and not so easily definable.

If literary style consists in the extent of linguistic choices an author makes, it is linguistically possible for us to define and describe the nature of the style of an author and say statistically in what exactly the author's style consists. In this process literature, linguistics and statistical methods come together. The literary work is analysed by terms of the major recurring language elements and structural aspects, and on the basis of such a statistical count the style of the author in the specific work can be described. This is also known in present day linguistics as discourse analysis, a discourse being a unit of language ranging from a simple utterance to a lengthy text. In all cases the essential method employed is the statistical count of the language forms and structural aspects employed by the author.

On its basis it is also feasible to have a comparative study of the different works of the same author as well as of the works of different authors. It is also possible to have stylistic comparisons of different ages by comparing the texts of representative authors belonging to the periods. In all these instances the style under consideration has bearing on the specificities of language used by the author or authors. The application of the tools and methods of linguistics to literature has considerably widened and increased the scope of stylistic studies. Discourse analysis has in recent years been receiving great attention. A greater advantage, of course, is that stylistics has proved to be the best testing-ground for the latest tools and statistical methods of linguistics. Stylistics has emerged today as a major field of linguistic enquiry which has more than ever brought together linguistics and literature into one fold.

5. Metalinguistics

'Meta' designates something 'beyond', and the term metalinguistics do not exactly tell us what this specialized field is all about. Metaphysics has nothing to do with physics, as it deals with the questions of ultimate reality while physics is concerned with the world of physical reality. But metalinguistics, unlike metaphysics, has everything to do with linguistics, and the field is concerned about aspects of language that are ordinarily dealt with in general linguistics.

Metalinguistics studies the structure of the suprasegmental features. The term 'meta' is applied because the suprasegmental features can be very well contrasted with and distinguished from the sets of segmental features that in fact form the whole language. Language consists basically of allophones, phonemes, allomorphs and morphemes which are segmental units with their own definable distinction features. What is thus ordinarily studied under linguistics are these sounds, sequences of sounds, words and their combinations. Sounds are said to form clusters and syllables; the meaningful combinations of sounds form morphemes; morphemes in turn constitute words; and words are ordered in to sentences. All these are considerations starting from the segmental level.

Parallel to the segmental level there is the metalinguistic or suprasegmental level (also known as the prosodic features). These include (1) features of stress, (2) pitch levels (3) tonal contours and (4) juncture. The levels of pitch and tonal contours put together are usually referred to as patterns of intonation. The usual segmental phonemes studied under linguistics consist of distinction features which are definable in terms of their physical or articulatory characteristics. | p |, for instance, is a unitary distinctive combination of several features such as bilabial, plosive, voiceless and aspirated (if initial) or unreleased (if final). It is possible to define and describe all segmental phonemes on the basis of similar features of production etc.

At the same time, the suprasegmental units are not definable and describable in the same manner i.e. on the basis of the criteria used for distinguishing segmental units. Stress is described in terms of 'peaks' of voice; and the levels of such peaks. In speech what is in fact audible are these peaks of voice which the listener is able to catch. A word is judged to be such on the basis of such peaks. The word desert is judged to be distinct from desert chiefly because the stress is placed differently on different syllables making the peaks of audition different. Stress is marked differently by different authors. But the usual way of marking stress features is the following.

1. Primary stress : definite
2. Secondary stress : continue
3. Weak stress : information
4. Sentence stress : ^{2}John ^{1}is ^{3}fine

Pitch levels consist in the rise of tone which mark different parts of an utterance differently in terms of the tone employed. Four pitch levels are usually considered in metalinguistics. They are:

1. ^{1}There is a ^{4}girl ^{2}behind the ^{3}curtain.
2. ^{1}There is a ^{3}girl ^{2}behind the ^{4}curtain.
3. ^{1}There is a ^{3}girl ^{4}behind the ^{2}curtain.
4. There ^{4}is a ^{3}girl ^{1}behind the ^{2}curtain.

Tonal contours consist in the rise and fall of voice at the terminus of an utterance enabling utterances assume new meanings as a result of the change in the tonal contours. Three such tonal contours are studied in metalinguistics:

1. Falling Tone : What are you planning to do ?

2. Rising Tone : Are you planning to leave ?

3. Falling-Rising Tone : He is planning to go.

Junctures mark the transition from one word into another. The usual example given are: black bird - blackbird or black board - blackboard. Junctures have a lot to do with the stress of the words. Junctures are structured on the basis of the word stress.

Metalinguistics is thus centered on the suprasegmental aspects of language. As such it is a complementary subject in the sense that metalinguistics attempts to describe features of language which are not normally included in linguistic description or which have not received enough specialized attention from linguistics. As a result metalinguistics adds much to the understanding of the suprasegmental features of language which are not so easily amenable to exact scientific description.

6. Mathematical Linguistics

It is interesting to note that linguistics suffer from a major methodological set back compared to any other discipline of its kind. Linguistics has as its object the study of language, just as psychology, sociology or anthropology has its own specific object of enquiry. All sciences except linguistics have the advantage of employing language in which their methodology and tools will be set. Linguistics on the other hand is compelled to employ the same language as its means of enquiry which itself is its object of enquiry. In other words linguistics suffer from a serious setback that it has to use language itself to define, state, analyses and describe the features of language as its object.

It is to counteract this setback in methodology that present-day linguistics has started employing mathematical models in linguistic description. What are the chief merits of mathematical models? As we have stated above, natural language is full of ambiguities and ambivalent features so much so that any linguistic description using natural language, however refined, is bound to cause various discrepancies. In natural languages no amount of mathematical precision is attainable. One word stands for several notions; one notion is symbolized by several words; semantic features essential to one word are shared by different words; and the same spelling sequence sometimes represents various sets of sounds. There is no end to the complex ambivalence which language gives rise to.

Mathematics, on the other hand is a language of precision. Mathematics is a kind of language i.e. symbolic sets of a representations in which the most qualitative features are precision and accuracy. Consequently models in mathematics have the advantage of representing a wide variety of situations which linguistic definitions do not. Mathematical formulas are capable of standing for 'n' number of situations feasible to be included in its scope. On the other hand linguistics definitions are semantically determined and their horizons are not open to several possibilities:

animate + human + young + male = boy

it cannot be any thing else; this formula does not function as a representative mould for serval such features in language. On the other hand : a + b + c + d = N
1 + 2 + 3 + 4 = 10

This mathematical formula may stand for any set of items such as dog, cats, houses, stars or the like.

Such a characteristic of mathematical models is exploited in mathematical linguistics. Mathematical linguistics is, thus, the application problems in linguistics with a view to attaining solutions which have precision and clarity. Transformational generative grammar is, perhaps, the first theory on language to employ mathematical models in the description of language. Transformational generative grammar aims at mathematical precession and rigorousness in the formulation of transformational rules so that each transformational rule will be in a position to generate 'n' number of sentences belonging to the natural language which the rule represents. Therefore each transformational rule is framed in the form of a mathematical formula. The following phrase-structure rule in transformational generative grammar will generate any number of sentences of English :

S → NP + VP

NP→ Adj. + N

VP→ V + NP.

in which s stands for the sentence which consists of a noun phrase and a verb phrase which in turn consists of smaller elements. Mathematical linguistics is intended to develop a linguistic description i.e. a theory of language which has mathematical precision and clarity. How far such a description is attainable is yet to see. One thing is sure that the application of mathematical models to problems in linguistics will certainly do away with much of the ambivalences that have been part of the description of language from the beginning.

7. The Teaching of Foreign Languages

In fact the teaching of foreign languages is the field where the principles and findings of modern linguistics are applied more than any where else. Applied linguistics proper is referred mostly to foreign language teaching and the role linguistics plays in giving shape to a methodology which is aimed at making foreign language teaching easier and more effective. From time immemorial the knowledge of the language and the way language was imparted had close relations. More or less the understanding of the nature of language formed the basis for the language teaching methods of all times. This is true even of present day linguistics and foreign language teaching methods. We find two categories of linguists: one is linguistic theory-oriented i.e. the predominant object of linguistics research is the development of insights into the nature of language; and the other group of linguists are theoreticians but for practical objectives such as foreign language teaching methods, computerization, programmed instruction, research into brain diseases such as 'aphasia' etc. Thus there are those trained in linguistics who have dedicated themselves to the cause of foreign language teaching. Linguistic researches by these specialized men are aimed at developing better techniques for foreign language teaching.

The fundamental principles laid out in general linguistics as well as the specialized accumulation of knowledge on language have paved way to deeper understanding of the processes involved in the learning of a foreign language. The basic dictum is if we know the way the native language of the pupil functions and the way the language is produced, well, the same should be the way a foreign language should be put in. Consequently the attention in recent years have been on the language acquisition process: how does the child learn its native language?

In other words, on the one hand the advancement of the general descriptive linguistics, and on the other specialized offroots like psycholinguistics, biolinguistics and socio-linguistics have helped the understanding of the process of native language acquisition and the structure of language as such. Insights at both these levels together have formed the basis of all present day foreign language teaching methodology.

After having examined various significant aspects of general linguistics and the fundamental principles of linguistics in Part I of the present work, we shall turn to Part II in which one considered the Psycholinguistic aspects i.e. the functional aspects including the process of language learning as well as what constitutes the production of language at various levels. These two parts together, as it has been stated above, will form the theoretical basis for all that we shall be discussing in part III on the methodological foundations and methods of teaching English as a foreign language.

A knowledge of the basic linguistic principles involved is a requirement not only for those who deal with the theoretical aspects of English teaching, but for the teacher who is to be fully involved as a practitioner in the classroom. His responsibility as a teacher of a foreign language not only lies in imparting knowledge or in enabling children master a few skills, but the teacher's greater responsibility is in making the foreign language learning a unitary, pleasant and fruitful a unitary, pleasant and fruitful experience not too different in essence from the way they learned their mother tongue.

6
Sub-disciplines in Linguistics

1. Methodological Approaches to the Study of Language

Linguistics as the systematic enquiry into language is always subservient to some methodology or other. No linguistic investigation in the proper sense of the term can be undertaken without a clear-cut and well-defined manner of doing it. In a very loose sense of the term this manner of doing some investigation constitutes the methodology of a science like linguistics. It is, at the same time, interesting to note that the entire outcome of some specific investigation depends on the methods of carrying it out and the tools which are employed for the purpose.

Man tends to observe things and processes or events around him and draw conclusions which befit a given situation. The primitive man developed all his rudimentary knowledge and beliefs about the worlds around from what he observed around. He had no ways of listing whether what he believed were true. Language for that matter used to be the object of human observation from time immemorial, and again man cherished rudimentary knowledge of his language apart from his concrete use of the language. In fact the earliest known systematic observations of language have come down to us from the Greeks and the Sanskrit grammarians of India. It was with a note of surprise that the West has accepted the fact that some of the earliest records of language study in India shows much more objective and rigorous method of analysis than of the contemporary Western counterparts, the type of analytic methods which the West was to undertake only much later.

With the Greeks language study always formed part of their preoccupation with philosophical questions just as with the Indian scholars who pursued language study as part of their preoccupation with the religious scriptures. This shows that in fact the study of language for its own sake is something very recent compared to the origins of the study of language which take us far back to the B.Cs. Just as philosophical or scriptural questions are debated and answers are sought, language figured in to take a dominant place. For Plato who enquired into the essence of the world of Ideas, or for Aristotle who investigated into the essence of reality subject to human experience, language became a philosophical topic of supreme interest. What is interesting to note is that one and the same ***speculative method*** of enquiry was applied both to the study of language and to other existential questions. Enquiry into human language, this became part of speculative philosophy with its stress on ***introspection*** and deductive reasoning. Since all normal human beings acquire and employ language for a variety of purposes, it was quite natural that the philosophers had to come to grips with the problems of language to find answer to the central questions relating to the working of the human mind.

Speculative studies on language formed the basis of early linguistic investigations. The philosophers of language, belonging to various schools of philosophy have made undeniably significant contributions to the rational understanding of human language. Recent developments in the in the transformational generative school of linguistics have recognized the significance of the contributions of Descartes and others of the rationalist school of philosophy. In fact, as Noam Chomsky points out (***Language and mind*** Chomsky. 1968), Descartes argued that the only sure indication that another body possesses a human mind, that it is not a mere automation is its ability to use language in the normal way; and he argued that this ability cannot be detected in an animal or an automaton which, in other respects, shows signs of apparent intelligence exceeding those of a human, even though such an organism or machine might be as fully endowed as a human with the psychological organs necessary to produce speech. Chomsky's *Cartesian linguistics* (1966) is based on the relevance of Descartes' philosophy to modern linguistics.

Just as in philosophers' speculative conclusions on language especially during the middle ages and the early modern period grammarians of these times for centuries were methodologically influenced by introspection rather than extrinsic analytic observations and study of language. So far as English language is concerned we find that King Albert and others, the earliest English grammarians, depended more on the content of language as such i.e. language material for analytic purposes and study rather than speculation on English based on some model which might have had no relations whatever with the language under consideration. It is later that we find exclusive speculative preoccupation with the nature of language and with the grammar of a language which the grammarians presumed would be thoroughly parallel to that of any classical language, like Latin in the West, and Sanskrit in India.

The classical ***grammatical studies*** of the 15th century (Ch. 15) and the ***Renaissance grammatical studies*** of the 16th century (Ch. 15) were based more on observed language data from the classical languages and the newly emerging regional languages respectively. It was with the so-called ***philosophical Grammar*** of 17th century (Ch. 10) that we find an exclusive pre-occupation with speculative methods. The very label indicates that the grammar of seventeenth century with its well-known *Port-Royal* school of France was philosophy oriented. All the same with the present day status which transformational generative grammar has achieved, we find a complete resurrection of the Part-Royal grammars of the 17th Century.

The pendulum always strikes the extremes. The speculative grammatical preoccupations of the 17th century brought its own reactions in one form or other, and we find that an approach to language study taking shape which rejected the speculative, philosophical approach. This was certainly the result of the grounds gained in later centuries by a thoroughly empiricist approach to the sciences set forth in part by the theories of Isaac Newton, Charles Darwin and others. Newton's theories of motion in physics and Darwin's theory of evolution in biology constituted the springboards for further empirical leaps in the fields of psychology and linguistics. A conviction dawned on scholars of language study that mere introspective analysis of linguistic aspects would not lay sufficient grounds for a thoroughly scientific study of human language as such or languages in particular. And interest shifted so to say from a preoccupation with the ***nature*** of human language to the ***structure*** of particular language.

Such is the background of what we know to day as the '***comparative method***' of the 18th and 19th centuries, a period of considerably fruitful research in linguistics in regard to the genetic relations of languages. As we shall be examining on the following sections, comparative method intensely dealt with language ***reconstruction***. The procedure whereby morphs of two or more sister language, considered so at an extrinsic level are matched in order to reconstruct the ancestor language is known as the comparative method. When a variety of changes including those of sound affect different parts of one linguistics community there is said to be an earlier stage (called Ancestor or ***proto-language***) and two or more later stages which we may call ***daughter languages*** with regard to the Proto-language, and ***sister languages*** with regard to each other. This is the result when a language splits chiefly on a geographical basis. But what is interesting for that matter presently is the 19th century preoccupation with language reconstruction on a universal basis taking into consideration specimen material of the languages of the modern times and those languages which have becomes extinct. Methodologically what is appealing is the new spirit to work in line with the empiricist principles rather than on the principles of speculative philosophy. The methods of linguistic analysis in language reconstruction meant dealing with concrete language data of one kind or other, and never departing or deviating in terms of conclusions from what the data reveal as inherent in the system of the given language. As the 19th century linguistic came to have the strong belief that a set of speculative postulates do not have the necessary foundation in the concrete data of the language.

The linguistic interests of the early twentieth century was based on similar principles, but in a more rigorous fashion. The language reconstruction of the 19th century linguistics was thought to be a ***historical concern*** rather than a ***descriptive concern*** in which the present-day languages and their present structure alone become the subject-matter for study. As it will be examined in detail in section 3 there developed a strong belief by early 20th century that genuine linguistic research is only descriptive research, which is supposed to take care of only present-day languages. Again it was not a speculative concern with the nature of human language and its working but a descriptive concern with a language spoken in modern times on the basis of some given data which invariably provide sufficient grounding for a set of more reliable and objective linguistic conclusions on the ***structure*** of the particular language under consideration. For this reason we label this trend in linguistics as ***structural linguistics***.

The methodological pendulum again swings back; and we find today a genuine concern for the speculative and introspective values in linguistics with the onset of the present-day transformational generative grammar. The transformational generative linguistics constitutes not only the dawn of a merely a new theory on language or a fresh theory on language or a fresh look into the age-old questions on language, but also it reveals a methodological evolutionary phase in linguistics. The values of speculative concern for the nature of human language is once again given priority over an enquiry into the structure of particular language which constituted the principal structuralist concern. It is a trend that is certainly welcome and will prove intensely more fruitful in the study of language than what have so far constituted part of modern linguistics.

2. Historical Linguistics

If the 17th century is looked upon as a period of 'philosophical linguistics' with its speculative preoccupations, the 18th and the 19th centuries constitute a period of intense preoccupation with what we shall call ***historical (Diachronic)*** *linguistics*. Divorcing philosophy from linguistics, scalars of language belonging to the period aimed at obtaining a thorough understanding of a given language (English for instance) by means investigations into its historical development and changes. Recognition of '*linguistics change*' as a phenomenon affecting all languages without any exception in line with the changes occurring in the linguistic community is a major contribution of historical linguistics as developed during this period.

Historical linguistics as an enquiry into the evolution and development of language has 'language change ' as its central concern. Change affects all aspects of human language as every speech community which makes use of a language undergoes considerable change with the change of time. As examined in Ch. 1. Sec. 6, the phonological, morphological, syntactic and semantic components of every language are susceptible to change. An interesting characteristic of language change is that it reveals only as a *cumulative effect* on a given language. It is difficult to record the insignificant changes which continue occurring at a given time. At the same time, examining the language material recorded a few decades ago and contrasting it with present-day language one comes to note significant changes in various aspects of a language. The history of English language as recorded by Otto Jespersen, Albert C. Baugh and Barbara Strang, for instance, exhibit the historic fluctuations which a language like English has undergone upto the modern period. Recorded in a highly lucid manner these histories of English language lead the student of English history through a variety of stages when the language was said to have the highest possible interaction with another language with consequent large-scale borrowings. These borrowings were expected to enrich the communicational efficiency of the particular language and enable the language to provide exacts linguistic counterparts for the shades and features of experience which a linguistic community has to take care of.

Language change as a universal phenomenon affecting all language constitutes, thus a major aspect of historical linguistics. But the historical linguist, unlike the writer of the history of a language (as those author mentioned above) is not concerned with the historical development of any particular language for its own sake. Instead, the concern of the historical linguist consists in the features of ***historical development of language as such*** which are realized in the development of particular languages. The ***alternations*** that occur in languages in time i.e. as a temporal rather than a geographical or spatial factor are features which the historical linguist attempts to define as part of the linguist's investigation into the historical development of languages. These alternations may be phonological, morphological, lexical, syntactic and sematic as mentioned above. Down the centuries we are able to notice sound changes with definable regularities and affecting the entire language so far as a given sound of set of sound is concerned. ***Sound shift*** in various forms has been a regular feature in the history especially of English. The famous 'Grimm's Law' as defined by Jacob Grimm in 19th century states the patterns of sound changes in early Modern English Period, which affected the Germanic group of the Indo-European Languages. Karl Verner redefined the 'Grimm's Law' later and added clarity to the pattern of sound changes as occurred in the Germanic languages. Any text on the history of English language provides the student of historical linguistics ample material to study the language changes as occurred in the various components of English language.

As examined in the preceding section the 'comparative method' of the 18th and 19th centuries, employed for purposes of what we have called '***language reconstruction***' has provided the most extensive material for the development of historical linguistics. The linguist concerned about the nature of the ***historical evolution*** of human languages attempts to spot varifiable relations among languages through the comparative method of language reconstruction. In a venture to build the ***hierarchy of world languages*** in terms of their relationships linguist tries to establish what are called the ***language families*** with the ***parent languages***, ***sister languages*** and ***daughter languages*** figuring in. In other words, the language reconstruction process of the historical linguist enables him successfully to establish the language families and highlight the language families and highlight the nature and direction of the development of human languages with the modern languages figuring in at the terminus.

Reconstruction would more specifically refer to the procedure whereby morphs of two or more sister languages are matched in order to discover the parent language or to reconstruct the ancestor language which is technically known as the *proto-language* (refered to earlier in Section 1). The linguist's reconstruction of a proto-language which does not exist either in speech or writing is necessarily partial and hypothetical. At the same time the language which was supposed to have existed was real and whole. Therefore the reconstruction of a proto-language by means of varifiable traces in the daughter languages figuring in the lower levels of the hierarchy can be said to be a partial representative system of an actual and historical language spoken once upon a time by a particular linguistic community. A reconstructed Proto-Germanic form, for instance, is formulated to represent a Germanic parent language which internally reveals the relations of Gothic, Norse, Old English, Old Saxon and Old High German to each other and establish a phonological and morphological formula to state the *consistency* which an evolution of this kind exhibited. A successful reconstruction provides the historical forms (phonemes and morphs) which had been central to the historical evolution that the languages undergo. Relations required *regularities* and *consistency* in the occurrence of such forms point out to the essential evolution which took place in course of the historical development of the language under consideration. If the regularities and the consistency of the occurrence of the forms are not sufficiently established, then the relations hypothetized may be a farce. This is where one of the principal setbacks of language reconstruction lies. To establish such consistent regularity what the linguist looks for one sets of *correspondence* between forms. If a phoneme |a| of the ancestor language in a given environment class appears as |m| in one daughter language and as |t| in the other daughter language, corresponding morphs in the two sister languages will be matched in such a way that |m| in one represents |t| in the other. Such a pair of phonemes, one in the first language and the other in the second give rise to a set of *correspondence* (t/m) which should then be verified by generalizing as a universal phenomenon true of all such instances in the same environment in the two languages. Thus once the regularity of the pattern of the phonemic occurrence in sets of morphs is established, the reconstruction at this level is complete. the reconstruction of the proto-language as the ancestor becomes easier when the ancestor language is independently known to the linguist. For instance the relation of the Indian languages Hindi and Marathi to the Sanskrit and further to a 'proto-Indic' language is apparent and the comparative analysis and reconstruction help establish the fact in a scientific manner. As the relations are established, the modern north Indian languages (Hindi, Marathi, Gujarati, Bengali etc.) are traced back to the Indic group of the *Indo-Iranian* and further to the main *Indo-European* common ancestor called the *Proto-Indo-European language*.

The world languages are traced back to their common

Family Tree

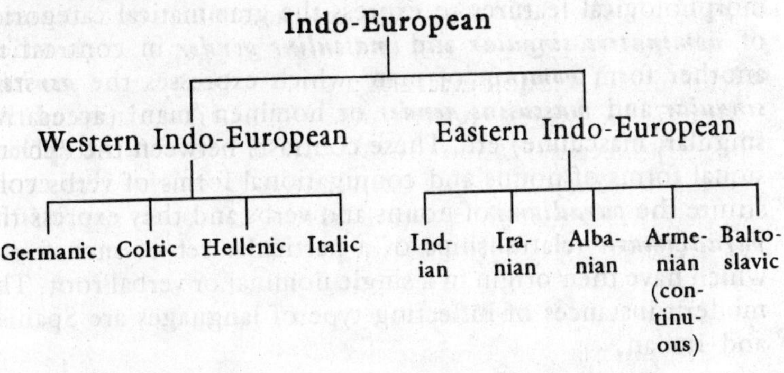

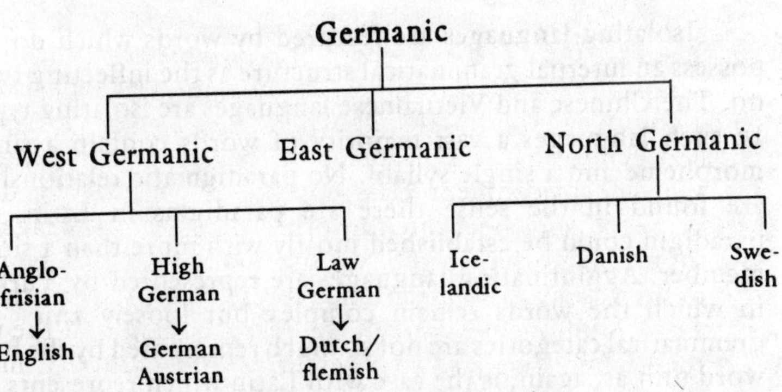

ancestors in the following manner:

The diachronic analysis of historical linguistics has also enabled the linguist to hypotheses in regard to the fundamental structure of languages. The 19th century diachronic studies of language attempted to classify languages on the basis of their structure features. There are said to be three classes of languages: (1) *Inflecting languages*, (ii) *Isolating languages*, and (iii) *Agglutinating languages*, grouped on the basis of the morphological structure of world languages. Latin is considered the best instance of the inflecting type because the inflectional features of prefixation, zinfixation and sufixation and most predominant and we part of the very structure of the language. The word is a centred, tightly structured and rather complex unit and contains in it several basic grammatical elements and expressing basic grammatical categories. The Latin word ***homo*** 'man' or ***puer*** 'boy' contain within as part of its structure morphological features to express the grammatical categories of ***nominative singular*** and ***masculine gender*** in contrast to another form ***hominis*** 'of man' which expresses the ***genitive singular*** and ***masculine gender*** or hominen 'man' (accusative singular, masculine) etc. These contrasts between the declensional forms of nouns and conjugational forms of verbs constitute the ***paradigms*** of nouns and verbs and they express the ***paradigmatic*** relationships of a particular set of such forms which have their origin in a single nominal or verbal root. The modern instances of inflecting type of languages are Spanish and Italian.

Isolating languages are featured by words which do not possess an internal grammatical structure as the inflecting types do. The Chinese and Vietnamese languages are isolating types. In such languages a vast majority of words contain a single morpheme and a single syllabi. No paradigmatic relationships are found in the sense there are paradigms in Latin. No paradigm could be established mostly with more than a single member. Agglutinating languages are represented by Turkish in which the words remain complex but loosely knit. The grammatical categories are not so much represented by the basic word unit as, again, is the case with Latin which represents the inflecting type. The morphological structure of the word in Turkish differs significantly from that of a word in Latin. The notion of paradigmatic relationship is, as in the case of isolating languages not applied to the agglutinating languages. But most modern languages cannot certainly be classified neatly into any of the type mentioned above. A language like English falls between these types because it shares several of the 'inflecting', 'isolating' and 'agglutinating' characteristics as part of its basic word structure and sentence construction.

A more modern view tends to classify languages into 'synthetic languages and 'Analytic languages' Latin being the best example for a ***synthetic language*** and English for ***analytic languages***. Again the grouping is based on the morphological structure of the word. The grammatical features in synthetic languages are expressed by inflectional endings, and those in analytic languages expressed by independent, free morphemes called the grammatical parties. The Latin ablative ***hominis*** (singular) and ***homines*** (Plural) expresses the same semantic contest as the English possessive 'by man' or 'with man'; the particles doing the same grammatical function as the inflectional endings in Latin. All the same, at best, these traditional classifications may be considered as '***theoretical types***' with more than any one such type realized in most languages.

Historical linguistics by and large has contributed significantly to the understanding of language change as a universal linguistic phenomenon, the reconstruction of world language into members of language families, and lastly to the construction of several 'theoretical types' under which languages could be classified in some way or other based on features (chiefly morphological) which are predominant in a language.

3. Descriptive Linguistics

As we have examined, historical linguistics with its ***diachronic analysis*** attempts to state the changes a languages registers in its speech habits from time to time and takes into account the cumulative difference a language reveals by contrast to various preceding stages of development. It attempts to establish the fundamental relations that existed between the modern languages and their relationships with ancestral languages. As a final goal historical linguistics attempts to state the nature of the development of language as such from its phylogenic viewpoint, modern languages being the terminal points of a vertical linguistic evolution which had its origins in some pre-historic, unrecorded language (s) whose even remote traces are not available as a source, for diachronic study. The main preoccupation of the historical linguists of the 12th century, as noted in the preceding section was linguistic reconstruction for which they made use of what we have called the ***comparative method***. Since diachronic analysis involves the use of written records and the reconstruction of extinct languages involves the use of available written records only, the method from that viewpoint has often come to be known as ***philological method***.

In all this the concern is with the different stages of evolution that languages in general or particular languages undergo. By the first half of twentieth century the concern for the historical evolution of languages dwindled and linguistics began to be more aware of the ***structure*** of contemporary languages. Even though diachronic studies involve description of the various stages of language, the term ***descriptive linguistics*** (synchronic linguistics) has been applied exclusively to refer to the description of the structure of a language at a given time without any reference to the earlier phrases of its development. With the structuralist linguistics descriptive linguistics, further, assumed a very narrow sense. By descriptive linguistics the structuralist linguists of the early half of the century meant the analysis and description of the ***speech habits*** of an individual on of a linguistic community with a view to explicating the phonological, morphological and syntactic structure of the spoken language. For the structuralists written records used by philologists presented no language at all; speech alone constituted real language which formed the content of linguistic analysis at all levels.

In present-day linguistics ***descriptive*** (***synchronic***) ***method*** means quite a few things, such as : (1) the construction of a body of description or what we shall call ***a theory of a particular language*** which accounts for the structural patterns at the levels of phonology, morphology, syntax and semantics, (2) the construction of a body of linguistic description i.e. a theory of language which is so universal as to account for the structural patterns of human language as such as realized in all languages. In fact as it is conceived in present-day linguistics, the ultimate goal of descriptive linguistics is to construct a ***universal theory of language*** which will duly account for the nature of human language. In descriptive linguistics it has been a movement from a very narrow approach the study of language to an approach that intends to take care of the universals of human language. This shift in emphasis in descriptive linguistics is caused by the differences in the analytic methods as noted in the first section. The structural linguists adhered to their operational approach to linguistic description (***operational theories***) in which the role of the language data is predominant and no significant departure is made in terms of conclusions from what the data reveal. The entire process of 'theory making' here is dependent on the linguist's operation on the data, and the amount of information the data can reveal. Introspection plays absolutely, as if, no role in the development of the body of description. On the other hand, with the onset of transformational generative grammar, present-day linguistics has come to depend on what is called ***explanatory theories*** i.e. explanatory approach to linguistics description.

The structuralist linguists following behaviourist dogmas of the period in behaviourist psychology revealed what we may call an essential weakness in their approach to explanatory description. This was based fundamentally on the belief that the ***mind*** is not essentially different from its biological substratum, the ***brain***. The mind as such must be far simpler in its structure than any other physical organ of the human body because it is supposed to be only an abstract projection of the complex working of the human brain. Thus on the basis of this assumption the structuralists too for granted and placed exclusive stress, on factors such as the 'habit structure', 'associative connections', 'repetition and training', the motor activities and so forth. Accordingly they thought that knowledge of a language for that matter should develop in course of time through mere habit formation and by means of repetition and training, rather than on the basis of deeper principles of mental organization which would pose greater complexity than any other superfluous aspect of language acquisition.

As seen above, descriptive linguistics has a double goal : the construction of the theory of particular language and a universal of language which accounts for the nature of language. In other words descriptive linguistics involves the study of the grammar of a particular language which will finally lead to the study of ***universal grammar*** which will include particular phonology, morphology, syntax and semantics, and such as study must yield the phonology, morphology, syntax and semantics of universal Grammar. Referring to Chapter 7 of the present work we find these elements presented in a slightly different manner. Descriptive linguistics, according to the scheme presented in the present work, will attempt a description of the *Grammar*, *usage* and *use* of a particular language, and as the final goal will develop a theory which will adequately describe the *Grammar*, *usage* and *use* of human language in general. A detailed presentation of the scheme is reserved for the following chapter. The notions of a particular grammar and of universal grammar become part of the present scheme.

Descriptive linguistics has special significance in ***transformational generative grammar*** just as it had in ***structural linguistics***. It is pertinent to make clear in this context the notion of structural linguistics. In present-day linguistics the term 'structural linguistics' is usually referred to the post-second World War school of linguistics or known also as the Post-Bloomfieldian linguistics whose traces gradually go back from the Bloomfieldians to Bloomfield himself and further back to the beginning of the American school of linguistics with Franz Boas and Edward Sapir at the helm of it. But the term structural linguistics has no exclusive reference to their particular trend in language analysis. What is significant is that with the Post-Bloomfieldians begun an exclusive concentration on the ***structure of language*** than on aspects which used to receive attention from their predecessors. Structural linguistics must be considered that aspect of descriptive linguistics which studies language as an ***objective***, ***structured system*** with the mosaic of phonology, morphology, syntax and semantics figuring in. In this sense descriptive linguistics is much broader than structural linguistics and its scope is tremendously vast. Apart from structural linguistics which should include all the language studies concerned with the structural features of language (all grammatical models including in the part even Chomsky's transformational generative grammatical model and Halliday's

'Scale and Category' Model for which see Halliday, M.A.K.), descriptive linguistics includes ***psycholinguistics***, ***sociolinguistics***, ***biolinguistics***, ***stylistics***, ***metalinguistics***, ***mathematical linguistics*** etc. Every one of the disciplines mentioned above is directly concerned with the description of human language from a specific viewpoint as explicated in chapter 5. Everyone of these discipline is legitimately part of descriptive linguistics since these disciplines are concerned with the working of human language as subject to present-day observations. They equally fulfil all the criteria required by the norms of descriptive linguistics as examined in the present section. We might draw proper distinctions between the field of linguistics and the field of psychology where language too becomes the object of study for gaining better insights into human behaviour, between historical linguistics and descriptive linguistics as seen above, between structural linguistics and non-structural linguistics such as psycholinguistics or sociolinguistics, and within structural linguistics between the Post-bloomfieldian linguistics and transformational generative grammar.

Coming back to the special significance that generative grammar attaches to descriptive linguistics, we might say that principally it is a difference in methodology and in directions, in contrast to the structuralist understanding of descriptive linguistics. Transformational generative grammar considers human language primarily as a generative mechanism. The intricacies of such a generative mechanism has underlying principles which even introspection cannot reach, but an explanation of human language can be arrived at only by accounting for these underlying principles, the mind being the focus of such a study. For this reason present-day generative linguistics has keenly turned to an understanding of the mental principles underlying the language process. Again, for this reason the generative linguistics employs explanatory approach to the study of language and the mind. For the structuralists descriptive linguistics was meant to account for only the phonological, morphological and syntactic structural intricacies of particular language without attempting an accounting of the same for human languages in general. In fact adherence to operational theory making was the root cause for this descriptive restraint. This restraint is overcome with the generative grammar which has resorted to developing explanatory theories. The ultimate goal, again, of descriptive linguistics is to develop an adequate explanatory theory which will account for the acquisition, development, production, and structural features of human language in general from the viewpoint of the universals of human language. This can be achieved by obtaining greater insights into the working and structural features of particular languages. In other words the proper output of descriptive linguistics is the construction of theories of particular languages as well as the construction of a theory of human language.

4. Contrastive Linguistics

Contrastive linguistics makes use of contrastive analysis as its method of language study and as a method of linguistic analysis it is of recent origin. A contrastive study compares the language habits of different individuals groups or of larger linguistic communities and tallies the similarities and differences regardless of the past history, or geographical differences of the material brought under study. Contrastive linguistics must be distinguished from the comparative method of historical linguistics as discussed in section 2. 'Comparative method' is a technical term employed to designate the method of linguistic reconstruction in historical reconstruction, while contrastive study is of recent origin and is used fruitfully as part of descriptive linguistics for comparing different sets of language data.

Contrastive study formed part of the structuralist approach to language analysis and structural linguists made considerable use of this method. Again, contrastive study involved the study of the structural components of languages as such components are isolated for contrastive purposes. As seen, contrastive study is undertaken when language material or more specifically speech habit belonging to different individuals or groups are to be compared for greater comparative insights into the structure of the languages, dialects or idiolects involved. In other words, contrastive study can make use of material from two idiolects, dialects or languages. Comparative study could be made of the speech habits of people belonging to two different professions or occupations, say, farmers, in contrast to fishermen belonging to the same dialect or language. The idiolectic usage of farmers will yield quite a lot of contrasts when compared to the idiolectic usage of fishermen. Again, the language of lawyers could be contrasted with the language of teachers which will yield material for fruitful contrastive study. Contrastive study can be made of two geographically different regions belonging to the same language which might show aspects of dialectical differentiation.

What is known today as 'area linguistics' or 'geographical linguistics' takes care of the contrastive peculiarities and features of the speech habits of sections of population belonging to different well-defined regions. On the basis of such studies ' linguistic atlases' are featured which tremendously help research in linguistics. In such studies centred on geographical differences fruitful analysis can be made of the gaps which language creates in different pats of the same country even though the differences spotted may be minor. Area linguistics can be of great help to highlight the 'linguistic complexity' of a given region from the viewpoint of the number of dialectical and register-wise and idiolectical variations found in the region.

Contrasts of language material requires a component-wise analysis of the pairs of data at one's disposal. Such a study involves, detailed analysis of the components of both the languages. If the study involves the speech habits of people belonging to two different dialects or regional varieties, say for instance the kind of English spoken by the Indians in the Southern and Western parts of India or the kind of English spoken by Indians on the one hand and the people of Shiv Lanka on the other, the first aspect of the study will take care of the phonological differences of the English speakers in India and in Sri Lanka, or the phonological differences of the English speakers in the Southern and Western India. The phonological level itself is something complex when undertaken as a separate analysis. It means a description of the phonological elements of English Spoken by South Indians and compare it with the phonological specificities of the English of West Indians. For any such analysis some definite sample is required to make the description as objective, scientific and specific as possible.

Again, the sample of speakers chosen for the purpose should represent the population which the sample is expected to represent. This is where a contrastive study of the kind mentioned here poses considerable problems. Against the multilingual background as India has, it is not at all easily to spot clear-cut region and specifications as representative of a large region. Such specifications being mostly related to individual regional languages, the linguist is faced with a set of variations that is beyond his capacity to handle for effective comparative studies. Therefore extreme care need to be taken when a sample of English speakers is selected as a group to represent a wider region with a rather complex population.

It is possible to choose a set of Malayalam speakers of English to represent the kind of English spoken in South India. The problem, then, is that there are regional specificities of pronunciation and usage in Tamil Nadu which a speaker of English from Kerala does not in fact represent. The word | b ɔl | *ball* when spoken by a Malayalam speaker has a predominant | 0: | sound in place of the regular English |ɔ| vowel, while the same word is spoken by an English speaker from Tamil nadu with a predominant | g: | vowel. In both instance it is a deviation in either way away from the norm of Received Pronunciation. All the same, for purposes of contrastive study between the language specificities of different larger regions as the south or the West it is better to choose a group which would properly represent sub regions where the pronunciation and usage would have considerable difference. It would also be possible to choose such representative study samples from two groups belonging to the contrasting regions, for instance a group of speakers from Kerala and a group from Gujarat. Then the contrastive study of the phonology of English from Southern and Western India would consist of the phonological contrasts drawn from the language of a Malayalam and Gujarati speaker of English. The Generalizations which the linguist draws must then be true of ***Southern Indian English*** in contrast to ***Western Indian English***. At a later stage the contrastive study could be more specified and made fruitful by a contrast drawn between a group of Malayalam speakers of English and a sample of Tamil speakers of English, and group of Marathi as well as a sample group of Gujarati speakers of English. The contrastive study would then be more complete, specific and detailed.

Drawing Phonological Contrasts: By phonological contrasts would mean the contrastive description of the English phonology of the sample group of south Indians and the sample group of West Indians. The phonological contrasts would include the following specific aspects : (1) the *vowel system* of English as produced by both the study groups. More specifically this would include the study of the monophthongs spoken by the groups; (2) the diphthongs of English as produced by both the study groups; (3) the *triphthongs* if at all they figure in the speech habits of the study groups under consideration (4) the *consonant sounds* as they are specifically produced in the speech of the study groups; (5) the aspects of *stress*, both primary and secondary stress; (6) the *intonation* with attention on the *pitch levels* and tonal contours of their utterances, especially the questions; and lastly (7) the features of *transition* (qualities of *juncture*) as can be distinguished in the speech habits of both the study groups.

Drawing Morphological Contrasts: An examination of a set of sentences produced by the study groups in contrast to each other enable the linguist to compare elements of phonological contrasts and thereby discover features which will be characteristic to each sample and can later be extended in fact to the whole population. Similarly, the investigator then moves on to drawing morphological contrasts as produced by the speakers of both the sample groups. By morphological contrasts we mean the difference that occur in the sentences in regard to especially the process of *affixation* and *compounding*. The morphological contrasts may be less significant than the contrasts in phonology, as aspects of pronunciation will be common both the elements in phonology and morphology. The word | ɔiz | boys produced by a speaker from the South (Kerala) with a predominant | s | phoneme at the end. It is a morphological error just as in the case of a speaker from the West (Gujarat) who pronounces the same word with a predominant | dz | in place of the R.P. | z |. In either case the error is morphological because the speaker either totally deviates from in the latter case, and displaces in the former case the *allomor-*

phic alternations of [–iz, –z, –s] which are the allomorphs of the ***plural suffix morpheme*** {–Z_1}. The same occurrence takes place in the ***genitive morpheme*** {–Z_2} as well as in the ***third singular morpheme*** {–Z_3}. Again the word | ʤʌʤiz | judges, for instance, is spoken by a speaker from the South (Kerala) with a predominant | ʌ | phoneme in place of the regular | i | and thus the allomorphic realization in the specific instance becomes [–ʌs] instead of the regular [–iz]. This is chiefly caused by the shift of the primary stress from the first to the second syllable. In contrast a speaker from the West (Gujarat) produces the same word with a similar shift in the primary stress with a predominant | i: | instead of the regular | i | phoneme transforming the allomorph into an [–i:z] rather than an [–iz]. What is examined here are merely two typical instances of a definable set of such words in which departure from the regular morphenic alternations is spotted.

Lepcical contrasts: Similar contrastive statements could be drawn in regard to the lexical items predominantly employed by the speakers of English in the regions examined above as represented by both the sample groups. The lexical contrasts are not essentially different from the morphological contrasts since lexical (words) treatment is part of morphology and usually known as ***lexical morphology*** as contrasted with ***inflectional morphology***. All the same as part of the contrastive study liberty would be allowed to make use of a morphological treatment as distinct from one at the level of lexical items as used by the speakers under consideration. Lexical contrasts of this sort can be chiefly drawn from the loan words into English which the speakers of the representative groups might be using. As part of the Indian English speech in the South as in other parts of the country peculiar words are often in use which are not necessary found used in other parts from the L_1 background. Closer examination would help us spot several such lexical items which are most commonly used by the speakers of both the regions, for instance.

Syntactic Contrasts: Similarly, any contrastive study of two representative groups which belong to two different idiolectic groups, dialects, regional varieties or languages would yield considerable number of contrasts for the investigators pursual and study. Such syntactic contrasts between groups of speakers would mostly consist of certain predominant patterns of English, Expressions and peculiar usage. This exclusively could constitute the major bulk of constrastive study, provided the specimen sentences are available from the representative group. Syntactic contrasts are greater as one moves away from the idiolectic groups farther to regional L_1 varieties such as, say, the American and British English, or L_2 varieties as in the case of Indian and Ceylonese English. As we examine the L_1 syntactic contrasts of the language of merchants and sailsmen, one is certainly able to find a set of patterns and expressions that are predominant in one group and another set in the second group. Syntactic contrasts are expected to make a very interesting constituent part of any comprehensive contrastive study.

Semantic Contrasts: Another interesting aspect of contrastive linguistics consists of the semantic component of the material in question. By semantic contrasts we mean the differences in the *meaning specifications* of the language spoken by the sample groups. The lexical items which the English speaking Indian's in the south and in the West employ in speech differ considerably on the basis of the connotations that go with the words and expressions. The words *sister* and *brother* as used both in Kerala and in Gujarat are bound to have differences in the speaker's emotional attachment or attitude to the specific meaning content because the meaning content is expressed in every local personal name which in the case of men will carry the suffix *'bhai'* meaning 'brother', and in the case of women will carry the suffix 'ben' meaning 'sister'. It would be in fact an offense to address people by the first name without using these suffixes. This would indicate that the lexical item *brother* and *sister* do possess a much more universal connotation than would be in the use of the same in the South. Again contrastive analysis would indicate (West) can get into the semantic texture of '*smoking a cigarette*' because he is habituated to '*drinking a cigrarette*' as the L_1 equivalent for the same designates '*drinking*' rather than 'smoking'.

Constrastive linguistics as based on the contrastive analysis of languages or levels of languages is chiefly oriented to the *teaching of second* or *foreign languages*. Contrastive linguistic studies have been of considerable help to language teaching since such a study as outlined on the preceding pages comes to the aid of the teacher and the students to recognize the areas of difficulties in the second language. One of the such fundamental pedagogical purposes of contrastive linguistics is to lay bare the areas of *help* and of *difficulty* to the second language bearer in the L_2 in contrast to the L_1 as seen above. It is possible to develop for purposes of teaching a detailed parallel, contrastive description of the L_1 and the L_2 from the aspects we have just noted, and bring to the notice of students these contrasts on the one hand, and pay special attention to the problem areas in the second language which the learners find difficult to master. Apart from the pedagogical implications for the teaching of second languages, contrastive linguistics aims at developing contrastive structural descriptions of dialects, regional varieties or languages as part of the grammar of a language. Research has in fact not fully tapped the resources of the contrastive method of developing theories of language.

7

The Grammar, Usage and Use of Language

1. Vertical and Horizontal Dimensions

Language as a rule tends to overrule the limits that linguists usually set for it. It is a very complex phenomena and stretches far and wide in terms of the viability that it poses for life. Language as employed by humans for purposes of social communion and so on possesses a double dimension in its working, and this double dimensions affects the integrity of any attempt to study it as an object of human observation and introspection. These two dimensions which are so interlinked are (i) the *historical* and (ii) the *spatial* dimensions of human language. The historical dimension is *vertical* while the spatial dimension is *horizontal* by nature. By the historical or vertical dimension we mean that language is a changing and evolving factor even though the aspect of 'language change' is rather looked down at in present day descriptive linguistics. Language as *human behaviour* on the one hand and language as an abstract *structural system* on the other is subject to historic development or degeneration because the entire spectrum of human language is dependent on a community which develops it and makes use of it as a speech system for a variety of purposes, and again, depends on agents who makes use of the language as a system of writing. A language survives as a writing system, even after the active use of the language in a community ceases to be, so long as there are written records which preserve the codified material of the language. The survival of the language for centuries in its speech system and its subsequent survival exclusively in writing as in the case of most classical languages (Ancient Greek and Sanskrit for instance) is typical of its historical susceptibility. It is one thing to concentrate on the present structural features of a modern language, English for instance, and to study only the structural features as it is relevant to the present-day speech communities, and it is quite another to view language from the historical perspective of its changing and evolving development, if we call the process so. It is not that the descriptive structural linguist should always pay attention to the historical implications of the structural description which he undertakes, but a historical consciousness will permit the linguist to view structural complexities from a much broader perspective especially as a result of the complex structural evolution that a particular language undergoes. The structural features of phonology, morphology, syntax and semantics which the investigator examines at a given point in history must certainly be seen as the end result of a complex evolution parallel to the sociological evolution which the linguistic community undergoes. This is the vertical (historical) dimension language that the investigator at a given period of history must be conscious of.

Language as spoken by a vast community has yet another parallel dimension which the linguist pays attention to: this is the spatial dimension of language. The complexity of language with its variety and change can be properly understood only in relation to the double dimension: vertical (historical) and horizontal (spatial). By spatial dimension of language we mean the geographical (extended) spread of a language in terms of the extensiveness or density of population which speak the language. Just as a language is spread in time in terms of its development and existence from a particular period to another in history, a language is equally spread spatially in terms of it geographical extension. In so far as descriptive linguistics is concerned this spatial extension of language which we have presently called its horizontal dimension is significant. Language in concrete is spoken by individual members of a community. This individual has a set of roles to play i.e. he is at a given time, say, a professional, a friend, a husband, a father, a brother, a neighbour etc. depending on the social environment in which he finds himself. Everyone of these roles has got much to do with the specification of his language. Whether he makes use of the formal, informal, standard non-standard, or general language depends on the particular situation he finds himself in. The language that the person speakers as a professor in teaching his class or as a professional in formal situations in bound to be different from what he speaks at home with his wife or daughter. Several of these specifications are part together in what we call the idiolectic use of a language. This will be more technically and elaborately treated in Sec. 4. of the present chapter where we shall be dealing with the *use* aspect of language.

We may refer to the term 'idiolectic group' since by idiolect we mean the linguistic specifications of one individual speaker in contrast with that of another speaker. Any structural description for that matter can be legitimately undertaken on the presupposition that there are linguistic aspects considerably common between two speakers of the same language. If only is this presupposition correct can any linguistic research be undertaken. All research is based on the presumption that there are enough of patterns basic and common to the individual speakers of a community. Similarly, in the same manner, the speech habits of individuals vary so much in specifications that we are permitted to talk of idiolects. The term 'idiolectic group' becomes relevant as there are several intermediary stages of linguistic patterning between the dialect of a language and an idiolectic specification. There stages are dependent on registorial groupings such as a professions and occupations, economic groups, ad so on. Since such registorial grouping can not be distinguished from the idiolect of an individual, I have used for present purposes the term 'idiolectic group' which should include all individual language specificities within a given dialect or regional variety of a language.

The bases of the hierarchical spatial distribution of language constitute the idiolectic variations which cannot be easily subjected as such to any investigation for its own sake. The horizontal (spatial) dimension of language, in other words, consists essentially of an indefinable set of idiolects, virtually as many idiolects as there are the speakers of a language. The next higher level in the hierarchy of the linguistic community falls between the idiolect as used by the individual speaker and the dialect spoken by a large section of the community which is more or less geographically distributed. This is the idiolectic groups we have spoken of. Therefore the *idiolects*, the *idiolectic groups* (the language of salesmen as different from that of farmers) and the *dialects* constitute the most regular levels within a language, so far as the hierarchical spatial distribution is concerned. With language of an international nature we find that there is another level in the hierarchy on the bases of the regions or countries where the langauge is spoken. This is true of English for instance. This level in the spatial dimension falls between English as a language and any given dialect of English. We call this level a *regional variety* such as British English, American, Australian or Canadian English. Indian English we say is such a regional variety of English language.

We are so much concerned with the two dimensions of language which we have called vertical (historical) and horizontal (spatial) because the structure of langauge and the levels that we shall pose as constituting the anguage have much to do with these dimensions. Language changes not only historically but also spatially as we look at it from these perspectives. As we shall examine in the following sections, the structure of human language is complex enough to elude any escapist or biased explanation that we shall ascribe to it. Language is not constituted of any one level on any one aspect; nor is it on the one hand a mere *process* to be explained out by 'habit formations' or 'stimulus-Response-associations', or on the other a mere *formal system* (structured system) to be accounted for merely by a few structural levels. Any biased one-sided explanation of human language will not necessarily account for all the complex features that language manifests. The structuralist linguist's identification of human language with a few structural features, and the behaviourist psycholinguists identification of language with a few aspects of language behaviour will tend, essentially to leave and the 'substantiality' on the one hand and the 'animosity' on the other of language as it becomes susceptible to study by the linguist. The living language must not lose its living-touch by becoming subject to study by the linguist.

It is with the distinctions DE Saussure drew between la langue and la parole that a water-light figuration began developing between what he called the language (la langue) and speech (la parole), and the so-called la language became the formal object of descriptive linguistics (for further discussion on this point, see Ch. 6 : Sec. 3). But with the on set of transformational generative grammar we are once again drawing closer upon closer association between the two dimensions of language. These two dimensions of human language are labeled in my earlier works as the *aspects* (1) and *aspect* (2) of langauge: language as a *process* (human speech) and langauge as the *content* of this linguistic process. Both these constitute part of descriptive linguistics in contrast to, say, historical linguists, and within descriptive linguistics we shall certainly, for the sake of clarity is treatment, distinguish between structural linguistics and psycholinguistics, for, instance. As stressed in ch. 6., Sec. 3. The functional aspects of language acquisition, development and production constitute the formal object of psycholinguistics, and the structural aspects which Saussure called 'language' proper become the formal object of structural linguistics. Descriptive linguistics must therefore be kept open to include all these sub-disciplines whose formal object is one or other aspect of human language studied for its own sake in contrast to a science like psychology which studies language as a means to the exploration of human behaviour.

Descriptive linguistics therefore has to concern itself with the totality of human language experience and an adequate description of the structural features of language will necessarily include aspects of language behaviour in line with say for instance generation and transformation as processes have become part of the generative transformational grammar which is in fact concerned with structural linguistics. Again the terms 'performance' and 'creativity' designate processes and constitute essential aspects of human speech (aspect 1 above) and at the same time have become integral part of present-day structural description of language. In an attempt to provide an explanatory theory of universal langauge behaviour and a description of the particular language as it is subject to our observation and experience, present-day linguistics tries to account for linguistic facts which on the one hand include dimensions of ***linguistic behaviour*** such as 'voicing' or 'verbalization in sounds or 'mapping' or 'transformation' in grammar, and on the other hand include dimensions of linguistic ***structural aspects*** such as the structure of the sound | k | or | g | or surface-deep structure in grammar.

An accounting of the multiple structures: phonological, grammatical and semantic, multiple levels: the Grammar, usage and use, multiple dimensions: historical (vertical) and spatial (horizontal) and multiple aspects. The behavioural and structural aspects renders the theory of language exceptionally complex. There is not use shutting one's eyes on aspects of language which we find problematic or beyond the scope to account for or do the same for petty methodological reasons that cannot be substantiated. If the structuralists were blamed for exclusive preoccupation with phonological and morphological analysis' of languages, the transformationally grammarians are equally blamed for their syntactic attempts that have not taken them further than the analysis of a few sentences. All attempts of this kind have their limitations, all the same a comprehensiveness of treatment in an explanatory direction cannot fail to evoke some sense of intellectual satisfaction in our approach to the science of linguistics.

2. The Grammar of Language

The distribution and spread of language in space and time and the variation that is essentially part of language in these double dimensions and right across the phonological, grammatical and semantic components of human language calls for the introduction of three distinct levels in the structure of language. These three levels as we shall see below cuts right across what we usually call the components of language: phonology, grammar and semantics. To avoid greater intricacy a division between morphology and syntax at this level is avoided. The morphological and syntactic aspects are conveniently treated together under grammar for the time being. The three levels a discussion are:

The *Grammar*, *Usage* and *use* of language. These three will be labeled throughout as the level of the grammar (with capital G), the level of usage and the level of use. Level (i) : the grammar consists of all aspects of language and all structural components which constitute the *core* of human language. By core aspects we shall mean all structural elements in language which is unchanging and permanent and form the very foundation of human language, in contrast to those elements which are more and more accidental, peripheral as well as the elements which are susceptible to change in the vertical and horizontal dimensions discussed in section 1. So far as the nature of language and its behaviour are concerned we shall have to properly distinguish between the permanent and the accidental, deeper and the peripheral changing and the unchanging elements of language. Therefore the three levels we are posing will account for all these elements as mentioned above and attempt to reflect the unity that language essentially has as one and the same mode of human behaviour.

While level (1): the grammar accounts for all that is permanent and substantial in language, level (ii): usage and level (iii) : use account for whatever is changing, accidental, and peripheral and what in fact in directly related to the spatial and temporal stretch and distributions with all the variations that are part of language. All the three levels: the grammar, usage and use, we said cut right across the three major components of language : (1) the phonology, (2) grammar, and (3) semantics. It means that every one of the three levels has constituent components as figuring in the structure of language in its entirety. The level of the grammar consists, thus, of what we shall call (a) core phonology, (b) core grammar and (c) core semantics; the level of usage consists of (a) phonology, (b) grammar and (c) semantics and lastly the level of use comprises (a) phonology, (b) grammar and (c) semantics. It is thus one and the same set of major components distributed as constituents of the triple levels posed here. The phonology of the Grammar, of usage or of use is not *different* in any way from the ***phonological component*** which maps the surface structure sentence on to the phonetic representation. The distinction drawn in the present and in the following chapters is merely one of levels and to find adequate explanation for the linguistic complexity which we are facing including the two-dimensional variation that is apart of language.

The *Grammar* of language (level i) comprises all elements which render the language permanent and stable. On the on hand we attribute to human language the characteristic of change, and on the other, we know that human language exhibits a functional stability and *substantiality*. When De Saussure speaks of *la langue* and *la parole* he is attributing to language a fundamental substantiality in terms of the *la langue* which constitutes the language proper as an objective structured system with a permanence of its own, in contrast to *la parole* (speech) which has essential fluctuating and peripheral nature. 'Speech' is a relatively passing phenomenon and what the linguist can catch hold of for description is the 'language'. This must be the background of Saussure's concern with la language as the formal object of linguistics. Composed, again, to the features which are stable both in the process and system of language, the changing elements are so minute and insignificant. What at this point we mean to stress is that human language has some level of substantiality which undoubtedly make language somehow independent of the speaker. Speakers come and go; speakers use or do not use a language, but the language remains and is passed on from generation to generation. This is a characteristic which places language certainly *above* the speaker as an individual.

Whatever constitute this central core of language and whatever renders language the substantiality we call the grammar of language. This is not the whole thing. There are levels within the Grammar which are the same in all languages. In other words at the innermost core of language we find aspects, levels, dimensions and components which make language a universal phenomenon posing the type of essential and fundamental unity that we find between the languages of the world. This level of the grammar which renders language a universal phenomenon is labeled as the *level of universals*. On the other hand, there is a level within the Grammar of a language which renders the language unique and different from all other languages. Language is a universal phenomenon; all the same every community speaks language with some sets of differences which are both ***behavioural*** and ***structural***. This level of the Grammar of language is called the ***differential level*** indicating that this level is responsible for the differences between languages and for their uniqueness.

The two levels: universal and differential, again cutting right through the three major components yield the following sets: (1) ***universal phonology*** and ***differential phonology***, (2) ***universalgrammar*** and ***differentialgrammar***, and (3) ***universal semantics*** and ***differential semantics***. All these aspects together constitute the grammar of language. A comprehensive description of the nature of the grammar of a language must also include two perspectives from which these levels and aspects should be viewed (1) the ***behavioural*** and (2) ***structural*** perspectives of universal phonology, differential phonology, universal grammar, differential grammar, universal semantics and differential semantics. Language is not a share mosaic of forms and meanings; language as has been said is a rule-governed behaviour; the levels, aspects, components and dimensions which the linguist labours to account for are in continuous interaction with each other as part of this behaviour. There are structural and behavioural components which the linguist will not neglect as the following sections and chapters of this book aim at explaining.

Universal Aspects of the Grammar

We shall have to ask a very fundamental question at this point: what makes a language like English what it actually is and different from all the rest of the languages in the world? This is key-question and if and when we are able to find solution to this problem, we shall have found a substantial answer to the puzzling nature of human language. Certainly the present book is not even to be taken as attempt for a solution; it is only an attempt to provide a direction to the solution a remote possibility. A discovery of the entire structure of what we have labeled the ***grammar***, I believe, will provide the cue to the problem mentioned above. The human language, as we have seen it, has certain universal properties which make a language identical with what all the rest of the humanity speaks. These properties enable us to speak of 'human language', and somehow or other make 'human language' different from the particular language which the individual speaks. Such an account of the universal grammar will consist primarily ***abstractions*** of rules, levels, components and properties which are concretely shared by and realized in a particular language. These abstractions, again, which of themselves are not explicitly part of the linguistic competence of an individual speaker so long as he does not term his attention over to the universality of language which he shares in, constitute the ***theory of language*** (in the extinct sense of the term) which the linguist is concerned with. Again, the same set of abstractions which function as the abstract properties of the individual speaker's linguistic competence constitute the 'theory of language' in the individual speaker's cognitive structure. The difference are significant; the linguist is concerned with the theory of language from two perspective: the set of abstractions that constitute only the universal properties of language, and the set of abstractions which constituent both the universal and differential properties of a language. The former will be what we call the ***universal theory of language***, and the latter will form the ***theory of a language*** (say, English). There can be no theory of a particular language without the basic universal aspects figuring in as shared by that language.

Our search for the universal aspects of the Grammar of language will certainly meet with considerable material which belong to this dimension of language. The role of a ***syllabic unit*** as something which makes speech itself possible can be taken as a typical instance of the ***phonological*** aspect of the ***universal*** dimension of the ***Grammar*** of language. The structure of syllable as a unificatory level between the segments and the word takes the central place in the phonological component of language. It is a matter of differential phonology whether the syllabic unit of language is structured by a combination of two or three consonant sounds and a vowel sound, one consonant and one vowel, a vowel alone or by a syllabic consonant alone. But the fact that a vowel as carrying sound, as a sonorous sound, is at the heart of a syllable and that the syllabic unit of word is structured around it is something essentially part of the phonological component itself and most basic to language. We are concerned with the fact that the structure of the syllable, as making the very phonological component possible must be part and parcel of the Grammar of all languages constituting part of the phonology of the universal dimension shared by a particular language.

'Nominalization' and 'verbalization' as two very basic constituent parts of a sentence in human language can be taken as a typical instance of the *grammatical* aspect of the *universal* dimension of the *Grammar* of language. The very structure or organization of an ordinary sentence of the human language requires that the sentence attempts to signify one way or another, a subject who (or which) undertakes or undergoes some experiences or is predicated of some qualitative or quantitative feature of experience. The nominalized element of the sentence takes care of the *subject* of the experience and the verbalized element takes care of the *experience* itself. There can be absolutely no human language whose sentence structure one way or other expresses these two elements in terms of the two contrastive units: (1) the NP (Noun Phrase) and (2) the VP (the Verb Phrase). We have here an example figuring in the *grammar* of the *universal* dimension of the *grammar* of a language, which the grammar shares with the grammatical properties of all languages.

The notion of the universals at the levels of the semantic component is far too complex. At the semantic component of language the universals consist of the semantic units and specifications. The complexity of this level comes from the fact that it is at the level of semantics that language as a formal systems of signs and the world of conceptual content of the mind meet (For details see *psycholinguistic Foundations*). One and the same component is viewed at this level on the one hand as the *linguistic content*, and on the other as the *conceptual content* of the mind. One is able to enlist *experiences* which are most basic to man everywhere in the world. Linguistic (conceptual) contents related to food-habits, housing, parts of the body, social behaviour such as marriage, various basic human relation etc. are aspects of the very life of man belonging to any community. These linguistic contents constitute the ***semantics*** of the ***universal*** dimension of the ***grammar*** of a language.

Differential Aspects of the Grammar

The counterpart of the universal aspects of language is the ***differential dimension*** of every language which as we have seen renders the language particular and unique. The initial question as to 'what makes English language exactly what it is? Can only be talked with at this level. It we are in a position to isolate those differential features of English, and say that exactly these features are unique to English language and not in tauto founds else where, thus we will have found the answer to the question. An accounting of the differential features of a language along with those universal aspects which are realized in the particular language will yield the ***theory of a particular language*** or what is today known as '***the grammar of a particular language***'. Those aspects of the phonology, grammar and semantics of a language which will figure in at the level of the grammar constitute what is most fundamental to the language and we have called them core phonology, core grammar and core semantics. The differential aspects of these we shall call ***differential phonology, differential grammar*** and ***differential semantics.***

The phonological organization of English, for that matter, is an aspect that belongs to the differential phonology of English. English language in a specific and well-defined manner shares in the universal phonetic system by means of a system of phonetic representation that consists of, say, forty-five phonemes with which the entire phonological organization of English takes place. So far as the structure of particular phonemes is concerned English shares in the universal phonetic system, but again what makes this language unique is the sequences of these phonemes to form the lexicon of English which as such it does not share with the lexicon of any other language in the world except for the loan words the language has from a variety of other languages.

The set of inflections the English language makes use of, and the specific word-order with the use of a set of prepositions are unique to English language the way they function to form the sentences of English. The English prepositional phrases such as ***on top of the mountain***, ***in the same manner***, ***at 7-00 a.m. on Monday, 6th January 1979***, etc. following the English verb are unique features in the syntax of the language. The differential grammar of English (the grammar of the differential dimension of the Grammar of English) will account for these features.

The differential semantics of English (the semantics of the differential dimension of the grammar of English) should include the ***semantic specifications*** which determine uniquely the socio-cultural experiences and relations of the English-speaking community whichever variety of English we may refer to : British, American or Canadian. Such unique features constitute the differential semantics of English. Certain aspects of the differential features could be repeated (found to occur) in certain other language also; but the fact that such features of phonology, grammar and semantics ***do not*** constitute part of the universal dimension of language makes item differential by nature and add to the uniqueness of the language in question.

3. The Level of Usage in Language

Among the three levels of language which is said to cut across the components of phonology, grammar and semantics, we have seen that the ***grammar*** figures in as the first and the innermost, ***usage*** as the second and ***use*** as the third and the most extrinsic of the three insofar as a language is concerned. A distinction of this kind in terms of the levels of language does away in fact with considerable confusion that has arisen in regard to the relation or difference between grammar and usage. We have so far distinguished between the ***grammar*** (with a capital G) and ***grammar*** the first constituting the core of language and whatever is relatively unchanging and most fundamental, and the second constituting part of all the three levels: the Grammar, usage and use.

What in fact do we mean here by usage? We could say that among the three levels usage is most worthwhile to consider because it is directly related to the two dimensions we were concerned about in the beginning of the chapter: the vertical (historical) and the horizontal (spatial). If the grammar of a language is the principle for its stability, oneness and unity, usage is the principle behind language change on the one hand and variation on the other. As the principle of change in course of the historical development and evolution of language, the usage level of language subsumes, to itself the impact that temporal variation can have on language. While the grammar with its core components of phonology, grammar and semantics sustains the stable and substantial nature of language, usage permits changes and variation in language. The term *change* we may employ to designate historical change and *variation* to designate spatial differences as we will see identical below and have explained in section 1 of the chapter. The historical existence (survival) of a language calls for adjustment with and accommodation to the changing and evolving community which uses the language. For a language to survive the list of historical flux it has to be by nature accommodate to the demands, on the one hand for stability and substantiality and on the other for evolution and change. If a language cannot keep up to these demands, it breaks sooner on later and entirely new developments will take place. What therefore enable a language to keep up to the demands of stability and change are respectively the two levels of the grammar and usage. The level of usage therefore allows the language enough flexibility to change in line with the socio-cultural developments taking place in a community.

On the other hand, usage is also the principle which permits the language to succumb to the variation which is part of the spatial distribution of a language. By spatial distribution we have meant the geographical spread of a language in regard to its idiolectic groups, dialects, and regional varieties. English language for instance is not one simple language spoken by a homogeneous community of people. The basic idiolectic groups of limitless variety, a number of dialects, and further as a typical instance, a number of regional varieties (Natural Varieties) constitute what we call the English language. Here again we face a serious dichotomy: What constitutes these variations, and what still provide us the sense of substantiality in regard to the oneness of language ? It is a dichotomy between ***linguistic substantiality*** one of the one hand, and ***linguistic variations*** on the other. The term 'substantiality' has been used so far in the same sense as used in the present context to mean 'the intrinsic unification' of language as an objectively structured system relatively independent of the speaker as an individual. This dichotomy, again, is resolved in regard to the relevant features of the linguistic structure only by postulating the two distinct levels of the grammar, on the one hand, and usage on the other. As in the case of historical changes (vertical variation), in spatial (horizontal) variations too and ***in particular***, the grammar of a language functions as the principle of unity and substantiality while the level of usage functions as the principle of variations. While the grammar sustains the need for unity in the geographical spread (distribution) of language, usage sustains the impact effected on the language by the fact of variation.

Looking into the details of what we have called 'spatial distribution', we find that usage penetrates all aspects of language and cuts, again right through the three major components of language: phonology, grammar and semantics. This would mean that usage as the changing and variant aspects of language includes all the three components as mentioned above. Thus usage includes whatever aspect of a language that is susceptible to change. An examination of the historical development of English and an investigation through the Old English, Middle English, Modern English, and contemporary English will provide material on the basis of which a description of the usage level of English language can be established, so far as is historical dimension is concerned: 1. The ***phonology*** of the ***historical aspect*** of usage may be illustrated in terms of the phonological alternations that the history of English has reveled throughout. English words as we use them today have a traceable phonological history. The Great Vowel Shift was concerned with the 'long stressed vowels' of English during the middle ages. The high vowels became diphthongs. The middle English ride | ri:d | became modern English ride | raid |. This vowel shift affected hundreds of English words such as ***life***, ***hide***, ***wide***, ***side*** etc. The Sound | e: | became | i: |, | o: |

became | u: | or | u | in words such as *reed*, *heel*, *queen*, *deep* and so on, *mood, shoot*, *cool* and *fool*, and took, *look* etc. affecting the vowels of hundreds of vowels in English.

2. The *grammar* of the historical aspect of usage can be illustrated in terms of the morphological and syntactic alternations which have occurred in English in course of its historical development. The grammar of English changed in several aspects from Old English to Middle English, and further to Modern English. So far as usage is concerned these grammatical changes are most significant. Structural items (function words) such as the pronouns and the definite and indefinite articles underwent changes. Significant changes occurred in English inflections and derivations. New compounds came to be formed to designate new meanings. There has been a constant shift from 'strong' verbs to their weak forms (ending with -ed suffix). Certain developments took place in the area of tenses and in the structure of the verb phrase. The older '*What they do*' became present-day *'What they are doing*. The model auxiliaries (should, might, must etc.) underwent considerable changes in their structural role.

3. The *semantics* of the historical aspects of usage can be illustrated in terms of the semantic alternations that English language has undergone in course of its history. Semantic alternations occur by way of (i) addition of a meaning specification to the semantic content of a word in the form of an additional conceptual element. The word *cloud* designating the clouds in the sky assumes an additional conceptual element when the same word comes to mean 'a clouded mind', a states of mind. It could be (ii) the addition of another concept while retaining the existing meaning. The word *trunk* apart from all that it means in terms of 'an elephant's trunk', 'tree trunk', etc. has come to designate the concept of 'a trunk-call'. There are a large variety of ways in which semantic changes occur as part of the change at the level of usage (See *Psycholinguistic Foundations* ch. 12 for details).

4. The *phonological* aspect of the second dimension: the spatial distribution of usage can be illustrated in terms of the phonological variation which we are able to spot in the regional

varieties of English language, chiefly British and American English. It is the level of usage, it should be noted, that renders a variation of this kind possible, yet keeping English language itself unified and different from, say French language (the function of unification provided by the grammar) as elaborated in the present chapter. Clear instances of the phonological aspect of the spatial distribution of usage are available in the differences of pronunciation including stress and intonation that exist between the L_1 varieties of British and American English or Between the L_2 varieties of Indian or Ceylonese English. The British variety of ***either*** | aiðə |, ***neither***, | naiðə |, ***ate*** | eit |, ***patron*** | peitrən | or ***glance*** | gla:ns | is contrasted to the American variety of ether | i:ðə |, ***neither*** | ni:ðə |, ***ate*** |ɛt |, or ***patron*** | pəetən | or glance |gləens | while the British employes only predominant primary stress in words such as ***secretary***, territory or laboratory, Americans put a secondary stress on the penultimate syllables of such pollysyllabic words in the form of ***territory***, ***secretary*** and ***laboratory***. These are some instances of the regional differences that are part of the phonological component of language as exemplified from English.

5. The ***grammatical*** aspect of the spatial distribution of usage can be illustrated in terms of the grammatical differences we find between two dialects or regional varieties of a language. Lexicon differences are present in British and American English. While words such as ***insane***, ***gas***, ***truck***, and ***interval*** are predominant in American English, their counterparts ***mad***, ***petrol***, ***lorry***, and ***intermission*** are predominant in the British variety of English. So far as the syntactic element is concerned, the English use more plural verb forms for collective nouns such as in ***The public are*** or ***The government are***..... by contrast to the American use of the singular verb forms as in ***The public is*** or ***The government is***. There are considerable differences in the use of prepositions and often of auxiliaries apart from the differences present in the pattern on intonation.

6. Lastly, the ***semantic*** aspect of the spatial distribution of usage can be illustrated in terms of the semantic differences that are found in the dialects or regional varieties of a language. An examination of a parallel list of words from, again, American and British English would provide us with ample instances of

differences of semantic specifications in terms of conceptual elements that are ***more***, ***less*** or ***different*** in either side. The use of ***gas*** for ***petrol***, ***second floor*** for ***first floor***, and ***rise in salary*** for ***raise in salary*** by the Americans point out to not mere lexical innovations, but to differences in thought and attitudes which require linguistic adaptations to reflect different level of conceptual organization.

The six aspects we have examined indicate the structure of what we have come to call usage in contrast to the grammar on the one hand and use on the other. Differences in all aspects of language are not only a property of language as a historically evolving thing but also a property of a language as used by people belonging to geographically separate regions and different nations. This is a diachotomy we have to account for in our understanding of the nature of human language. As usually come to be explained, usage does not merely consist in the few words, idioms or expressions which change in language, and grammar in a few fundamental rules which are dear to the school teacher. The grammar and usage as seen so far are integral levels of language and penetrate an take care of all the three fundamental components of language" phonology, grammar and semantics. This enable use to see the substantiality and unitary nature of language on the one hand, and the change and variation of language on the other. These are structural principles which control the behaviour of human language.

4. The Level of Use in Language

If the Grammar of a language consists of whatever is fundamental, stable and substantial, and usage consists of whatever undergoes change and variation in language, by use, lastly we mean the individual speaker's freedom ultimately (i) to employ one form or expression for another as situationally determined, and (ii) to deviate considerably within the scope of the norm which permits greater individual variation. Use is the level of language exercised by the individual speaker. The grammar and the usage levels of language come to bear upon the level of the individual speaker's 'use' of language because language becomes a reality only at this level. The grammar assigns in its turn the fundamental and essential rules pertaining to the construction of a sentence and usage specifies the choice of alternative forms and expressions as indicated by the dialectical or regional variety. While the Grammar assigns to the sentence, for instance, the rules of 'passive construction', the level of usage assigns to the sentence the set of forms and the semantic content as specified by one variety of language in contrast to another variety. The grammar assigns to the sentence the essential and obligatory rules of phonology, grammar and semantics pertaining to the production of the sentence, while usage assigns the phonological, grammatical and semantic rules which specify the particular variety of language as against other varieties. While the basic phonological structure of the word *laboratory* is governed by the rules of the grammar of English in terms of the distinctive features which constitute every phoneme, and the sequence of phonemes which constitute the word, the placing of the strong primary stress on the second syllable and a weak secondary stress on the penultimate syllable by British speakers, as against the placing of the primary stress on the second syllable along with a considerably strong secondary stress on the penultimate syllable of the word by American speakers are governed by the differentiating rules of English usage as determining both the varieties of English.

Use, on the other hand, is built on the foundations of the grammar and usage. Use is the specific business of the speaker as one who actuates language behaviour. It consists primarily in a set of determinations and specifications which, as we shall say, the *idiolect* of the individual imposes on the construction and production of a sentence. If whatever is obligatory and fundamental to the construction of the sentence is assigned by the grammar level, and whatever specifies the individual's sentence as part of a particular dialect or variety is assigned by the level of usage, then whatever the individual speaker's *idiosynchratic specificities* (phonological, grammatic and semantic) which govern the final production of the sentence is assigned by the level of use.

There are several aspects of idiosynchratic specificities which constitute the individual's idiolect. No structural description can encompass the idiolectic variation of a language since such a thing varies from idiolectic group to group and further from individual to individual. As noted in detail in Ch. 3. Sec. 4, idiolects constitute the final building block of a language and the level where human language is actuated as a physical reality. At the level of use (as we may call it ***idiolectic use***) the human individual who possesses the creative, generative language mechanism (faculty) produces the sentences of his language (collectively and situationally called a discourse). In the creative production of the sentences of his language he functions at three levels as seen above : (i) he adheres to the fundamental and obligatory rules of the Grammar of his language (ii) he employs the options that he is granted at the level of usage so far as his dialectic, regional specificities are concerned, and (iii) he exercises the domains of idiolectic variations and departures permitted to him as an individual speaker governed by features such as the particular situation, the speaker's state of mind, the physical environment, and the physiological specifications of his physiological specifications of his peripheral (speech) mechanism. The sentence that the speaker constructs is determined by all these conditions. This is the domain (level) of 'use'.

There are ***phonological*** specification which characterize the level of use as exercised by the individual speaker. The word ***laboratory***, for instance, governed at the level of usage by the two major regional variations: British ***laboratory*** and American ***laboratory*** from the stress viewpoint will consist of several further variations at the level of the use as actually spoken by individual Englishmen and Americans in varying situations. The two forms of regional variations which we are able to reproduce as one against the other, are infact ***abstractions*** of the large number of idiolectic variations among both groups of speakers. These specifications at the level of phonology will occur in the form of, for instance, alternation in the distinctive features of vowels and consonants, differences in stress placement, changes which occur as a result of pitch differences, changes which result from the alternation in the 'speed' of sentence production as specified by the situation, and above all the changes resulting from the placement of the particular word in the sentence as determined by the lexical (phonological, morphological environments).

There are *grammatical* specifications which characterise the level of use of exercised by the individual speaker. The individual language is characterised by idiomatic expressions, slang elements, dialectic and collegial features which considerably influence the grammar of the individual's speech. There are mannerisms such as 'you know' 'you see' or 'you under stand' which people sparsely make use of, especially when the required fluency of speech is not the required fluency of speech is not obtained by the speaker in a particular moment. Then there are linguistic deviations of serval kinds including structural errors, errors in the use of pronouns, articles and prepositions which though known to the speaker correctly, one used erroneously. These are aspects of the use level of language which do not ordinarily form part of the structural description of the language, but are intimate aspects ogf the language of the speaker. A contrastive study of the so-called 'colloquialism' of a language with the standard language would reveal the intensity of such idiolectic specificities.

There are lastly, *semantic specificities* which characterise the level of use as exercised as the individual speaker. The semantic component of the individual speaker's language, of the sentences he constructs are characterised by considerable conceptual differences. The individual's concept of (the meaning of) a particular feature, thing or event is highly determined by the socio-cultural and geographical environment in which he lives. A farmer's concept of 'cosmetics must be very different from that of a film actress; or a village woman's notion of 'fashion' is considerably different from that of urban lady. These are extreme instance. But there are *more or less* of conceptual elements which constitute the meanings of one individual's sentence as against another's. The level of use is what thus relates language with the individual speaker and enables language to be actuated in the form of physical sentences.

5. Universals and Differentials

The notions of *universals* on the one hand and *differentials* on the other can cause us some concern. After having seen the scope of the levels of the grammar, usage and use, it will be helpful to dwell upon these two properties of language. Our ability as investigators into the nature of language is not questioned in so far as the questions which are investigated belong exclusively to a particular language and so far as the conclusions are not carried over from the one language investigated, to all languages in the world. An attitude of this kind is detrimental to the growth and the very possibility of any science, especially of one like linguistics. What is our rational behind extending a conclusion either theoretical or practical from a ***sample*** consisting only a very limited number of members to the ***populations*** which will be incredibly larger than the sample? An extension of this kind is possible only if the behaviour of the sample with which we are concerned is established as belonging to or proceeding from the very nature of the sample which constitute part of the larger population. In every type of research this is what happens. The scientist who examines the property of some chemical deals only with some speciman of it; or one who subjected water to hydrolysis for the first time did so only with a awfully little quantum of water and found it composed of H_2O. It was somehow possible for the scientist who examined the property of a particular chemical or of water to move towards making a statement which was descriptive of not just a few ounces of water or a few grams of chemicals but of the immeasurably vast world of water or of the particular chemical. Some logical principle of an existential implication is certain at work in drawing conclusions of this kind; and we shall call these ***universal conclusions*** arrived at through a process of what is known an inference. But once the inferential conclusion is drawn on the basis of some feature of experience, the scientist then bases all his further conclusions and whole world of theory on some such simple experiment or experience. He doesn't in fact every time go back on his experiment or experience for every further statement that he is able to make. In fact, this is a world of ***conceptual organization*** posited against the world of human experience which enable us as theoreticians to make any progress at all kind is just a starting point on which the human mind is capable of constructing a whole body of conceptual organization. This is what we call a ***theory***. The same is true of the ***theory of human language*** and the ***theory of a particular language***.

For reasons which are examined above, it will be groundless for any one to question our ability to move from a particular thing to a universal characteristic which we believe that the particular thing partakes. The rationale behind such an extension lies in that the characteristic noted in the particular thing constitutes part of the very nature (proceeding from what the philosopher's called the 'essence') of the thing under study. The entire world of language as spoken by individual speakers through out the world is inaccessible to any enthusiastic investigator. Just as, therefore, an investigator examines some simple language data and legitimately extends his linguistic conclusions to the particular dialect, regional variety and further to the entire language without hesitation, the linguist can legitimately extend his conclusions from one language which he examines to language on earth so long as the characteristic or rule that has become subject to his study is seen as belonging to the very ***nature of human language***.

In other words, there can be no denial of the legitimacy of the linguist's conclusions moving from his exclusive study of just one particular language to what we call the ***universals*** of human language, just as any investigator extends his conclusions from his examination of some data of a language to the patterning of the whole language. Language as a property of human behaviour and its content has dimensions which on the one hand renders it a universal phenomenon, and on the other a phenomenon which is unique and particularly restricted to a linguistic community. This is a dichotomous character of human language just as it has other dichotomous properties as its temporal (historical) and spatial extensions. Whatever characteristics and aspects render it a ***universals*** of language, and on the other hand whatever makes it particular and unique as different from other languages we will label as ***differentials*** (This is a distinction already drawn in The ***Psycholinguistic Foundations***).

While the universals (or universal properties or dimensions) make all language on earth one and the same, the differentials (or differential properties or dimensions) make a language different from all the rest. It is a blend of universals and differentials what constitutes the human language as on the one hand a set of universal abstractions at several levels, and on the other a set of concrete and physical properties. The dichotomous properties of one and many, of concrete and abstract, of matter and concept are all resolved only in the distinction between the differential and universal properties of language. All the same an absolute demarcation of these two dimensions of language in one particular language will be impossible. There are several reasons for this. The two properties are so blended and have so much of overlaps that we are required to postulate a number of gradations. This would means first of all that there are properties of language (structural and behavioural) which belong absolutely to the very nature of human language with no language an exemption to it. This would mean that if something is to have the label of 'language' (in the sense we understand human language) it will retain these properties) as basic. We may take the 'vowel-consonant distinction' as such an instance which undoubtedly belong to the very nature of language. The distinctive features which distinguish a vowel from a consonant or rather the organization of distinctive features which distinguish vowels from consonants belong essentially to human language without which speech as such becomes impossible. The vowel- consonant combination constitutes the syllable which in turn forms the basic unit of human speech.

Secondly the gradation that is postulated would mean that there are properties which will be true only of most human languages, and not all. We shall not legitimately call these universals, because even if true of most languages these properties cannot constitute universals in the right sense of term as these do not belong to the very nature of language. Among the vowels the phonemic distinction between | i | and | i: | or between | ə: | and | ʌ | may be found in most languages, but an investigation might reveal that there are languages in which a phonemic distinction (with meaning contrast) between these vowels is not made. And we will be in the wrong box by labelling these as universals. Now, properties of this kind as they do not necessarily belong to all languages must be regarded as not universals but differentials because they are differential properties shared by most language, as against the few languages which do not share in such properties.

Thirdly, the gradation that is postulated would mean that differential properties will be shared by many languages which add to their uniqueness and particularity. The | z | and | ʒ | sounds with phonemic distinctions or with distinctive features closer to these are found in most Indo-European languages in one form or other, but these sounds do not form part of the Dravidian languages of South India, in which there is a predominance of S, Ṣ and Sh sounds. These phonological prop erties are not shared by not even *most* languages, but only by a comparatively limited number of them.

Lastly, the gradation of differential properties would mean that there must be found some set of properties which renders a language unique so as to enable us to call one language 'English' as against another, 'Tamil'. The essence of this basic differentiality consists in the specific phonological, grammatical and semantic organization that English has developed as against, say Tamil. Apart from possessing the *universal* properties of human language, a particular language possesses a set of properties it shares with *most* languages, another set of properties which it shares with *some* languages depending on the affiliation it has got with other languages, and another set of properties the particular language possesses as uniquely *its own*. The structure of a particular language comprises all these four levels of properties in the form of a hierarchy with the universals at the base of the hierarchy and the unique differentials at the apex of the hierarchy. The specific phonological, grammatical and semantic organization realised in the particular languages constitute the set of unique differentials which form the apex of the hierarchical structure of a particular language that is postulated in this book.

8
Phonology of Language

1. The phonological component

Language as we have seen is an intrinsically complex form of human behaviour with considerable number of *component-habits* figuring in on the one hand, and a very complex set of *structural features* constituting what we have called the content of this linguistic behaviour i.e. the language itself as a *formal system* of components on the other. Throughout the study we have attempted to make clear that human language in its wholeness may be understood and tackled with only as a unified system consisting of these two aspects: (1) the habit-predominated *process of language* and (2) the *structural system* which forms the content of this process. While psycholinguistics proper studies the former aspect, structural linguistics takes care of the latter aspect. Both must form part of the general descriptive linguistics. Any biased and exclusive concern for either language process or linguistic structure only will not meet the broader issues that the study of human language poses. Similarly, structural linguistics cannot help taking into account the aspect of *writing* in contrast to *speech* both necessarily constituting parts of what we call language. Therefore the system developed and presented in the present word is an attempt to take care of whatever is mentioned above.

There is no wonder that the structuralists of the first half of the present century got so much engrossed in pursuing the study of the phonological features of language; and there is not wonder that the 19th and early 20th century saw the intense development of the ***science of phonetics***, especially the acoustic and articulatory phonetics. All this happened because it is only the features of sound articulation and their organization in relation to the production of the sentences of a particular language that we can have immediate access to. In the production of sentences what the speaker utters and what the listener receives are in fact only a definite sequential ***set of sounds*** and apparently nothing else. Therefore of all the complexities of human language what is immediately accessible to a linguistic investigator, just as in the case of an ordinary listener, are only the sequential set of sounds. It is on the basis of the ***sets of sounds*** as produced by speakers of the large variety of languages all over the world that the 19th century phoneticians developed what we call today ***universals phonetics***. Ch. 2. has outlined the discipline of phonetics and drawn a distinction between phonology and phonetics, which will not be dealt with here. Universal phonetics lists and describes the structural features of the distinctive, definable sounds which constitute the phonetic system of all human languages without entering into the organizational specificities of these sounds in particular languages. Abstracted from the large variety of human languages the universal phonetics has established or rather developed a ***universals phonetic alphabet*** (known generally as the ***International Phonetic Alphabet***), and a system of laws governing the phonetic behaviour of languages. The alphabet as developed by universals phonetic system defines the set of possible sounds which are in part shared by and realized in a particular language. These sounds, again one defined and described in terms of their complex structural features (articulatory features) which are known as ***distinctive features*** including properties that make | p | different from | k | and both different from | r |.

The most apparent ***level*** and one most susceptible to observation, as seen, is the ***phonetic level*** which explains the significant advance the science of phonetics has achieved. The English sentence ***The boy did not understand the message***, readily yields a conspicuous set of sounds which can be distinguished as distinct units by empirical means. The phonetician has been able to define the particular units in the sequence in terms of the ***place*** and the ***manner*** of articulation of the sounds in the mouth. This level in which the sound sequence (the entire sentence as a sequence of sound units) is actuated in the production of language is called the ***phonetic level or representation***. Universals phonetics has been able to isolated the sounds units of languages and develop the universal phonetic system at the phonetic level of language. By means of a detailed description of the distinctive features of the sounds and the rules which take care of their occurrences in the phonetic representation of a particular language, the ***phonetic theory*** of a language is developed; and the ***universal phonetic theory*** is concerned with, as seen above, the comprehensive description of the distinctive features of the sounds which are shared and realized by all languages.

The phonetic representation, all the same, is only extrinsic actuation of a still inner and more abstract level of language which is called the phonological representation. By ***phonological representation*** more specifically we mean that level of language which assigns the phonetic representation to the surface structures of language. In other words the phonological representation as a level of human language ***relates*** the phonetic representation with the surface structures of sentences. Both the phonetic representation and phonological representation together constitute the ***phonological component*** of language, which is the concern of the present section. The sentence examined above ***The boy did not understand the message*** is at the most extrinsic level the product of surface sentence represented first at the phonological level in terms of the phonological rules of English language, and then represented at the phonetic level in terms of the phonetic rules of English language as part of universal phonetic system.

As the level that takes care of the output of the surface sentence that the syntactic structure yields as a result of a process of transformation on the deep sentence, the phonological component assigns rules to represent the sentence at the phonological level and further at the phonetic level. In other words the phonetic representation of a sentence yields the phonetic rules of the production of the sentence in terms of the actual ***articulation*** of the sound sequences which constitute the sentence, and the phonological representation which is more intrinsic and relatively abstract governs the organization of the sound units according to the phonological rules of English language, for instance. The two sets of rules (phonological and phonetic) are relatively distinct and constitute the phonological representation of the sentence in question. Therefore every English sentence, for that matter, as discourse units of English language has (1) the phonological representation governed by phonological rules and (2) phonetic representation governed by phonetic rules and both together constitute the phonological component which specify the relation between the surface sentence as sequence of abstract units and the concrete articulated auditory, sequence of units which the listener hears.

The transition of the phenologically represented and constituted sentence with its surface framework into phonetic representation by means of articulation of the sound sequences governed by the distinctive features of the units we shall call ***phonation***. In other words phonation must be seen as the process of transmitting into the ears of the listener a phonologically represented sentence according to the phonetic rules of the language giving actuation to what we have called the phonetic representation of the sentence. Therefore phonation is the linguistic process which actuates the phonetic representation of a given sentence according to the phonetic rules of the language. The speaker's role, thus begins with the most intrinsic organization at the level of semantic representation and ends with phonation which is the starting point of the process of the starting point of the process of ***communication*** in relation to the listener.

The phonological component, again, is in fact a junction where some significant departure takes place. The phonological component is a turning-point from which an individual either turns over to speech (phonation) or writing. There is no essential sequence between speech and writing; one can speak first and write later or one may write without in fact speaking ór speak without writing. But there is a very fundamental relation between speech and writing since both essentially constitute language activity, both produce language as the content of the process of speech or writing. This essential relation, as both are apparently different language activities, must have its basis at some level. It is at the level of ***phonological representation*** that speech and writing meet. Upto this level of language what goes behind speech and writing are the same. The individual as a speaker or writer has his language structured upto the level of phonological representation where the surface sentence is phonologically organised in terms of the ***abstract representations*** of the sequences of sounds which in fact the phonological representations is). Once the sentence is set according to the phonological rules of the particular language, the individual as a ***speaker*** unaware in fact of the underlying process, proceeds to phonate the sentence by further representing the sentence according to the phonetic rules of the language, and the individual as a ***writer*** instead proceeds to represent the sentence according to the ***orthographic rules*** of the language. This level actuated by the writer we shall call ***orthographic representation.***

In other words, the production of language at the extrinsic level involves a level of 'obligatory' and a level of 'optional' representations which together constitute the phonological component we have in mind in the present context. The phonological representation as such constitutes the obligatory level within the phonological component; the phonetic representation and the orthographic representation together constitute the optional level within the phonological component, since within the phonological component the phonological representation most necessarily constitutes the background and starting point for either the phonetic representation (speech) or the orthographic representation (writing) which between themselves do not have any necessary sequence as seen above.

The basic rationale for the conclusions arrived at above in regard to the relation between the representation at different levels as presented above is provided by the thoroughly studied presence of ***vocalization*** and ***sub-vocalization*** not only found in the reading habits of individuals, but also found present when we write. The almost chocking experience of sub-vocalization (not to mention vocalization) which individuals as a whole experience in writing and in reading must not be overlooked as mere erasable accidental habits, but must be seen as a constituent part of the language activity and as conclusive proof for the fact that the phenetic and orthographic representations respectively proceed from the basic one and the same phonological organization we have labeled as phonological representation which must be looked at as the obligatory level within the phonological component of language. What the writer experiences as sub-vocalization must be the organization of the abstract representations of sounds at the level of the phonological representation as constitute part of the phonological component of language.

2. Behavioural Features of Phonology

It has become clear how language is looked at from three major levels: the ***grammar***, ***usage*** and ***use***, and every one of the three levels is a complex of three constituent elements: ***phonology***, ***grammar*** and ***semantics***. Consequently we spoke of the core phonology, core grammar and core semantics to designate the three constituent levels of what we called the *Grammar*, the phonology, grammar and semantics of the level of ***usage***, and the phonology, grammar and semantics of the level of ***use***. Further we saw that the grammar (the core aspects of language) is constituted by a ***universal dimension*** and a ***differential dimension*** by which it is meant that what constitutes the core aspects of language (the grammar) consists of linguistic elements of phonology, grammar and semantics which are universal and true of all languages, and there is a dimension in every language as part of the grammar which renders the particular language unique and different from all other languages.

The concern in the present section is the phonology constituting part of the Grammar, which we called core phonology. It must be borne in mind that the phonological component we discussed in the preceding section is all-pervading and consequently the phonology of the grammar, the phonology of usage and the phonology part of the level of use together constitute the phonological component. But in all the cases and the same language and one and the same level is viewed from different perspectives. Compared to the triple aspects of phonology, grammar and semantics of the grammar the triple aspects of the levels of usage and use are less significant because the grammar constitutes the major level of language.

The phonology at the level of the grammar of a language represents two dimensions following the double dimensions of the grammar: the ***universal*** aspects and the ***differential*** aspects. In other words we shall have at a given time to account for a universal dimension of the phonology of a language which makes the language same as other languages of the world, and differential dimension of phonology which makes the language phonologically unique and different from other languages. Just as in the preceding section we could speak of ***universal phonetics***, now we shall speak of a ***universal phonology*** meaning that there is a certain level at the phonological representation of language which is universal just as it has counterpart in ***differential phonology*** which makes the phonology of the language unique.

Universal phonology should include all aspects of the phonological component of language which are realized in all languages in the same way. This means that it should take care of both (1) the process aspect and (2) the language (content) aspects. There are universal phonological principles which governs the ***phonological behaviour*** of language and there are principles which govern its ***phonological structure***. The phonological behaviour corresponds to the process aspect while the phonological structure corresponds to the language as content aspect. Just as universal phonetics accounts for the phonetic behaviour (e.g. voicing, valorization) and the phonetic structure of human language in general, and particular phonetics accounts for the participation of a particular language in the universal phonetic behaviour and phonetic structure, universal phonology should account for the phonological behaviour and structure at the level of language as such as realized in all languages while differential phonology do the same in regard to the phonological behaviour and structure of particular language. In short universal phonology will provide an explanatory account of (the theory of) the universal phonological component while the differential phonology will describe the nature of those aspects of the phonological component of a particular language which renders the language unique and different from the phonological component of other languages. Both these theories should include the behaviour and structure of the phonological component at specific levels.

As we have seen the phonological component has certain well-defined functions so far so its relations to the surface structure on the one hand which is part of the syntactic component, and on the other to the phonetic representation which constitute part of the phonological component itself. Attention must be drawn to the structure of the phonological component (Sec.1) and we have seen that the ***phonological***, ***phonetic*** and ***graphic*** representations (as obligatory and optional levels respectively) together constitute the phonological component. The phonological component as a level of language meets certain functional requirements; by phonological behaviour we have exactly meant these functional requirements governed by a set of psycholinguistic laws subject to the process of human language. The phonological behaviour of universal phonology therefore designates and includes all that goes on in the phonological component of language so far as it ***maps***, as generative grammar tells us, the surface structure sentence on to the phonetic representation. The syntactic component of language generates, as we have seen, an infinite set of pairs of deep structure and surface structure sentences. The language assigns a semantic representation to the deep structure which undergoes a process of transformation and the resulting surface structure is subsequently assigned a phonetic representation to the sentence generated at the deep level. By mapping we means assigning a phonetic representation to the surface structure in line with the laws of universal phonetics.

The exact function of the phonological component therefore is to relate the surface structure and the phonetic representation (or graphic representation as an optional level) by an application of the rules of universal phonology by mapping a phonological representation on to the phonetic level to produce the phonetic representation of the sentence. The sentence ***The boy did not understand the message*** must for the time being the viewed as a surface structure sentence which need to be mapped on to phonetic representation by means of its phonological representation. The surface sentence is yet a sequence of abstract entities (formal units) which have not yet found any form of articulation (phonation). The sentence is still only internally conceived at the surface level. The function of the phonological component is therefore to provide the sentence with a proper phonetic mapping (or otherwise a graphic mapping). This is the key function of what we have called the phonological representation. Phonological representation is the process of ***organizing*** the phonological entities (units) which we call the ***phonemes*** (see Sec. 3) according to the rules of universal phonology in general and of differential phonology in particular. The sentence ***The boy did not understand the message***, therefore, receives the respective sequences of phonological units (phonemes). The phonological representation in terms of concreteness falls between the abstract surface level and the most concrete and physically determined phonetic level. As such what is required is a concrete mapping of the abstract units of the sentence on to their physical counterparts. By physical counterparts we mean the articulated (phonated) units of sound i.e. the phonemes articulated according to the phonetic rules of the language.

The language employes the phonological rules for the organization of phonemes to translate the abstract units of the surface structure to the concrete phonetic representation. If attempt an analysis of the phonological representation of the sentence mentioned above the following may be found:

| ðə # b ɔi # did # n ɔt # ʌndəstænd # ðə # mesidʒ

In the above representation the symbol # represents the junctures, the juncture as featured here being significant a part of the phonological representation and further at the phonetic level. As we examine the above description we find the keynotes of what we have labelled as phonological organization of the sentence for the final mapping on to the phonetic representation. The instance examined here is relevant to our explanation of ***behaviour universal phonology*** only from the following perspectives and should be considered central to the universal phonological representation of sentences in language: The phonological representation of a sentence is a ***sequence*** of semi-concrete, inarticulated, unhonated ***phonemes*** which stand midway between the corresponding abstract formed unit at the level of the surface sentence and the concrete (physical) formal unit at the level of phonation. The sequence of phonemes which are assigned by the phonological component invariably assumes a kind of *linearity* in which only one phoneme or a sequence of phonemes can occur in a given unit. This linearity has been recognized as a fundamental principle of language structure from the time of sanssure. The sequential organization of the semi-abstract phonemes at the phonological level is governed by the a number of phonological rules which constitute part of the differential phonology of the language. These rules specify (i) the placing of junctures in lexically determined positions, (2) the number of such phonemic units that should go into the structure of one lexical unit by contrast to another such unit, (3) the organization of phonemes to constitute the lexical items which together in their sequence constitute the sentence, and so on. The list can undoubtedly go on.

The phonological behaviour of the universal phonological component lastly consists of *converting* all the constituent *distinctive features* of phonemes (+ - values in terms of place and manner of articulation, voicing etc.) into their corresponding *phonetic values* by assigning their physical, articulatory features to effect the final phonation. The whole behaviour of the phonological component with its constituent parts is oriented thus to its actuation into the phonetic or otherwise graphic representation.

3. Structural Features of Phonology–I

We have examined the grounds for distinction between the *behavioural features* and *structural features* of the phonological component of language. The preceding section has the role of the number of phonological representations which constitute the phonological component of language, from the viewpoint their phonological behaviour at various sub levels. The phonological component is also a level of language with highly intricate structural features which require explanation. The sentence *The cat has a red mark on the head*, thus exhibits a phonological structure which, again, has its *universal* and *differential aspects* which we do not enter into at this point. The sequence of sounds which constitute the sentence shows that apart from for theoretical purposes it is difficult for us to demarcate the *beginning* and the *end* of every single unit especially where the sequence does not break for the juncture. The sequence of sounds is so much interlinked that one requires meticulous analysis to isolated one sound from another. As we contrast the sequences in the sentence with another set we find some features emerging: Let us contrast *cat* with *cap, has* with *had*, *red* with *bed*, *mark* with *shark*, and *head* with *knead*. The structuralist linguists developed a comprehensive system of contrasting sounds and their sequences and attempted in their linguistic analysis the phonemes and morphemes of particular languages. The contrast we have drawn between *cat* and *cap*, for instance, yields, a set of units | t | and | p |, the pair *has* and *had* yields another set | z | and | d |, the pair red and bed yields | b | and | r |, and further pairs give us the units | ʃ | and | m | , and | h | and | n |. Every one of the above units by its presence in a sequence provides the sequence with a new *meaning*. In other words every sequence which is technically called a morpheme (see Ch. 9) is representative of some conceptual element, concept or conceptual organization (Ch. 12) merely because of the presence of a different sound in the sequence by contrast to another sequence which has another meaning with a different sound. The pairs of sequences (words, morphemes) we have examined: *cat: cap:, has: had, red: bed, mark : shark, head: knead*, are called *minimal pairs* which constitute Paris with only minimal sound differences but with a difference in meaning. Such minimal pairs are considered the starting-point of phonological analysis to extract individual sound units.

The sound units which by their presence in a sequence have been able to signify some meaning are called *phonemes*. In continuous speech (discourses of any kind) a specific form (sequence of phonemes) does not occur in isolation. As constituent parts of discourse, set of forms can be called only relatively similar or identical as these forms occur in a given phonological environment, perhaps preceded and followed by other forms which exert certain definable influences which will be discussed in the section on morphophonemics (Ch. 10).

Therefore even minimal pairs can be called so only in so far as a contrast of one phoneme stands out from any other insignificant contrast which will not be marked in a phonological representation of a words. All the same it is interesting to note that the concept of phoneme is an abstraction and that the ***phoneme*** itself is an ***abstraction***. In this sense every sound (phoneme) which is represented in the universal phonetic alphabet is such an abstraction. Human language in all its complex variety informal elements and in the infinite environments of their occurrence consists of very minimal differences all of which can never be represented in terms of their actual variations. These concrete occurrences of phonemes in their minute phonological differences is known as ***allophanes***. In fact what occurs in actual utterances are the ***allophonic alternates*** (varients) of phonemes. The sentence ***The cat has a red mark on the head*** thus consists of allophonic sequences. In contrast to the [k] with its initial occurrence in ***cat***, the medial [k] in ***hicup*** and the final [k] in ***pick*** possess phonetic features as part of their phonetic structure, which make the initial, medial and final alternats different in terms of some specific features. The initial occurrence of [k] in ***cat*** has a full-fledged ***plosion*** and ***aspiration*** with a release of breath which make it different from others. The initial [k] spoken in front of a candle will flicker the flame while others do not. The test of aspiration in initial occurrence is common with all plosive sounds. The [k] allophone in ***hicup*** is made much less powerful by the presence of the preceding and following sounds. This is true more especially in forms like ***actual*** where the [k] sound is softened by the following sound [t]. Similarly, and more especially the final occurrence of [k] like other plosive phonemes is extremely weak. The final [k] in ***pick*** or ***smock*** is an unaspirated unit and the speaker makes special efforts to release the sound. When such words occur as part of a continuous discourse the final plosive like [k] tend to lose even whatever little release of breath naturally possess as it is the case with the [k] sound in sequences such as ***Smock to your satisfaction*** or ***I like him for that***. In these sentences the occurrence of [k] before | t | on the one hand and | h | on the other extremely softens the sound.

Allophonic alternants are a reality not only in ***initial***, ***medial*** or ***final*** occurrence of phonemes, but also in a large variety of natural environments which we shall label as ***phonological environments***, the [k] in ***occurrence***, the [k] in ***sequence***, the [k] in ***discourse***, in ***milk van***, ***speak to him*** etc. will receive one and the same specific phonological description and have not received one and the same phonological representation. In all these instances whose specifications we do not intend to mark here in regard to their phonetic features, we have the occurrence of a large variety of ***allophonic alternants*** of the same phoneme | k |. The variants of a phoneme such as | k | or | m | are all represented through the single phoneme | k | or | m | principally for convenience of phonetic classification through the notations phonetic alphabet, and chiefly because in all allophonic variant of a phoneme we find one and the same fundamental realization of the ***distinctive features*** (phonetic features) of articulation with variation happening only in regard to their minute details. These minute details of the phonological organization of phonemes in their phonetic realization can be very conveniently left out in the representation of a sequence in phonetic notations, as these details would tend to complicate such a description beyond necessity.

In other words the building blocks of the phonological component of language are the ***allophones*** which find distribution in limitless sets of phonological environments. Its alright for us to say that the phonological component maps the surface sentence onto a phonetic representation by converting the semi-abstract phonemic units of the phonological level into the concrete phonetic units of the phonological level which the listener receive as part of his auditory experience. What is in fact mapped on to the formal units of the surface sentence are the allophoneic variants determined by their positions (initial, medial or final) distributed along the sequences of forms in a discourse. The major difference that makes one allophone (aspirated [p]) different from another allophone (unreleased [p]) consists in ***more or less*** of distinctive features entering into the formation of a given allophonic variant in a given environment. In some cases the phonetic (distinctive) features of aspiration is present while in other the additional feature may be that of release. The distinctive features which are as a rule assigned to a specific phoneme may not all be present in the structure of a phoneme in a particular allophonic position. An allophone as a ***positional variant*** in a sequence may retain only some of the very basic distinctive features which are assigned to it. The allophone [I] in ***pulp*** or ***bulb*** do not retain all the features that are phonetically assigned to the phoneme | i | in English. This is especially true as the unit of sound occurs in a particular idiolect or dialect or even in a regular discourse. The very basic features such as voicing labial or velar position will be retained as these determine the phonetic structure of a phoneme in contrast to that of another. Again in individual speech nasality may be present while a phoneme such as | p | does not have nasality as part of the phonetic structure of the sound | p |. Therefore a description of the phonological or phonetic representation of a sentence can only be done on the basis of some stable classification such as that of the phonemes.

4. Structural features of Phonology-II

If allophones are considered to be the building blocks of phonological representation, which are classified into phonemes as basic sound unit measured in their own rights, the ***distinctive features*** which go into the structure of an allophone, consequently of a phoneme, are to be considered the micro-units of the macro-segment, the phoneme. The particular phoneme | p | or | i: | should necessarily be traced back to the distinctive features which constitute the phoneme. The relation between the two levels: (1) the phonological representation and the phonetic representation should thus be defined in terms of these distinctive features on which ultimately depends the nature of phoneme as such and of the sequence which the phonemes build to represent the surface sentence.

The phonetic representation, as we have seen, is a sequence of symbols drawn from the stock of universal phonetic alphabet. Each such symbol whose representative value as an individual symbol and as a sequence is entirely governed by the phonological representation since it is this level that relates the sequence of symbols to the surface structure sentence which consists exclusively of abstract forms that await ultimate realization and concrete representation in the symbols of phonetic alphabet. For this reason we shall say that the value of the phonetic symbols and their sequences is immediately governed by the phonological representation so far as their relation to a particular language is concerned. In other words the phonological representation as constituent part of the phonological component governs the ***representative value*** of the phonetic symbols which enter into the making of the final phonetic representation as the pairing constituent part of the phonological component.

In other words we shall say that the phonological representation as a level within the phonological component has greater independence that than usually thought of. This level as one of a ***semi-abstract*** nature by contrast to the concrete (physical) phonetic representation (and graphic representation) and by contrast to the abstract surface sentence (consisting of abstract formal sequence) governs the function and value of the more remote representations mentioned above. It is important to note that the phonological representation is independent also because a sentence having formulated at the surface level can very well stop short of its phonetic or graphic representation as usually happens in case of those sentences which we are about to speak but do not.

There is such a strong point for argument in favour of the relative independence, as a level, of phonological representation, from the viewpoint of sub-vocalization of language. Human mind functions in close association with and more or less dependent on the linguistic categories with which a child grows up. The triple development of (1) ***sociological*** experience, (2) ***cognitive*** experience and (3) ***linguistic*** experience takes place so hand in hand that the mental development of a child cannot be seen as separated from the linguistic categories which he employs for functional purposes as he grows up. For this reason man has his very thinking organized in terms of the corresponding linguistic formal units, and the thought process is deeply linked to a language which the individual speaks as his own. Similarly, there is essential association between the ***abstract*** representation of forms at the surface level and the semi-***abstract*** representation of the same at the phonological level before the sentence get phonated in terms of articulation. It is again because of the independence of the phonological representation that departure and take place at this level either to phonetic representation or to graphic representation. Well, the common-sense 'thinking aloud', the consequent murmur certain people without anyone to listen to, the sub-vocalization or the "murmur in the brain" while writing, reading, and while we are *about to speak* but stop short, are perhaps, extrinsic proofs for the relative independence of the phonological representation of language not directed to actual speech or writing.

As mentioned above the distinctive features go into the structure of an allophone, consequently a phoneme. Ultimately what relate the two representations are the distinctive features. The phonological component with its universal and differential aspects infact can be said to convert the *specific values* attached to the distinctive features of the universal phonetic system for purposes of actual phonetic representation of the sentence in the particular language. This would mean that the phonological component with its constituent phonological representation functions as the representative family of the language so far as it converts the distinctive features of the symbols of universal phonetic system into a *more specific* set of values that the particular language requires. The values of the universal phonetic symbols are represented as '+ –' features. The + – features are vehicles of the distinctive features which constitute a phoneme such as + consonantal – vocalic + labial + plosive + voiced. Each symbol in the universal phonetic alphabet represents a phoneme in the articulated phonetic representation. In other words the mapping of the surface sentence on to a phonetic representation is undertaken in terms of the values attached to the +- features of the phonetic system, by converting these values of the system of symbols into distinctive features which are finer, detailed and more specific than what the symbols as such represent, and as would be required by the phonological component of the language as a vehicle of all the detailed *information* which the surface sentence contains.

At this point we shall have to see how the three things are related : (1) the information provided by the surface sentence or which stands to be phonologically and phonetically represented, (ii) the set of semi abstract phonemes which constitute the phonological representation, and (iii) the set of concrete (physical) phonemes which constitute the phonetic representation and which are symbolized by the universal phonetic alphabet. The surface sentence has a ***linear structure*** which is the end-result of series of ***hierarchical*** and ***branched*** representations at the levels of deep structure and of transformation. The linearity is the result of all the deep level structural organizations which the deep structure sentence(s) undergo. This property of linearity is important in our consideration of the relation between the three aspects mentioned above. It is such a linear structure or a sequence of such linear structures as in a discourse which is received by the phonological component for further representations. One thing is significant in our considerations: there is no point in saying that the surface sentence is assigned to the phonological representation and subsequently the phonetic representation in any manner other than in proper linearity. The manner of labeled bracketing and the hierarchical formation of the surface structure as the process is usually explained is perfectly consistent; while the application of the same features of structural formation at the phonological and phonetic level will only serve to complicate the issue more than explain the representation adequately.

We may therefore hold that the surface sentence as the find output of the transformational process is assigned to the phonological and further to the phonetic representation in ***linear fashion***. This position need not otherwise be substantiated since linearity is the fundamental property in the production of sentences at the phonetic level where it is our intimate experience that a sentence is articulated in a very linear sequence beginning in an ***absolute manner*** from one end to the other and producing only one word at a time. If the formation of the final phonetic representation (the same ***absolute linearity*** is true of the graphic representation) is susceptible to our direct experience, the same must hold true of the level of phonological representation since the association between the too levels is far too close and the differences merely a matter of the degree of concreteness.

As we have said, the phonological component takes up or makes use of the universal phonetic system with all the variety of values, and translate the values offered by the phonemes into finer, detailed and highly specified distinctive features as required by the phonological rules of the particular language. This means that a lot of deletion, addition and rearrangement need to be carried out on features assigned by the universal phonetic system apart from giving the above mentioned kind of specification to the + - values offered by the system. For example the sentence *All right, please do it* will consist of a sequential set of abstract forms as discussed above, at the surface structure level which is the final yield of the generative transformational process at deeper levels. The sentence is to be assigned a final phonetic representation. The sentence consisting of abstract forms is now assigned to the phonological component. The phonological component receives the sentence in its linear organization. The phonological component, first of all, assigns to it the necessary phonological representation and the sentence assumes a semi-concrete characteristic. This process, takes place in terms of a set of 'phonemes' which are semi-abstract by nature and are formed exclusively in the individual's cognitive structure, and have nothing to do at this level with the articulated, phonated, phonetic representation of the sentence. The sentence *All right, please do it,* now becomes a matter of '*interior utterance*' as we may call it, a representation which is so parallel to and intrinsically but not essentially related to the phonetic representation. The phonological component receives the sentence from one end to the other in a linear sequence as the representation is a process with some *duration in time*. The sentence at this level has merely a temporal dimension, not a spatial dimension. It has not become a reality (physical) in space. It will not be measurable by physical means just as a phonated sentence can be measured and represented on a spectrograph. It is a *unidimensional* sentence while the phonologically represented sentence becomes *bi-dimensional*: temporal and spatial. The sentence as a phonologically represented sequence *becomes* susceptible only to the individual speaker's cognition, and to the cognition only. In the whole process of the production (from generation to phonation) of a sentence, the speaker becomes aware of, the sentence becomes susceptible to the speaker for the first time at the phonological representation. The 'phonemic units' which constitute the signals of the phonologically represented sentence are not definable in terms of any constituent distinctive features as is the case with the regular phonemes at the phonetic representation. Just as a concept is simple, formal unit of the surface sentence is simple, the phonemic units of the phonological representation are simple by nature.

The sentence is finally assigned to the phonetic representation, where it is actually phonated. It is here alone that physically specified phonemes with their + - distinctive features figure in. Now the phonological component draws from the universal phonetic system of symbols and the sentence is linearly mapped to these symbols in terms of the distinctive features. The sentence *All right, come in, please* can have a large variety of meanings depending on the situation that has preceded the sentence. Whatever information the phonological component has received from the surface sentence is now accordingly mapped to the phonetic representation in all detailed specifications of phonetic values. In a certain variety of Indian English the universal phonemic sequence of | ɔ l rait | is specified and converted into a much *lower front flat vowel* ranging between | ɔ | and | ə: | in terms of its distinctive features. In a certain other variety of Indian English the same is converted into a greater specification of | O: | instead of the R.P. | ɔ |, again a *high back rounded vowel.* Again the sentence | rait | in its phonetic representation in certain variety of Indian English is converted into | rajit | with a *voiced palatal semi-vowel* almost dividing the diphthong | ai |. Similar conversions in the formation of | t | as well as in the stress intonation varying gravely between falling and rising depending on the situation expressed, can be found in Indian English. What is important at this point to note is that the phonetic representation by the phonological component by the phonological component of the language is undertaken by a greater, finer and *more detailed* application of the phonetic values of the universal phonetic system to the sentence. The symbols (phonemes) of the universal phonetic system are thus mere abstractions of the great allophonic alternations as realized in human languages. A speaker in producing an utterance by giving shape to the phonetic representation *draws from* this abstracted set of universal system of phonemes by assigning to the values of the phonemes greater, finer and more detailed specifications governed by the phonological rules of the language. The final sentence which is phonated and falls on the ears of the listener as the result of finally specified representation of the surface sentence.

5. Description of the Phonology of a Language

Exclusive analysis and description of the phonological component of particular language have largely been undertaken by the structuralist linguists of the period between 1930s and 1950s. The concentration on the phonology of particular language without ever attempt a comprehensive description the phonological component of human language as we have discussed so far was in particular a feature of the 1930s. Some of the very basic material on structural phonology (Post Bloomfielding phonology) was published during this period. By and large, unlike in present-day linguistics there was an atmosphere of certainty and the structuralist claims on phonology sounded authentic. The method and the directions were clear. But things became for too methodical and clear for the structuralists that there was hardly any dimension left of further descriptive progress until the Chomskyan period of transformational generative grammar came to develop. All the same the contributions of this early period in 20th century linguistics were remarkable from the view point of the phonological description of a particular language.

Phonemic analysis of a language is a considered the starting-point of phonological description. Phonological analysis as the method of *isolating grouping* and *defining* the segmental units of language provides the data for the phonological description of a language. In other words the aim of phonemic (phonological) analysis is to identify the phonemic units of a language and to classify them according to their function in the phonological component in the phonological component of the language. The phonemes in terms of their distinctive features are found to be *contrasting* in the 'minimal meaningful forms' (morphemes) of the language. The principle underlying the method of phonemic analysis is that the presence of a contrastive pair of segments in a set of words ordinarily indicate a contrast in meaning unless the difference in segments are mere sound fluctuations as are the case with ' free variation'. The sentences ***The boy saw a hat*** and ***The boy saw a rat*** differ semantically because of the mere presence a pair of contrasting segments in the sentences [h] and [r]. Having substantiated the meaning contrast of the words we are in a position to isolate two segments which alone contrast in the entire sentence : [h] and [r], presuming that the pitch two sentences are similar at the time of the production of the sentences.

Phonemic analysis of a given data by means of a detailed process of contrast at the very initial stage yields a number of contrasting segmental units. After having gathered an inventory of these segmental units the linguist undertakes a phonemic classification and groups together segments having the same fundamental phonetic structure. He makes use of the universal phonetic alphabet tally the segments and to group them together under separate phonetic symbols. A phonetic grouping of this kind brings together what we have called the ***allophones*** of the same segment. The initial occurrence of [k] in ***cup*** the medial occurrence of [k] in ***hicup*** and the final occurrence of [k] in ***pick*** are classed together under what we call the ***phoneme*** | k |. | k | is therefore considered a class, a phoneme, an abstraction which is a label for the allophonic alternants in a set of environments (see Sec. 3). The fundamental value of the language data for phonemic analysis is for isolating initially the possible variety of segments which constitute the data.

Once the segments are isolated and listed the linguist, we said, classifies the segments on the basis of the universal phonetic alphabet. The linguist will label such class on the basis of the phonetic criteria which define a phonetic symbol in terms of the ***distinctive features*** which constitute the particular symbol. Any variant of | p |, for instance occurring a variety of phonological environments will be classed under the ***unvoiced bilabial stop consonant*** | p | (these being the distinctive features which differentiable | p | from another class | b | the ***voiced bilabial stop consonant***). Any variant of | l | will be grouped together under the ***voiced alveolar lateral consonant*** | l | in contrast to the variant of | f | which will fall under the ***unvoiced labio-dental fricative consonant*** | f |.

The linguist as the *investigator* depends on the *informant* who provides him with the data necessary for the phonemic analysis. The only way to keep a record of the data from the informant is to transcribe the utterances at once into the universal phonetic alphabet. The investigator's acquaintance with the universal phonetic notation enables him through out the analytic work to use the notation as the symbols under which the segmental classification needs to be undertaken. Again the definition and description of the classified phonemes are required to be done in consonance with the universal phonetic system.

Since meaning change or contrast in utterances can also occur not only by contrast phonemes but by differences in what is called *prosodic features* (or supra segmental features or metalinguistic facts) such as stress, pitch levels, tonal contours and features of transition, phonemic analysis also includes the study of these features in a language. The treatment of *segments* and *suprasegments* together constitute phonemic analysis. Information about the occurrences of the supra segmental features of the data should be obtained as a result of a single analytic operation of the data into simultaneous components. These features are to be extracted out of the flow of speech as they constitute phonemes morphemes) themselves in simultaneity with the sequence of segments.

In the process of examining the language data the linguist come across a set of phonemes which are substitutable with one another and not in contrastive distribution, the two segments are said to be in *free variation*, and they are called *free varients*. In Gujarati, for instance the sounds | s | and | h | occur regularly as free variants of the standard phoneme | s |. The two segments are part of two distinct Gujarati dialects and words as a rule are available in which the two segments freely alter *without* any alternation of the meanings. In the language of children, especially such free-variation of segments is often found. Two sounds | p | and | b | are considered to be in *contrastive distribution* in sequences such as *pit* and *bit* as the occurrences clearly contrast both formally and semantically, as we saw earlier. Two sounds, on the other hand are said to be in *complementary distribution* in sequences such as *pot spot* and *top* as | p | has an initial medial and final distribution and as such one cannot be substituted placed in the phonetic environment of another. The initial [p] has characteristic features such as aspiration which will not found with the final occurrence of [p]. As these are in basic phonetic similarity and are classed under one and the same phoneme, we shall say that only allophonic alternants occur in complimentary distribution while a phoneme occurs in contrastive distribution with another phoneme as | d | and | tʃ | in *speed* and *speech*. The description of the phonology of a particular language thus begins with phonemic analysis and the ***phonological theory*** of a particular language begins with a concrete description of the sounds and this sequence which constitute the phonological component of that language.

9
The Morphology of Language

1. Morphology and Grammar

For the sake of a theoretical consistency in treatment, we have not so far been dealing separately with morphology in any manner. Ch. 7 is concerned with the three levels of language which we labeled as the grammar, usage and use and which penetrate the three components described as phonology, grammar and semantics. Phonology has been seen in detail from different perspectives including its universal and differential dimensions. A distinction is drawn between the Grammar (with capital G) and grammar, the first constituting the core aspects of language and the second constituting part of all the three levels of grammar, usage and use.

At this point we will draw upon the structure of what we have so far been calling merely 'grammar' for convenience in treatment. While by the term the *Grammar* we meant all the three core aspects of phonology, grammar and semantics, the usual and traditional meaning of the word 'grammer' is designated in the present treatment by the same term *grammar* without any addition or deletion in meaning. For this reason, to make the distinction clear we have throughout the present book used the word in the first sense with the definite article and the capital G. In the traditional sense, in present day linguistics and in the present work morphology is treated as part of the grammar of language, except that morphology is not explicitly distinguished from syntax in transformational generative grammar.

Morphology is concerned with the ***internal structure*** of words and their relationship to other words ***within the paradigm***. ***Syntax*** on the other hand treats the ***external functions*** (the organizational features) of words and their relations in a ***discourse***. The term ***grammar*** takes care of the treatment of both morphology and syntax. Wherever the term grammar is used it would mean that a specific distinction between morphology and syntax is not required at the point. Yet another level which has not figured in so far to avoid complexity is that of ***morphonology*** (known also as ***morphophonemics*** or ***morphophonology***) which is said to relate the levels of phonology and morphology. In present-day linguisties the trend has come to develop where instead of the three levels of phonology, morphophonology and morphology only one single level is postulated and that is the level of ***morphonology*** in contrast to syntax and semantics. But in the present book we shall adhere to the distinction between ***phonology*** (the study of the phonological component of language) as relatively and theoretically distinct from ***morphology*** with the treatment of a third level that can be posited between the two i.e. the level of ***morphonology*** (see ch. 10.). No one can seriously deny that it is not necessary for a theoretician to make distinctions between levels and aspects which are certainly not ***separate*** in the actuality of language but are perspectives which need to be posited for the clear understanding of a phenomenon such as language.

Under phonology we saw that a sentence such as ***The boys disagreed with the gentleman*** consists of certain sets of sequences of phonemes which figure in at two levels: the phonological representation and the phonetic representation which together constitute the phonological component: at level 1 as semi-abstract phonemes and at level 2 as physically specified concrete phonemes constituted by distinctive features. The sentence above has a large variety of aspects which yield valuable linguistic information: (1) the sentence is a linear sequence of segmental units definable in terms + – distinctive features; (2)

the sentence is a linear sequence of semi-abstract phonemes which parallel the physical phonemes, and by meaning of which the sentence remains present in the cognitive structure; (3) the sentence is a sequence of word-forms the structure of which can be studied separately from the structure of the individual segments which constitute the word-forms; (4) the sentence reveals a set of organizational features which relate the words in the sentence among themselves; (5) the sentence conveys some of meaning which is the result of a unification of the meanings of the words; and (6) the sentence as graphically represented is a sequence of graphic word-forms constituted by sequences of graphic representations of phonemes called letters. The linguist stands in need of postulating a variety of levels to account for a few instances as given above of a large variety of perspectives from which sentence of language can be viewed. These aspects requires an accounting of even levels which do not explicitly constitute part of the extrinsic sentence. Hence the need for explaining aspects of language separately which would apparently seen one and the same.

In the sentence ***The boys disagreed with the gentleman*** we initially looked for the ***phonemes as the minimal units of distinctive sound feature*** at the level of phonology. Having done this we move a step further into the units and look for ***the minimum meaningful units*** of the sentence. This would yield those smallest units which as sequences of phonemes would express some unit of meaning. The sentence would then yield the following sequence:

> The # boy # s # dis # agree # ed # with #
> the # gentle # man #.

Upon examination of the above sequence we find that the units separated by the symbol which stands for juncture features, are simple units which are further indivisible into smaller ***meaningful*** units. We find that these are ***minimal units of form and meaning***. Such units of a sentence which constitute the sentence at large we call a ***morpheme***. Thus, the boy, -s, dis-, agree, -ed etc are morphemes. The sentence, thus is structured of an ***organized sequence of morphemes***. The morpheme | ðə | the which occurred before ***boys*** needs to be constrated to | ði | the with a vowel alternative which would precede a vowel sound as in *the egg*. Here we have two units occurring in different *morphonological* environments (the preceding vowel sound as determined by the initial sound of the following morpheme).

In this we have a typical case as found in the pair [ði] and [ðə]. The meaning (which is purely syntactic) is the some in both. A pair of *morphs* of this kind we call *allomorphs* of the same morpheme. The units [ði] and [əə] as they are independent and not assigned to any morpheme, are called *morphs*. A morph is such a formal unit which is not as yet assigned to any morpheme; or rather one looks at it independent of any morpheme. Thus *the, -s, -ed,* or [ði], [–z], [–id] looked at independently one all morphs of their own rights as occurring in different environments. The sentence above again yields another sequence *boys* which we have divided into boy # *s*. The form *boy* is found occurring independent of any other forms as in *The boy is clever*. Such free-forms are called *free morphemes*. *The, boy, agree, with, gentle, man* etc. are free-morphemes. On the other hand, the forms *-s*, *-ed*, and *dis-* in the sentence one not found to occur independent of other morphemes, and are bound to other morphemes as in *boys, walked, displeasure* to convey their meaning. Such forms are called *bound morphemes*. Traditionally these known as free-from and bound-forms. The terms free and bound morphemes can be traced back to Bloomfield (1933).

Just as we spoke of the *complementary distribution* of allophones, now we are in a position to speak of the *complementary distribution* of *allomorphs* in various morphonological environments. Allomorphs of the same morpheme, we say, in such a way that one allomorph, for instance [–z] cannot occur in the morphonological environment that belongs to another, for instance [-iz] going with *bus*. The morphonological contexts of allomorphs for that matter remain fixed. Therefore we may label allomorphs as the *positional variants (alternants) of the same morpheme*. In this sense, the occurrences of *-s* in I bɔiz I *boys*, I Kæts I *cats*, and in I wɔtʃiz I *watches* (respectively –z, –s, and –iz) are the positional variants (or *allomorphic alternants* or *allomorphic variants* or *morpheme alternants*) of the same morpheme {–S}. For the sake of clarity in representation the morphemes one enclosed in *braces* while the allomorphs are enclosed in *brackets* just as phonemes are enclosed in vertical bars and allophones in brackets. But to avoid complexity wherever possible all these diacritic representations are avoided and the forms are presented in normal letters.

Coming back now to the relation between *grammar* and *morphology*, we may say, morphology constitutes the beginning of the study of grammar, which would lead to *syntax* both being constituent parts of grammar. There is nothing therefore wrong in assigning an independent status to the study of morphology so long as its close componental relation to morphonology and phonology on the one hand and syntax on the other, is kept in mind and left open. As we move closer to either end in the study of any specific linguistic aspect such as above, the distinctions become considerably dim and aspects begins to overlap. But a rejection of any one linguistic level or aspect is no solution to the problem of overlap. A very detailed examination of the grammar of the levels of the grammar, usage and use would yield descriptions of morphology and syntax at the levels of core grammar, the grammar of usage and the grammar of use. But these distinctions hold greater validity for theoretical considerations and it would be certainly helpful to know that these distinctions do correspond to levels within language as postulated by the system outlined in the present book.

2. Lexical Morphology

As we examine the following sentence *The boys were disinterested in the information provided by the gentleman*, we find that the sentence as a not merely a sequence of morphemes, but a sequences which consists of several kinds of morphemes. That a study of the morphemes which constitute the sentence above would yield different *aspects* of morphology; namely *lexical morphology* and *inflectional morphology*. The word *disinterested*, for instance is a complex unit which call for an explanation different from what the word the requires. *Disinterested* if undergoes a *componental analysis* would yield the forms *dis*-, *interest*, and -*ed* which is ordinarily achieved in morphemic analysis by a process of contrast of the relevant word (s) with another set of words. Contrasting *disinterested* with *disappointed*, and *dismantled* we are in a position to isolate the morphemes *dis-* and *-ed* as distinct from the forms *interest*, *appoint* and *mantle*. As indicate above we label the forms *dis-* and *-ed* as bound morphemes and the rest as free morphemes.

Interest, *appoint* and *mantle* as indivisible lexical forms of modern English are called *roots*. Roots are the minimal indivisible free morphemes which further *formatives* will be added. A *formative* is a general term which stands for a bound morpheme that is employed to change the functional status of a free morpheme. In attempting a division between a root and formative we should take care that both the elements as a result of the division should retain some sense in modern English. What has lost its sense in modern English should not come under the label of formative or a root. If we attempt a division between *in-* and *-terest* we find that while *in-* is an active formative in modern English, *-terest* as such do not mean any thing to us. Hence, we consider *interest* as a simple free morpheme which will function as a root in *lexical formation*. But the word *disinteredness* is still more than a root and a formative. We shall distinguish a *stem* (base) from a *root* and a *formative*, in the form *disinterested* which functions as the base of the word *disinterestedness* with a further formative *-ness* added to it. We may consider *interested* as the base of the word *disinterested* with the formative *dis-* added to *interested*. If the most indivisible morpheme will be regarded as the root of a word, an addition of a formative in front or after it makes it a base. A base (stem) in this sense is an *expanding* thing with the addition of two, three or more formatives and is relative to every additional formative, as in '*disqualifiability*' which consists of a root (*quali*-regarded so as relative to either-fy or -ty) and five formatives respectively, dis-, ify, -able, -ly, -ty.

In the description above our concern with the *root* form and the *base* forms as *simple stems* (meaning the roots) *complex stems* and *compound stems* etc. we call *lexical morphology*, while morphological description of the various aspects of inflectional formations will be treated under *inflectional morphology* (Sec. 3). In the linguistic terminology the same distinctions of roots and stems as above are made also in terms of *simple roots* (simple stem), *complex roots*, and *compound roots* without employing the words 'stems' or 'base' for the purpose. Inflectional morphology is concerned with the functions of inflectional formatives as we shall examine in detail in the following section. Instances such as ***walk, walks*** , ***walking, walked*** are said to be members of the same ***paradigm*** because everyone of these belongs to the same grammatical category of verb, and are the results of inflectional formatives added to the root, the verb, ***walk***. Such formatives which are added to the end of a root are called ***suffixes***, and the process of such a formation is known as ***suffixation***. Those formatives which are added at the beginning of a root in order to 'derive' a new word are ***prefixes***, and such a process is called ***prefixation***, as we find in ***devalue*** (de+value), ***unaccounted*** (un+accounted) and so on. There is a third category of formatives called ***infixes*** which are not commonly found in English. To some extent, although all may not agree with it, we can consider the formation of ***father-in-law*** or ***charge-de-affairs*** as cases of ***infixation***. The process that goes on in all the three cases prefixation, infixation and suffixation are known as ***affixation*** or the formatives of prefixes, infixes and suffixes in a generic sense will be called ***affixes***. All these considerations are part of lexical morphology. The process by which a word is derived from its root or stem by the addition or an affix is ***derivation***, in contrast to ***inflection*** where as seen above the formation does not yield another word by only some functional alternations.occur in the word as between ***walk*** and ***walks***. Care must be taken to misinterpret inflection also as a case of 'derivation' since the word is 'derived' from ***walk*** to ***walks***. But for the sake of interpretational consistency such a tendency could be brushed aside.

Inflection and ***word-formation*** thus constitute the two major subfields of morphology. Inflectional morphology studies the formations ***within a paradigm class***, while word formation is concerned with the formations ***between paradigm classes*** or outside a paradigm class. Word formation consists of two subfields: ***derivation and compounding. Back, backs backed, backing*** constitute inflectional formations; ***back bite*** is a new word formed from ***back*** and therefore this process falls under word formation, in which ***backbite*** itself is the result of compounding (the form being a compound) while ***backward*** is derivation just as ***movement*** is a derived form. These are all well established terms and no confusion is bound to occur in our understanding of such technical terms in morphology.

'Inflection' is studied under 'inflectional morphology', while as seen above, 'word-formation' is dealt with under the subtitle 'lexical morphology'. A rather detailed treatment of derivations and compounding within the scope of the present book is formed in section 4 of the present chapter. In the present context we are concerned more with the lexical structure of morphology and more especially the aspect of word-formation is general.

The description of morphology as concerned with the 'internal structure of words' and their relation 'within the paradigm' has been the concern of grammarians in one way or other for several centuries, though not within the texture of the present-day linguistic terminology. The past attempts to formulate a theory of morphology to account for the morphological features of language have produced a few ***models*** of morphological description (see Hockett: 1954, P.H. Mathews: 1974) which will provide insights on the present position of morphological description. With the onset of transformationalism especially grammatical models came to have a prominent place in structural description since a model provides a firm basis as a blue print for a more rigorous kind of representation of a structural description of a component of language. A study of the grammatical models originally provided by C.F. Hockett traces the excellently the course of development morphological studies have taken. These models have further been developed and specified by R.H. Robins and P.H. Mathews. Of these three models we may regard as first what has been called ***Word and Paradigm Model.*** This model provides the frame work in which traditional grammarians treated morphology (for obvious reasons many of the present day linguists believe that the traditional treatment of grammar was principally morphological with seldom any insights provided on syntax. For this reason liberty is taken at this point to call these models 'morphological models'). The word is the central unit of study with the study of grammar centred on the grammatical categories with grammatical words as minimum elements to deal with. The word and Paradigm Model is the classical (Greek, Roman) model of grammatical description for which the word as ***the unit*** of language study posited the problem chiefly of classification. This is how we have the 'parts of speech' which have come down to us as the main contribution of classical period. The parts of speech consisted of a classification, definition and illustration of the elements of a sentence from viewpoints which often do not tally. The categories of tense, voice, number etc which occupied the central attention in the traditional model of description is known today as 'morpholosyntactic categories' since these categories occupied a role in the description morphological and syntactic elements of a sentence. These are interesting categories which have the function, in the particular model, of governing the framework of a paradigm. These arē especially applicable to Latin with its regular declensions (of Nouns) and conjugations (of Verbs). The paradigm of a Latin verb consisted of a list of word forms with case endings assigned to tense, voice number, persons, etc. (as the form ***amat*** 'he loves' represents the third person, singular, active, present tense in contrast to ***amatur*** 'he is loved' which represents the third person, singular, passive, present tense). The classical model which is centred around the paradigm has lost its relevance to a language like English because the paradigm itself has a very limited basis in this 'word-order' predominated language. By contrast to a Latin paradigmatic class which consists of dozens of members based on tense, voice, persons and number an English paradigm has very few members as in ***walk***, ***walks***, ***walking***, and ***walked***.

The second model under consideration as schematized has come to be known as *Item and Arrangement Model*. The entire model is centred around the concept of ***morphemes*** which occur in a sentence as sequential organization. All that we have seen so far in relation to the structure of the morpheme and the allomorph fall under this model of grammatical description. In item and arrangement model morphs are regarded as the basic unit of structural description, which are in turn assigned to morphemic items as allomorphs of different morphemes.

The third model is known as *Item and Process Model*; the implications of this model will be dealt with in section 5. This constitutes a morphological description centred on what are called ***morphological processes***. A sentence is not merely looked at as a sequential 'arrangement of items' but as the result of a generative process which yields morphological processes at the level of the surface structure. This notion has come to develop as 'generative morphology' as part of the transpirational generative grammar in present-day linguistics. The development that have taken place in the study of morphology could be summarized in a way in the three models presented above. As a sheer sketch the above accounts are intended only do draw some theoretical contrasts as to the most basic approaches to morphology as developed by traditional grammarians, the structuralists of the mid 20th century and the post-Chomskyan linguists. It may be noted that unlike in the fields of phonological, syntactic and semantic studies, no significant and drastic innovation has occurred in the study of morphology which somehow marks a gradual development in our understanding of the morphological structure of language.

3. Inflectional Morphology: Noun Inflections

The two major sub-fields in the study of morphology, we said, consist of (i) inflectional morphology and (ii) word-formations which is sub-classed into (a) derivations and (b) compounding. Inflectional morphology is defined as the study of the formations within a paradigm while word formation is concerned with the rotation between formations which belong to different paradigms or rather formations outside a paradigm. In other words inflections are the formal relations that exist between the members of a paradigm while word-formation is concerned with formations outside a paradigm or with relations between paradigms. The examples which we have examined make the distinction clear. So far as we are concerned with the structural features of a form like ***walked*** as against another form ***walking*** we are the domain of what is known as ***paradigmatic relations*** which is the proper concern of inflectional morphology. The moment we further step into the relation that the form ***walked*** establishes in the structural context of the sentence ***They had walked a fairly good distance*** we are in the domain of what is known as syntagmatic relations. While paradigmatic relations keep us in the domain of morphology, syntagmatic relations take the investigator right into the field of syntax.

Inflectional morphology offers considerable scope in our understanding of ***inflecting languages*** or rather we might better say that a study of the morphological structure of inflecting languages offers great scope in our understanding of the inflectional features of human language. The morphological structure of inflecting languages is contrasted to the morphological structure of ***agglutinating*** and ***isolating*** types of languages (see Ch. 6 Sec. 2.). The inflecting structure of a language such as Latin offers considerable complexity as Latin lexemes are highly inflected. The Latin noun has a ***declension*** while the Latin verb has a ***conjugation.*** A student who learns Latin, in other words, is expected to master these declensions and conjugations so as to be able to employ the proper case-form in the construction of sentences. The five declensions of Latin can be distinguished by the endings of the genitive singular :

1	2	3	4	5
–ae	–i	–is	us	li
viae	servi	legis	portus	rei
(road)	(slave)	(law)	(gate)	(thing)

A Latin declension, for instance, would read like the following :

		Form		Mean		Function
S	Nom.	terra	:	land, (the, a)	:	Subject
	Gen.	lerrae	:	of the (a) land	:	possessive
	Dat.	lerrae	:	to or for the land	:	indirect object
	Acc.	terram	:	the (a) land	:	direct obj.
	Abl.	terra	:	by, with, from the (a) land	:	agentive etc.
Pl.	Nom.	terrae	:	lands, the lands	:	subject
	Gen.	terrarum	:	of the lands	:	possessive
	Dat.	terris	:	to or for the lands	:	indirect obj.
	Acc.	terras	:	lands, the lands	:	direct obj.
	Abl.	terris	:	by, with, from the lands	:	agentive etc.

The Latin verbs are connjugated to show ***voice, mood, tense, number***, and ***person***. There are four conjugational classes in Latin which can be distinguished by the endings of 'the present infinitive active.'

1	2	3	4
–āre	–ēre	–ere	–īre
laudare (praise)	monere (advise)	mittere (send)	audire (hear)

A Latin conjugation runs in the form of ***laudo, laudas, laudat, laudamus, laudatis*** and ***laudant*** the present instance indicating the active voice, indicative mood, present tense singular and plural forms of ***praise***. The instance shown above reveal the complexity of the Latin-type of inflection in inflecting languages. In fact English retains only a fraction of its original inflections (as found in old English) which has lost all the rigorousness of the Latin type paradigms. We will distinguish all inflectional formatives of English under two major heads: ***regular inflections*** and ***irregular inflections***. Regular inflectional class will be concerned with the regular ***plural***, ***possessive*** and ***third person singular*** suffixes, and ***past tense***, ***past participle***, ***gerendial*** and ***present participle suffixes***. All the rest (irregular forms of the above) will come under irregular inflections.

Regular Plural Suffix $\{-Z_1\}$:

All inflectional classes could well be considered ***morpheme classes*** as usual or inflectional classes of suffixes or inflectional formative classes. In fact every inflectional occurrence is regarded as a morpheme (Sec. 1) which comprises what we have allied ***allomorphs*** (morpheme alternants, allomorphic variants) of the same morpheme. These are often described as ***morphosymtactic categories*** along with all traditionally held grammatical categories of case, number, gender tense etc. They are termed morphosymtactic because of the syntactic role these categories play in the sentence while these categories are expressed not in the word-order but in the structure of the word itself, for instance the past tense function of the word ***walked*** is formally expressed in the structure of the very word through the suffixal past tense formative -***ed***.

The regular ***plural suffixes morpheme*** is morphologically symbolized in terms of $\{-Z_1\}$. The symbol $\{-Z_1\}$ stands for the normal orthographic representation of the plural morpheme ***-s*** as in words such as ***chips, cuts, eggs, buns, churches*** and ***benches.*** No other letter is used in English for this purpose. Plural morphemes in Latin take different orthographic representations in all five different declensions. The forms are :

(i)	terr–a	: land	(ii)	serv-us	: slave
	terr–ae	: lands		ser-i	: slaves
(iii)	bell–um	: war	(iv)	lex	: law
	bell–a	: wars		leg–es	: laws
(v)	flumen	: river	(vi)	port-̄us	: gate
	flumin–a	: rivers		port–us	: gates
(vii)	res	:a thing			
	re̱s	: things.			

The fiv̄e declensions receive seven forms governed by their ***gender*** characteristics as gender, unlike in English, plays a major syntactic role in Latin. By contrast, the English plural morpheme receives only one regular orthographic representation *-s*. The plural morpheme $\{-Z_1\}$ has different allomorphic distributions in terms of allomorphic variants of [–s], [–z] and [–iz]. The allomorph [–z] is arbitrarily chosen to represent the plural morpheme in $\{-Z_1\}$. These allomorphic variants are respectively realised to words such as ***chips*** [–s], ***bags*** [–z] and ***benches*** [–z]. The following is a schematic representation of the regular plural morpheme in terms of its allomorphic variants:

$\{-Z_1\}$	[–s]	:	cats	I kǽts I.
	[–z]	:	boys	I bɔ iz I.
	[–iz]	:	benches	I bentʃiz I

Irregular Plural Suffixes

The irregular occurrences of the plural morpheme $\{-Z_2\}$ also are regarded interims of theoretical considerations as the allomorphic variants of the same plural morpheme which expresses one and the same concept of plurality. The different variants of the plural morpheme in various forms has always been troublesome for the linguist to explain. There is considerable disagreement among linguists as to the way in which these irregular plural morphemes are to be grouped under a given set of labels. 'Sheep' and 'mere' are to be regarded as instances of the same plural more occurring as allomorphic variants of the same plural morpheme. It is ice this context that the concept of zero-morpheme was introduced. 'sheet-sheep' (as in the verb form came-come) a zero-variant of the plural morpheme is at work. This was the possible explanation Bloomfieldian Linguists resorted to which gained considerable acceptance is later period. Actress like P.H. Mathews considered such occurrences as cases of the proportionality within paradigms, syntactically speaking 'mean' is an occurrence based on MAN+PLURAL. Representative suffixes are found in: foot-feet, man-men, mouse-mice, woman-women, child-chidden, roof-roofs, cloth-cloths, and ox-oxen.

$$\{-Z_1\}\ x\ \{\upsilon\}\ x \rightarrow x\ \{i\!:\}\ x\ \text{foot-feet}$$

Genitive Suffixes

The genitive suffixes of –iz, –z, and –s orthographically represented by 'S and S' has a unique function in English language. Functionally this morpheme is different from all the rest of the suffixes. Randolf Quirk (1976:95) provides 7 categories of usages the genitive, all represented by the same English morpheme as indicated above. There is the possessive genitive as in 'my son's wife', the subjective genitive as in 'the boy's application, the objective genitive as in 'family's support', the genitive of origin as in 'the girl's story', descriptive genitive as in 'a women's college' and the genitive of measure as in 'ten days absence'.

The genitive morpheme $\{-Z_2\}$ has almost the same distributional feature as the noun morpheme $\{-Z_1\}$, and the third singular morpheme $\{-Z_3\}$. It is held that the genitive morpheme has fewer variations including a zero alternant where the -s is not present in the spoken form. The distribution may be given as below:-

1. X — {Z_2} → X — [–iz] : mouse–mouses

2. X — {Z_2} → X — [–z] : Jim – Jim's

3. X — {Z_2} → X — [–s] : Pat – Pat's

4. X — {Z_2} → X — [θ] : boys – boys'

Replacement Pattern

In Bloomfield as well as Post-Bloomfieldian theories of morphology the pattern of inflectional replacement became a matter of considerable importance. In formations like 'man-men' 'woman-women', 'foot-feet' etc the formative element in the base is considered a plural morpheme having the function of a plural suffix. Both structural and functional morphemic description consider this element a replacement having the function of a plural suffix. This has originated from the idea of a suffix having an alternant in the nucleus itself. There have been linguists who treated 'man-men' occurrence in terms of a zero alternant. But this has not received wider acceptance as replacement theory. In such explanations it would be wiser also to take into consideration the historical development of the forms to provide greater significance to the morphological accounting. Keeping X for the phonemes that are constant the following representation helps the description in terms of replacement:-

1. X {ϑ} X → X {i:} X foot – feet.
2. X {∂ǝ} X → X {e} X man – men
3. X {υ} X {∂} X→ X {i} X {i} X woman – women
4. X {θ} → X {∂z} clothe – clothes
5. X {KS} → X {Ks∂n} ox – oxen

4. Inflectional Morphology : Verb Inflections

The Third Singular Suffix

The inflectional suffixes of the English verbs occurs in a variety of morphemic contexts introducing characteristic meanings. These are: a definite present with a subject in the third person which is called Third Singular as in 'He ***works*** hard', as simple past in 'He ***worked*** hard' as a gerund as in 'working keeps healthy' and as past and present participles as in 'I have ***worked*** hard' and '***working*** persons remain healthy.' We shall represent in Third Singular Suffix in terms of $\{-Z_3\}$ with the three allomorphic variants of the morpheme as : [–iz], [–s] and [–z], as exemplified by kisses, likes and loves. The allomorphs are phonemically defined alternants of the same morpheme.

	1. [–iz]	: occurs after s, z, sh (sibilants)
$\{-Z_3\}\rightarrow$	2. [–s]	: occurs after voiced non-sibilant phonemes.
	3. [–z]	: occurs after voiceless non-sibilants phonemes.

	1. [–iz]	: She washes clothes in the morning.
$\{-Z_3\}\rightarrow$	2. [–s]	: He likes eggs for breakfast.
	3. [–z]	: She loves dogs for company.

The morphological values of the above allomorphs are determined on the basis of the recurring phonological environment as found in the examples. The third person singular is more or less regular in its occurrence in the phonological environment indicated above.

The Regular Preterit Suffix

The best way of systematizing the verbs of modern English is the division into two sub-classes: the regular and irregular preterit or past tense suffix. The regular verbs manifest no change in the kernel itself. The base receives the past tense suffix $\{D_1\}$. Iespersen called thus the preterit form. This suffix combines with the base in three distinct phonetic forms, and linguistically speaking we have three distinct morphological variants of the same morpheme $\{D_1\}$ the Past Tense Suffix:

	1. [–id]	– John wanted some fruit.
$\{D_1\}$	2. [–d]	– He waved his hands.
	3. [–t]	– She pumped in a lot of air.

The Participle Suffix and its Structure

The regular Past Participle Morpheme is represented as $\{D_2\}$ and it is realised in three allomorphs realised in different phonological environments. These three again become allomorphic variants of the same past participle morpheme. They are as above : [–id], [–d] and [–t].

1. [–id] – wanted, hinted
$\{D_2\}$ 2. [–d] – moved, rubbed
3. [–t] – slopped, dripped.

The irregular occurrences of both the Past Morpheme and Participle Morpheme are described with reference to the replacement mechanism (see Replacement in the same Chapter)

5. Derivational Morphology : Noun Derivations

Pattern Derivative Noun Prefixes

Derivatives are inner formations occurring close to the core, changing the form-classes of words by their presence. Derivation and compounding constitute word-formation. Morphology has the two major divisions: 1. Inflections and 2. Word-formation as seen earlier in the chapter Derivative prefixes and suffixes are statically more with more restricted distribution. In the formation 'un-employment' the first morpheme 'un' | ʌn | is called a prefix. Three important negative prefixes are: un-, in– and an –(a–). Traditional grammarians used to speak of productive (eg. pre-) and unproductive prefixes (eg. a–) as occurring in 'amoral'.

Pattern of Derivative Noun Suffixes

Derivative Noun Suffixes can be more easily isolated and classified than prefixes. Noun suffixes are identified chiefly as:- -ment, -tion, once, -ty, -once, -ician-, ners, al, -ic etc. Suffixes have the characteristic of recurring productiveness. Suffixes such as -ment, -ant, -ship, -tion etc are known to be very highly productive. One the other hand there are several unproductive suffixes such as -archy, -kin, -ok, -dom, -hood etc.

Homophonous Morphemes in English

Linguists like Eugne Nida (1948:266) considered homophonous morphemes as correspondingly belonging to different distributional classes. Forms such as 'spring' (N) meaning 'season' and 'spring' (v) are two different morphemes on the basis of the parallel semantic and distributional classes.

These words cover two different arrears of meaning and belong to different grammatical (distributional) classes. All the same there homophonous forms with formal identity and particle semantic resemblance as well as similar distribution in word classes. Forms like 'run: run' (to run factory/ to run two miles) belong to this category.

Formally Identical Noun and Verb Morphemes

Traditional grammarians were concerned with identical forms of 'object' (w) –object (v)' for their characteristic occurrence. This phenomenon in language came to be described as 'conversion': this meant assigning a base to a different class without changing the form of the base. With the origin of the concept of the zeromorph this was assigned to the formation mentioned above and these occurrences came to be explained in terms of zero morph i.e. a morphemic process of affixing a zero morph to the base keeping the base unchanged. Modern English enjoys plural freedom in the formation of verbs from Nouns and vice-versa without a change in the form.

6. Derivational Morphology: Verb Derivations

Prefixation of English Verbs

As we have seen the character of derivation is that this process renders not merely a change in the grammatical function as in the case of inflections (walk-walks) but introduces altogether a new word. Inflections are said to be inner formations while derivations are outer formations. It is characteristic that the presence of any derivational suffix always keep the inflections away from the root of the word. Hence inflections are always outer formations enabling these to express these unique syntactic functions.

eg. {[dis–] [abi] × [–ty] [–s] }

A distinction is to be made between prefixes and formulas in English Occurrences as in predetermine (prefixed), prepare (formulaic). The following sketch can be exemplified for a representation of prefixation of verbs:

Pattern of Derivative Verb Suffixes

dis	qualify	credit	in	fuse	un	tie
	arm	grace		carnate		do
	charge	like		tend		cover
	close	solve		scribe		lock
	cover	miss				veil
						fold

In the discovery of productive suffixes a clear norms to be used in that a root or the base to which the suffix is added is used as an independent word in modern English. –fy is an English suffix. But a form like 'defy' does not include this suffix and we call such forms formulas which do not carry the function of suffixation. It is not possible to separate the base de-and isolate-fy as the two elements are bound together to form what we have called a 'formulaic expression'. In all the verb formations through suffixation the stress of the word is preserved on the root without a shift: 'test-' testify, visual-visualize, agony-agonies etc. The affix formations of English words have become so much blended in the historic development that the norm indicated above need to be employed for the isolation of prefixes and suffixes for any linguistic description.

10

Morphonology and Suprasegmental Features

1. The Notion of Morphonology

Having seen in detail certain fundamental aspects relating to phonology and morphology, we come down to few of the much debated questions on the relation between phonology, morphology and syntax. As componental aspects of languages which is so simple an activity for a common speaker involving absolutely no technical problems, levels as mentioned above pose no problems when taken in isolation and examined separately. As componental aspects of language, again, which is a unified activity, each of the levels mentioned above gets easily merged into other levels as to battle the investigator easily. For this reason it is in fact different for us as investigators to set easy distinctions between the level, demarcate one from another and provide a definition which would properly and specifically take care of only the level concerned. As we examine the following sentence *It's all right for you to do the work*, we come across a number of features which are not yet accounted for by means of an exclusive description of phonology here. The phonological component with its obligatory phonological representation and optional phonetic and graphic representations as seen in Ch. 8, is the level of language which should account for (i) the segmental phonemes which constitute the sentence above (ǀ itsɔ·lraitfɔ ju : -------ǀ) , (ii) the features of *juncture* which characterise the production of the sentence, (iii) aspects of the *stress* which mark individual words, (iv) levels of *pitch*, and (v) *tonal contours* which contribute to the texture of the sentence. In the production of such a sentence as above we find there are serval instances where the particular environment (vi) whether we shall call it lexical, phonological or morphological alters the shape of the phoneme one way or other. Serval forms become so weak that they almost get lost in the sentence while others might assume a new shape especially in the idiolectic context of use.

Now, a straight forward segmental description of the sentence above can only taken care of the segmental phonemes and their organization in the language. For the post-Bloomfieldian linguists in particular the phonology of language is chiefly description of the segmental phonemes of language. They started with the assumption that phonology and morphology should be kept strictly compartmentalised that a truly scientific description is possible. But language constituents not only of *segmental phonemes*, but also *suprasegmental* features. By suprasegmental phonemes we mean the aspects ii, iii, iv and v of the sentence examined above, i.e. all those specifications of the sentence such as stress which characterise its production (phonation). They are called suprasegmental because there features are juxtaposed to the segmental phonemes. The post-Bloomfieldian linguists in some cases, rather arbitrarily classified the suprasegmental (prosodic) features with the phonemes and labeled stress, pitch, tonal contours and juncture as *suprasegmental phonemes* arguing that as part of the phonology of language these features signify meanings of some kind and be found in contrastive distribution. The form *'export* (iv) with the first syllable stressed is contrasted in meaning with the form *ex'port* (v) with stress falling on the second syllable. While in some other cases it happens that one and the same suprasegmental features are classified as morphemes and labeled them as *suprasegmental morphemes* arguing that these features function as 'minimum meaningful units' which is the definition attached usually to morphemes. Thus we spoke of *stress*, *pitch* and *juncture phonemes* on the on hand, and stress, pitch and *juncture morphemes* on the other.

The reasons for grouping the suprasegmental features nude either phonology and calling them phonemes, and under morphology and calling them morphemes are clear and well understood. But which level (phonology or morphonology) should they belong to ? In other words aspects such as these cannot easily be classed under one level or other and there is bound to be some arbitrariness in their treatment. Such are aspect that get as we said easily merged into more than one level of language.

The aspect (vi) of the sentence examined above which included ***phonemic alternations*** of one kind or other (result in also from sandhi) pose a problem similar to the one discussed above. While the aspects of phonology seen above do not necessarily form part of the segmental phonemes, phonemic alternations do necessarily affect the shape of phonemes, change one phoneme into another for reasons of change in the environment. Such phonemic alternations in phonological environments is usually dealt with under ***morphophonemics*** (morphophonology). Although in some cases morphophonemics is regarded as part of phonology proper, most post-bloomfieldian linguists consider it a separate level of treatment which falls between phonology and morphology. In some instances suprasegmental features are thought of as part of morphophonemics, again in most cases suprasegmental features hang between phonology and morphology receiving a separate treatment.

To avoid the confusion and to deal with the six aspects of the sentence we saw above which includes suprasegmental features on the one hand, and morphophonemic features on the other in present-day linguistics there is a move to include all these relevant aspects under one level which we may call ***morphonology***. The move to include the study of phonology, morphonology and morphology under one level of morphonology apparently looks fruitful and would do greater justice to the unitary nature of language. But the author strongly feels that a move of this kind in fact would add to the complexity of linguistic treatment since under one hand, morphonology, again we will be compelled to deal with the phonological, morphophonemic and morphological aspects of language separately. Linguistic theory cannot overlook the different manifestations of human language and study levels which have sufficient grounds to be dealt with separately as in the case of phonology and morphology. Therefore the wisest thing would be to posit ***morphonology*** only as an ***intermediary level*** between phonology and morphology, which takes care of what has so far been called morphophonological and suprasegmental features of language. In other words for present purposes the study of morphonology would include morphophonological and suprasegmental features as aspects which are uniquely bordering-cases between phonology and morphology. In our present understanding of the ***components of language***, morphonology is regarded as part of the phonological component, and morphology is part of the syntactic component for which the term 'grammar' (as against the Grammar) is also employed all through the book.

It is movement in the study of language therefore from pure phonology to morphonology which is the relating intermediary field and further to pure morphonology which takes us already into the level of syntax. Morphonology, thus deals with all sorts of phonemic alternations which do not occur strictly in morphology proper, including the rules of what has come to be called ***Sandhi*** on the one hand, and suprasegmental features on the other. Again a distinction between sandhi proper and other forms of phonemic alternations would create problems, just as phonemic alternations would in several cases take us right into the heart of morphology proper. What is expected is only that a student of linguistics must be aware of such problems.

2. Morphonology and the Phonological Component

The phonological component as we have examined in Ch. 8, is the level of human language which achieves a conversion of the surface structure sentence into its phonetic representation. The intermediary level which obtains this conversion or mapping is the phonological representation which along with the phonetic (and/or graphic) representation constitute the phonological component. There are two aspects of the phonological component which relate us at once to the points we are considering here. The phonological component is blend of the two aspects : (i) an organization of ***segmental features*** (vowels, diphthongs, triphthong, and consonants) and (ii) an organization of ***morphonological features.*** An analysis of the phonological component of any sentence would led us ultimately to these two aspects. The sentences of a language if listened to by someone other than the native speaker, who is not conversant with the language would consist merely of (i) a set of sequences of the segmental phonemes on the one hand, and one the other (ii) of a set of morphonological features including the suprasegmental features which occur in simultaneity with the segmental features. Only a native speaker or one who is conversant with the language alone with have the deeper communicational value for the sentences. It is a set of sequences of a variety of sounds for the vest.

The sentences ***It's all right for you to do the work*** consists thus of the sequences of segmental phonemes and an organization of simultaneous morphonological features. What do we exactly mean now by the term morphological features? This includes as we have said (i) phonemic alternations and (ii) suprasegmental features. Phonemic alternations consist of (a) regular sandhi on the one hand and (b) other forms of phonemic alternations. The first we may call ***Sandhi type*** and the second ***non-sandhi-type*** phonemic alternations as we shall see below. Suprasegmental features consist of (i) ***stress (accent)***, (ii) ***pitch levels***, (iii) ***tonal contours***, and (iv) ***transition (Junature).*** The pitch levels, and tonal contours together are known by the term ***intonation.***

Phonemic alternations of both sandhi-type and non-sandhi-type one common to English language too, though the occurrence and significance of sandhi rules in English cannot at all be paralleled with those of Latin or Sanskrit especially. Phonemic alternations of any type occur when a phoneme falls in a particular phonological environment in the precedent or following phoneme with its characteristic distinctive features influence and change the stricture of the phoneme in question. An environment which effects the phonological shape of a sound is known as the ***phonological environment*** when the occurrence is merely considered as a phonological occurrence (that of a sound). The same is known also as the ***morphological***

environment when the occurrence is regarded as morphological i.e. the affecting and the affected phonemes form part of or constitute morphemes which are the investigator's morphemes which are the investigators focus of attention. The alternations of *-s* in terms of the variants *-s, -z* and *-iz* occur in the environments of phonemes such as *-t* (*cats*), *-n* (*pens*) and *ch* (*churches*). These environments (*-t*, *-n*, and *ch-*) may be considered ***phonological*** when the focus is only on the sound as the unit under consideration for phonological purposes, or ***morphological*** when the focus is on the morphemes as the unit under consideration for morphological purposes.

Instances of phonemic alternation are easily available in English. The morphene ***hint*** when followed by *-s* becomes ***hints***. What happens here is characteristic. [*Hin–*] being a stressed nasal environment of [–t–] followed by the invoice alveolar tricative [–s] affects the distinctive features of the stop [–t–] and what results is a ***dissimilation*** of [-t-]. This is typical case of phonemic alternation where in the [n-s] environment [–t–] disappears. Its a regular feature in English exemplified by words such as ***tents***, ***tends mints***, ***minds***, ***winds*** etc. where both the voiced and voiceless stops are equally subjected to dissimitation in the [n–s] environment. An instance of dissimitation as illustrated above forms part of what we know as ***sandhi*** (The process of sandhi or the rules of sandhi). Dissimilative where a phoneme disappears in given phonological disappears in given phonological environment is one form of sandhi, which may be called ***dissimitative sandhi***.

Another instance of sandhi can be found in the word houses | housiz |. *House* | haus | being a morpheme with a voiceless alveolar fricative ending undergoes a phonemic alternation when followed by the plural morpheme alternant [–iz]. The phoneme assumed its voiced nature as part of modification in the distinctive features and becomes a voiced phoneme {-z] in the sandhi process resulting in the word | huziz |. The sandhi process my be presented schematically as the following:

$$[\text{haus}] + \{-Z_1\} \rightarrow [\text{hauz-}] + [\text{iz}] \rightarrow [\text{hauziz}]\ \text{houses.}$$

The process of sandhi as present in the above instance we will call ***replacive sandhi*** as the phoneme [-s] is replaced by [-z] in the combination of ***house – s.***

A third aspect of sandhi is known as ***assimilative sandhi*** where two phonemes of the same phonetic features when occurring together would undergo a process of assimilation and become one in the event of speech production. When, for instance two morphemes ***mid*** and ***day*** join together the final voiced unaspirated alveolar stop of ***mid*** undergoes an assimilation with the initial voiced aspirated alveolar stop of ***day*** and forms the word midday | midei |.

[mid] + [dei] → [midei]

Assimilation is what is happening in compound-words such as ***missuit, misspell*** etc. Assimilative Sandhi consisting of vowels is a very uncommon feature in English while most common in languages like Sanskrit and Sanskrit influenced Dravidian and Indo-Aryan language.

But phonemic alternations are not restricted to, nor are such alternations identical with the sandhi processes. There are a variety of phonemic alternations which have nothing at all to do with sandhi in the proper sense of the term. But such phonemic alternations must become part of a description of morphonology which takes care of sandhi process also. It must be remembered at this point that morphonology in all its aspects is intimately forms part both of phonology and morphology and the present work for several reasons regards morphonology a constituent aspect of the phonological component while morphology proper is regarded as a constituent aspect of the syntactic component. These distinctions are absolute requirement for proper theoretical lucidity. The phonemic alternations which we deal here take us right into the heart of morphology proper while the features remain intimately phonological.

The following alternations may be called non-sandhi-type alternations. Such non-sandhi-type phonemic alternations occur in what we called ***morphological processes*** of a restricted type. Since the set of such alternations are elaborated in Ch. 9, at this point we may include only what is referential. Phonemic alternations of this kind occur in (1) irregular plural formations as between ***man*** and ***men***, [–ǽ]→ [–e–], ***child-children*** [–ai–] → [–i–], ***mouse*** and ***mice*** [–au–]→[–ai–], etc., and (2) irregular past tense formations as between ***bite-bit*** [–ai–]→ [–i–], ***fall*** and ***fell*** [–ǽ–] → [–e–], ***hang*** and ***hung*** [–ǽ–] → [–ʌ–], ***wind-wound***, [–ai–] → [–au–], ***bind-bound*** [–ai–] → [–au–], ***bend-bent*** [-d] → [–t], and ***ring*** and ***rang*** [–i–] → [–ǽ–]. Similar phonemic alternations occur also in past participle formations as in ***fell – fallen*** [–e–]→ [–ǽ–] or ***load-laden*** [–əu–]→[–ei–]. In all such phonemic alternations as examined above including the process of sandhi we have observed one regular features which makes it essentially a morphonological factor: a phoneme is ***added***, ***deleted*** or ***replaced*** in a particular phonological environment influenced by the structural features of the phoneme or phonemes which constitute the environment. This is characteristically true of the sandhi rules while in the non-sandhi types the influence of the environment in the morpheme concerned is not so much evident as we regard it from a synchronic perspective without taking into consideration the diachronic background of the morpheme.

The phonological component of which maps the phonetic representation on the surface structure by means of the phonological representation is thus a blend of the two aspects: (1) an organization of the segmental phonemes and (2) an organization of the morphonological features. The morphonological features, as seen above consist of (a) the phonemic alternations and (b) the suprasegmental features. The phonemic alternations, in turn comprise (i) the sandhi-type alternations and (ii) non-sandhi-type alternations.

3. Constituent and Phonemic Stress (tonic)

It is a universal feature of language that utterances are made possible in a language by means of a combination of vowels and consonant sounds. The union of vowels and consonant sounds due to their characteristic distinctive features produce what we call a ***syllable*** or a syllabic unit. The word ***information*** comprises a sequence of vowels and consonants distributed in such a way that the syllabic units of [in–], [–fər–] [–mei–] and [–ʃən] are formed. The presence of four vowels have yielded four syllabic units in the word. The words of a language are thus ***monosyllabic*** or ***polysyllabic***: consisting of one single syllable or more than one syllable. The sonority and the carrying power of the vowels and the obstructive feature of the consonants together constitute the syllabic unit; all the same a vowel alone can constitute a syllable as we have the English *I* [ai], the Latin ā [a:] (by) or the Malayalam [i:] (this). In other words, we say, the ***vowel*** constitutes the basis of the syllable.

With the occurrence of every vowel in isolation as in I |ai | or in union with the consonant as in you | ju: | we find the presence of a ***simultaneous features***, the ***stress***. Stress in a general and non-technical sense of the term is fundamental to every vowel. With the occurrence of every vowel comes the stress as a ***volume of voice*** which actuates the syllable. In the technical and specific sense of the term, stress designates the volume of voice which enable a particular syllable to stand out from the rest. The distinction which we are drawing here is significant. There are a large number of languages which the term stress is applicable to only in the first sense as seen above characterised by what we know as ***vowel length***. The Dravidian languages, Malayalam for instance, have stress only in this general sense of the term. Malayalam vowels (syllabic units) stand out in terms of what we know as ***vowel length***. A syllable in this case is long if it contains a vowel that is long by nature. The Malayalam morpheme ***jeevan*** | dʒi:ven | for instance contains a ***double-length*** vowel '<u>ee</u>' [ī:] which makes the first syllable of the ***word a double-length syllable*** in contrast to a ***long syllable*** in English as in ***eat*** | i:t |.

It is against the 'double-length syllable' as found in Hindi or Malayalam, and the 'long syllable' as in English, we have the notion of a ***stressed syllable*** found only in languages such as English, or other European languages. It is in the second sense, of the term, as given above that 'stress' is used here. Apart from the ***constituent stress*** of a syllable found in all syllables of all languages, languages like English possess regular ***phonemic stress*** which is a significant aspect of the phonological structure of English. Stress is thus an intimate feature of the syllables of English and it is features in a word in a graded manner. We may say that the linguistic texture of English requires that apart from the constituent stress of syllables which English shares with other languages as a universal feature, every English wor whether monosyllabic disyllabic or polysyllabic possesses phonemic stress which retains considerable semantic implica tions as we shall see below.

The gradation of stress is feature in such a way that a polysyllabic word is assigned three levels of stress: ***primary stress*** ['–] (known as the tonic) ***secondary stress*** [,–] and ***tertiary stress*** [≏]. The tertiary stress is also known as the ***weak stress*** of a word which is not usually marked. The brackets show the placement of the stress-marker (the vertical bar above and in fronts of the syllable for the primary stress and below in the same way for the secondary show) which is usually indicated before the particular syllable [–] on which the stress falls. Words such as ***man, book, wait, take, him*** etc. are monosyllabic which as usual carry the constituent stress. Words such as ***'able, 'enmity, 'envelope, 'evening, 'every , 'favour, 'father, 'package*** and ***'village*** carry the primary stress on their ***first syllables.*** Words such as ***a'bove, a'bout, be'cause, con'sole, dé'ceive, dé'light*** etc. have the primary stress on the ***second syllable.*** There are polysyllable words which carry the primary stress on the ***third syllable.*** Instances for these are ***education, calculation, entertain, understand*** etc. There are words in which the primary stress falls on the ***fourth syllable: intelligentia, individuality, interpretation*** etc. English words have the primary stress also on the ***fifth syllable*** as in ***individualistic, intelligibility*** and so on.

The words shown above indicate the position of the primary stress in the first, second, third, fourth and even on the fifth syllables. Again English words are characterised by a secondary stress as seen above. Words such as ***calculation, disappointment*** and ***individual*** indicate a secondary stress which is a important to the intelligibility of English as the primary stress. The weak stress is not indicated (marked) except in specific phonological representations where the weak stress have some significance. Therefore it is also customary to speak of only the primary and secondary stress and not the weak stress. In our context the weak stress is identical to the constituent stress so far as English is concerned as against the primary and the secondary stresses.

In an intonational language such as English as against Hindi or Malayalam, the stress features play a very significant role. The primary stress which is known as the tonic (or the *tonic stress* or the *tonic accent*) is the key to the intelligibility of an English word or the words of any language where stress and intonation is predominant. The language of the native English speaker becomes intelligible with reference chiefly to the stressed (tonic) syllable. The tonic syllable stands out of the rest in terms of the amplitude of the voice, intensity of effort and greater breath force. In fluent and fast use of language it happens often that only the tonic syllables of words are heard and the weaker syllabus may get lost. A proficient speaker of English is in a position to catch a word merely from the tonic syllable if the tonic is placed correctly. The same happens with regard to the intangibility of a word when the tonic is wrongly placed. The English of Indian speakers of English becomes often difficult to the native English speaker because in several cases the stress is not correctly placed. In such instances the intelligibility of the language suffers.

The tonic is regarded on the one hand as ***phonemic*** and on the other ***morphemic***. As seen in sec. 1. of the chapter, in some cases it has come to be called a ***stress phoneme***, and in other cases a ***stress morpheme***. Like any segmental phoneme the stress feature of a word, the pitch levels of a sentence, the tonal contours and the transition have contrastive characteristic. Just as the presence of | P | in place of | b | in an environment brings a contrast in meaning, the suprasegmental features above such as the stress bring meaning contrasts in stress dominant languages. Words such as 'object (N) — object (v), 'record (N)— record (V) 'increase (N) — increase (V) contrast in meaning principally due to the stress. The vowel shift that occurs is caused by the shift to stress. As a phonological unit which brings contrasts in meanings stress is regarded, thus a stress phoneme, while, as a minimum meaningful unit which brings contrast in meaning we can talk of stress as a stress morpheme. In either way stress becomes a significant aspect of the morphonological level of language.

Another important aspect of the tonic is the phonemic alternations (sound shift) that happens as a regular feature in stress dominant languages. The English vowel phonemes |ɔ,ɔ:, and ∂u | are often subject to such phonemic alternations as examined in Sec. 1 of the present Chapter. The phonemes mentioned above retain their characteristic distinctive features when they occur in the tonic syllable. For instance the words ***in'form***, ***'product***, ***im'pose*** and ***Omen*** have their tonic (the primary stress) on the respective syllables and as such the respective vowels (ɔ:, ɔ and ʌ) are strong vowels. When the stress shift takes place from ***in'form*** to ***infor'mation***, ***'product*** to ***pro'duction***, ***im'pose*** to ***impo'sition*** and ***omen*** to ***ominous*** the syllables which held the tonic in earlier forms become characteristicallv weak. Consequently we have the weak vowel | ∂ | replaced in the syllables which held the tonic otherwise. Phonemic alternation is simultaneous with stress shift as it happens in ***derivation*** and ***compounding***. The process of derivation by means of affixation causes stress shift in several cases. It is a regular feature in English that suffixation of ***-tion***, or ***-ation*** to verbal stems and of ***-lity*** to adjectival stems causes shift in stress from the root of the word to the penultimate syllable, as the in ***con'tinue – continu'ation***, ***al'ternate - alter'nation***, ***in'telligible – intelligi'bility***, and ***res'pectable - respecta'bility***. The same is true of compounding where one form of the compound alone will carry the tonic as found in ***'blackboard*** or ***'earthquake***. The morphonological character of stress renders it basic in the behaviour of the phonological component of language. As a feature organized in a graded manner, stress also like segmental phonemes specify the morphonological behaviour of language.

4. Constituent and Phonemic Inonation

It is a basic characteristic of language that words as constituent units of sentence are ***linearly*** organised. A man is capable of uttering only one word at a time, not two. The second comes strictly after the first, the third after the second and so on. Corresponding to this strict linearity we find that we do not produce a sentence all in one and signal ***level of voice***. There are natural ups and down in our speech; some words have a higher level of voice than others depending on the context where the sentence is uttered. This is true of all human languages; the difference lies chiefly in the intensity of the stress put on the words at a given context. We saw that stress is primarily a feature which is strictly a constituent part of the vowel and the *constituent stress* as such forms part of all languages as against the *phonemic stress* which is restricted to some languages only. Similarly a distinction need to be made between *constituent intonation* of all languages as seen above and the *phonemic intonation* which is a characteristic of only some languages. Languages like Malayalam, Tamil, Hindi or other Indian language for that matter can be said to have only this basic constituent intonation. On the other hand English or other European languages possess what we have called phonemic intonation. Though the constituent intonation in language such as Hindi causes considerable change in the 'levels of voice', a change in the meaning of the sentence does not occur by that; in other words, there is no significant meaning contrast taking place. The constituent intonation is only part of the texture of the language under consideration. But a change in the levels of voice (intonation) in languages which possess phonemic intonation causes a contrast a meaning. Because such a change causes a contrast in the meaning of the sentence we have labeled such intonation as *phonemic intonation*.

The 'levels of voice' we have mentioned as referring to intonation need to be examined. What happens in intonational change is essentially a change in the level of voice. By this we mean to say that intonation is essentially a superimposed factor on the phonemic stress just as the phonemic stress is something superimposed on the constituent stress of a syllabic unit. It will be impossible for the phonetician or the linguist to draw a clear demarcation of the structure of stress on the one hand and intonation on the other. Stress and intonation or if we wish to put it more specially, constituent stress, phonemic stress, constituent intonation and phonemic intonation are merely four *degrees* of one and the same *pitch of voice*. For the sake of analysis considerations we may call all the four degrees of the pitch of voice by different names as seen above.

As such, the pitch of voice that features a particular syllable as different from other syllables of a word is the phonemic stress; the pitch of voice that differentiates a word (originally centered on the stressed syllable) from other words of the sentence we know by the technical term ***pitch level***; and the pitch of voice that differentiates the ***end of a sentence*** (centred, again on the stressed syllable of the last word) from the rest of the sentence and also from the ends of other sentences we know by the term ***tonal contours***. It is all the more necessary to keep in mind that the phonemic stress (the tonic), the pitch level (the highest pitch being the ***tonic of the sentence***) and the tonal contours are built on the foundations of the constituent stress, and that these are more a theoretical manner of viewing the same fundamental feature of the 'pitch of voice' with all the accompanying amplitude, muscular effort and breath from the different perspectives of ***syllable***, a ***word*** and a ***sentence*** a and a ***discourse*** as a whole.

The ***pitch levels*** of a sentence differentiate the words of a sentence among themselves. We can say that the tonic is moving thing so far as we identify the tonic of a sentence with the syllable on which the highest pitch falls. While the phonemic stress of every individual word in the sentence stands, the ***tonic of the sentence*** which is often called the 'sentence-stress' is in a position to move from one word to another as the situation and the semantic specifications demand. Thus we speak of a ***static tonic*** (the primary stress) of the words in a sentence, and a ***kinetic tonic*** which is the moving pitch phoneme on the sentence (the highest pitch level) that specify the particular meaning of the sentence.

When we say that the placing of the pitch (that kinetic tonic) depends on the situation and the speaker's intentions, it means that the highest pitch (the kinetic tonic) will be placed on that part of the sentence (word or phrase) which the speaker wants to make most ***prominent***. This most prominent word in the sentence is often called the ***nucleus*** of the sentence. The following instance makes it clear:

1. ^{1}*Have you* ^{2}*seen the* ^{2}*boy* ^{1}*doing the* ^{3}*work?*
2. Have you seen the boy ^{3}***doing*** the ^{2}work?
3. Have you seen the ^{3}***boy*** doing the ^{2}work?
4. Have you ^{3}***seen*** the boy doing the ^{2}work?
5. Have ^{3}***you*** seen the boy doing the ^{2}work?

The five instances of the same utterance differ as seen only in the levels of pitch. The numbers are used to indicate merely the pitch levels of the syllables occurring in the sentence, as against or as superimposed on the usual phonemic stress (static tonic) which is part of every word in the sentence. By kinetic stress we have meant the highest pitch that falls on ***work*** in (1), ***doing*** in (2), ***boy*** in (3) ***seen*** in (4) and ***you*** in (5). In other words the highest pitch phoneme has been shifting from sentence (1) to (5) in various syllables depending on the word the speaker wished to make prominent. We shall be concerned only with the highest pitch which is usually indicated by the number 3 or 4, '3' in the case of ordinary sentences such as a question, and '4' in the case of extraordinary sentences such as an exclamation or when the sentence is emotionally pitched. The lower grades of pitch are identical with the phonemic stress and therefore need not receive a marking except if we intend to grade the phonemic stress status of a whole sentence as done above. In the five instances of the sentence given above the meaning of the sentence changes with the change in pitch. As in the case of the phonemic stress by means of which ***meaning contrasts*** occur in words, because of differences in pitch levels (kinetic tonic or the placing of the nucleus) meaning contrasts occur. For this reason we are able to speak of ***pitch as phonemic*** (or ***morphemic***) as against stress as phonemic (or morphemic).

Again distinction need to be made between pitch levels and ***tonal contours***. In the usual description of the two impossible to distinguish one from the other as both will be concerned fundamentally with 'the pitch of voice'. We have seen that all that we have examined are one way or other fluctuations of the pitch of voice viewed from different perspectives: the tonal contours based on pitch levels, and this in turn on 'constituent intonation' until we reach the ultimate basis of the 'constituent stress' which naturally goes with every syllable.

While the pitch levels are distributed on individual words, tonal contours refers to the 'pitch of voice' of the last stressed syllable of the sentence. Instead of referring to tones as relevant to the pitch fluctuations of the whole sentence, we must restrict the notion of tones (tonal contours) to the pitch fluctuation (kinetic tonic: fall or rise) of the ***end of the sentence***. Thus there are three kinds of tonal contours: (i) ***rising tone***, (ii) ***falling tone*** and (iii) ***falling – rising tone*** depending on the nature of the sentence. The significant thing in this regard is that the tonal contours of natural (ordinary) sentences are more or less have a regular pattern, and changes occur only when, again, any extraordinary sense is attached to the sentence by the speaker. Since tonal contours are relevant only to the final tonic syllable of the sentence, the there contours (or modulations) are marked by arrow marks:

1. Are you going home?
2. What is your name?
3. I know him well.

The three modulations marked here are the extremes of what happens in ordinary speech. An ordinary English polar question has a rising tone; an ordinary 'wh' question has a falling tone; while a normal statement has a level tone. Departures from these occur within the genial tonal framework of the language only when some extra ordinary sense is attached to the sentence in question.

Transition (Junoture) is another phonemic aspect of closely associated with intonation. It is a significant suprasegmental feature which is phonemic in the sense that transition also brings contrast in meaning. Transition as a technical term designates the ***features of pause*** that occur in speech in a variety of ways. The meaning of a sentence, of a whole discourse is somehow attached to the transitions we make in speech. It makes a phonemic (morphemic) difference between saying ***blackboard*** (compound) and ***black#board*** (a phrase), ***cross-road*** and ***cross#road*** or ***blackbird*** and ***black#bird***. Compounds have assumed some special, distinct meaning other than what the members indicate while the phrase above mean what is apparent. Because of the transition that is present [#] there occur stress differences. As a rule only the first component of the compound retains the tonic while the both the words in the phrases retain the tonics of both the words. Transition is considered a part of the morphonological structure of English along with other suprasegmental features because of its ability to contrast meaning. The same is applicable to other types of pauses such as commas or colon [, :] in languages because of their influence of the meaning of the sentence.

5. Semantic Features of Morphonology

Reviewing what has been seen so far we find that Morphonology is a constituent part of the ***phonological component*** of language. Morphonology comprises two subfields: (1) phonemic alternations and (2) suprasegmental features. Phonemic alternations consist in turn of two aspects : (a) sandhi-type alternations, and (b) non-sandhi-type alternations. Suprasegmental features consist of (a) stress, (b) pitch levels (c) tonal contours, and (d) transition. To distinguish stress dominated languages such as English from other languages we posited what we have called 'constituent stress' which all languages possess and 'phonemic stress' which is built on the basic constituent stress, the difference being only in degrees of pitch of voice. In the place of 'phonemic stress' in English, we have seen that language such as Hindi or Malayalam have 'double-length syllables' which functions almost like the stress pattern in English, as against the 'long vowels' in English. To distinguish intonation predominated languages such as English from other languages we posited the 'constituent intonation' which all languages possess as related to the basic linear structure of a sentence with the modulation that is part of the sentences of all languages. By contrast to 'constituent intonation' we have 'phonemic intonation' which brings within significant contrasts in meaning as part of the structure of sentences.

The ultimate aim of linguistics lies in discovering the pattern of regularities which relate sounds with meanings. What is immediately accessible to the listener is only the stream of sound units organized in a large variety of manner. The linguist enters into the investigation of a large number of questions as he attempts to find out how this stream of sound units expresses some unit of meaning. Thus it is apparent that at one extreme of language we have the sounds and at the other extreme there are the meanings which the speaker intends to convey. The phonological component of language is inclusive of the entire range of sound variations and organizations of sound units which constitute the stream of sound units that falls on the ears of the listener.

It is all the more important therefore to view every little element of this stream of sounds as contributing in one way or other to the function of the phonological component in giving expression to a complex semantic organization which takes place in the semantic component of language. It is easy for us to describe the phonological aspects of the phonological component because the segmental phonemes are by and large definable in terms of their distinctive features. The universal phonetic system provides a comprehensive alphabet which defines the segmental phonemes on the basis of their structural distinctive features. But the stream of segmental phonemes does stream of segmental phonemes does constitute only the most phenomenal features of the phonological component of language. There is this simultaneous (parallel) stream of sound units which we distinguish from the stream of segmental phonemes and have called ***suprasegmental features***, as seen above in detail.

The unique characteristic of the morphonological features as a constituent of the phonological component is that the morphonological features, especially 'the suprasegmental features', are structured, purely of what we have called 'the pitch of voice'. It is the ***pitch of voice*** alone that distinguishes the suprasegmental features of language from the stream of segmental phonemes. Making use of the device of ***modulations in voice*** human language is capable of adding extra semantic specifications to an utterance which is already specified in terms of its segmental organization. The level of morphonology, thus throws light on the intricate but considerably economic structure of the phonological component. By means of the modulations of voice based on alternations in the pitch of voice human language achieves what we may call a ***linguistic economy*** which aims exclusively at a simplification of the relation between sounds and meanings: the phonological component and the semantic component of language.

The morphonological features of language with its phonemic alternations and suprasegmental features can thus be called the 'suprastructure' of the phonological component as against the 'infrastructure' which consists of the stream of segmental phonemes in the ordinary array. The suprasegmental phonemes and the phonemic alternations as the suprastructure of the phonological component gains significance especially when we consider that it is the ***tonic*** (***primary stress***) of a word and a sentence in its ***static*** and ***kinetic*** form that carries the entire meaning of a sentence to the listener, as if the meaning of the entire sentence (conceived as a stream of stressed and unstressed syllables) is codified in the tonic of the sentence on which the highest pitch falls.

1. I like his ^{3}*painting.*
2. I like ^{3}*his* painting.
3. I ^{3}*like* his painting.
4. ^{3}*I* like his painting.

The tonic syllables in the four sentences are so remarkable that a wide variety of meaning contrasts in brought about by presence of the tonic in one syllable or other in the stream of stressed and unstressed syllables of the sentence. The kinetic tonic moves from the fourth syllable of the five-syllabic sentence to the very first as the speaker's intention gets more and more extraordinary. In the context of a discourse the syllable [ai] of sentence (4) alone in a unique manner with the suprastructure of the tonic placed on its ***conveys*** all that the speaker wishes to put across in sentence (4) : The discourse is already a painting, which is ***his***, with the emotional attitude of ***like/dislike*** in question, and now, the speaker asserts '*I*...........' meaning that ***he*** likes the painting even if all others do not. It is the placement of the suprastructure of the kinetic tonic over the infrastructure of the segmental phonemes with its usual constituent stress that enables the speaker to convey himself the greatest possible economy.

The two aspects of morphonology: phonetic alterations and suprasegmental features are highly correlated in the structure of the phonological component. The phonemic structure of the tonic syllable is morphonological by nature. The phonemic alternation of [ðu] in ***go*** into [ɔ] in ***going*** is a case where phonemic alternation and the tonic converge. The word *'estimate* has an [e] on the third syllable governed by the primary stress on the first syilable; a phonemic alternation occurs in the third syllable the moment the primary stress is shifted to the third syllable, from [e] to [ei]. The monophthong is altered into a diphthong. The two aspects of morphonology as seen above function together to give most effective expression to the infrastructure of the segmental phonemes on which the semantic phonemes on which the semantic component ultimately depend. The phonological component of the sentence of a language essentially is a blend of two organizational features : the organization of segmental phonemes and the organization morphonological features which work together to carry the meaning of the sentences across to the listener of a language.

11
The Syntax of Language

1. The Syntactic Component of Language

The interpolation of structural and behavioral components of human language has the greatest bearing on an explanatory theory of language at the level of the syntactic component. A theory of language must on the one hand account for the ***structural elements*** which constitute the syntactic component of human language as an objective and structured system, and on the other account for the ***behavioral features*** of language as ***creative and generative mechanism***. There can be no accounting go human language without taking care of its creative and generative properties. The ***syntactic component*** is, therefore the generative mechanism of human language which is behavioral mode with a structural content that we call the language proper. It is the most comprehensive description that we may assign to the syntactic component.

As the transformational generative school insists, human language comprises a ***generative process***. If we make an inventory of the natural sentences of which a six year old produces, we will find that out of set of a hurdred sentences produced in the course of a day or so, there are hardly a few repetitions and most of the hundred sentences in terms of their structural organization, patterns employed, and the grouping of words bear a mark distinctive ***originality***. This originality springs from the fact that the individual has not produced the hundred sentences from a memory of a set of sentences that he had committed to memory any more than these are sheer repetitions of sentences produced earlier in some other set of contexts. The phenomenon that the sentences as part of several discourses bear a mark of distinctive originality can only be explained by the fact that the sentences are the product of an underlying ***creative and generative mechanism***. This underlying generative mechanism employs the ***lexicon*** (lexicon inventory) of the language on the one hand, and a set of ***formative rules*** (structural rules) on the other in producing the sentences of the language.

The syntactic component which is the generative mechanism of the language, thus makes use of two ***finite sets***: (1) of lexicon, and (ii) of generative transformational rules to produce what is known as an ***infinite set*** of sentences in the language. This is the central aspect of language as a ***generative mechanism*** (the behavioural component) and as an objective, ***structured system*** (the structural component) which comprises three distinct sets : (i) the finite set of words, (ii) the finite set of generative transportational rules, and (iii) the infinite set of sentences which the linguistic community or an individual speaker is capable of producing. For these reasons we have said that the syntactic component constitutes the most comprehensive and significant component of language in contrast to the phonological and the semantic components. It is in and the through the phonological component that we are able to have a vision of the behavioral and structural features of language that enable a speaker to come out with creatively original sentences. For this very reason we may say that ***language is syntax*** if syntax is understood to cover all that we have meant by syntactic component. The structuralist (and traditional) understanding of 'syntax' as sheer 'word order' provides so limpid and limited a scope to the understanding of the working of human language. Only a vision, as seen above, which encompasses the behavioral and structural features of human language alone can truly contribute to the genuine theory of language.

The syntactic component as we have seen is a generative mechanism. The phonological and the semantic components, on the other hand are so merged with the syntactic component that the generative process as the basic sentence-producing mechanism has its deep roots in the phonological and semantic components of language. All the same, the three components working simultaneously towards the production of sentences assign rules which specify in effect the semantic, grammatical and phonological features of sentences. As the generativist linguists explain it, the phonological component of language ***assigns rules*** for mapping the phonetic representation in the surface structure; the syntactic component assigns rules for the transformation of the deep sentence into the surface sentence; and the semantic component assigns rules for the creative; generative production of the deep sentence which is in turn transformed into the surface sentence.

At the deepest level the ***cognitive structure*** (posited here as the seat of cogitative, sensitive and vegetative functions of man) is regarded as the principle (faculty) of ***conceptual organization***. This, being the fundamental linguistic activity at the deep level, can be viewed from two perspectives: as a mental (cognitive) activity and as a linguistic activity, referred to earlier as cognitive experience and linguistic experience as against the third sociological experience. We might therefore say that language activity begins with conceptual organization taking place in the cognitive structure. The cognitive organization is the meeting ground, as we shall see later, of ***mental activity*** (perspective i) and ***linguistic activity*** (perspective ii), the first seen as an organization of ***concepts*** and the second seen as an organization of ***meanings***: one and the same reality (component) seen from two perspectives.

The roots of the syntactic component as seen lying deep at the heart of the semantic component of language as we consider the role of conceptual organization in the production of language. This interpolation is what is meant when say that the mental activity of thinking cannot easily be seen as distinct from language activity. The ***syntactic organisation*** of the forms of the speaker's language and the ***semantic organization*** at the level of concepts are two perspectives of one and the same activity of ***organization*** which takes place in the cognitive structure. No man can sit down to do a bit of thinking work without involving a little of language work, however rudimentary the language work involved may be. The level of syntax thus penetrates deep into the level of semantics resulting in a blend which we shall label as the ***deep structure*** of language. Deep structure, constituted at the heart of the cognitive structure (faculty) is therefore a blend of syntactic organization of forms (abstract) and semantic organization of concepts (abstract and universal).

What takes place at the heart of human cognitive structure is therefore a generative activity which is a rule-governed, creative process. The interpolation of the semantic and syntactic organizations aimed at producing the sentences of language is a ***rule-governed process*** which permits the production of only the correct sentences of language. It is the blended presence of the syntactic component right deep at the level of semantic component that makes the production of the deep structure sentence a rule-governed process. In a bilingual context of becomes necessary for the speaker to exercise, say, two parallel rule-governed activities or rather an activity governed by two sets of rules pertaining to the syntactic components of two languages, get worked out on the basis of one and the same fundamental conceptual (semantic) organization. It is not necessary for an individual to exercise a shift in his fundamental thinking process even though at a given time he may be required to speak (understand) two languages. The apparent dichotomy present in this context can be resolved by a detailed examination of a bilingual situation which the scope of the present treatment does not permit. We may therefore postulate in the case of bilingualism one and the same semantic (conceptual) organization with a parallel process of 'conceptual accommodation' in the line with two syntactic organizations (in the case of two languages) which figure in at the time of the bilingual which figure in at the time of the bilingual production by a speaker.

The semantic organization of concepts in simultaneity with the syntactic organization of forms yield what we know as the deep structure sentence. It is impossible to posit the two organizations as happening at distinct levels for the production of the deep structure sentence. The semantic organization as one of concepts and conceptual elements, and the syntactic organization as one of the lexical forms (the abstract lexemes) can be posited only as a simultaneous process in the cognitive structure. The human creative potency gets actuates through the cognitive structure with the mind and the constituent faculties as its operational center. In other words the cognitive structure functions like a ***generative mechanism*** which is essentially oriented to the 'creation' of language in order to meet the individual's communicational requirements. There is a very significant parallelism which we notice at this point. It is the parallelism between the ever creative organization of thought (which consists of organised streams of concepts) and the creative organization of language. Since human thought is essentially creative with its infinite possibilities for novel expressions, language which has thought as its content is bound to be creative with the same infinite possibilities for creative expression of human thought. The deep structure sentence is therefore, the output of the fundamental creative, generative process taking place in the cognitive structure.

All the same, we have said, the syntactic organization in simultaneity with the semantic organization produces a deep structure sentence which consists of abstract linguistic forms. There abstract ***lexemes*** constitute the basis for the individual lexical items later to be concretised phonologically set and phonated for lexical organization at the deep structure level is governed by the ***phrase-structure rules.*** The phrase- structure rules are regarded as central to the transformational generative grammar, and the phrase- structure system is traced back to Leonald Bloomfield (for details see Ch. Trends in Linguistics). The phrase-structure rules which consists of the ***hierarchical organization*** of Noun Phrase (NP), Verb Phrases (VP). Prepositional phrases (PP), and particles, form the skeleton of the deep structure sentence. The set of phrase structure rules of the language govern the rule-governed creative production of sentences; this set of rules constitutes the '***syntactic structure***' of the speaker's linguistic competence. The syntactic component of language, thus, comprises several behavioural and structural components all of which are oriented to the production of the ***surface sentence*** to be phonologically and phonetically, set for the listener to receive. The deep structure acquire elaborate treatment in the context of linguistic competence and linguistic performance as will be taken up in the following section. What is significant is that the syntactic component converges on the semantic and phonological components of language as unitary activity.

2. Generative Features of Syntax

The syntax component of human language is seen here as a ***generative mechanism*** which by and large converges on to the phonological component on the one hand and the semantic component on the other. The cognitive structure of the individual which ultimately functions as the generative mechanism for language production is essentially a ***human factualty*** which may be described as the infrastructure of all that is going to be the individual speaker's ***built-in ability***. What is this built-in ability, as transformationalists call it ? ***Linguistic competence*** is the technical term used to designate this built-in ability. The child's generative mechanisms as we call it is the principle of the mind with its component faculties of the intellect and the imagination which we do not wish to discuss at this point. To avoid unnecessary complication the term 'cognitive structure' has been employed throughout to include all the component faculties of the mind and the brain. We must be clear in regard to one important distinction : (1) the ***cognitive faculty*** (cognitive structure) which is an in-born principle in the individual, and (2) the ***linguistic competence*** which is the built-in ability for a particular language. The actual exercise of this competence is known as the linguistic performance.

Linguistic competence as the built-in linguistic ability chiefly consists of two aspects: (i) the finite set of the lexicon of the language, and (ii) the finite set of the generative transformational rules of the language. These two finite sets acquired by the native speaker (the child) in a progressive and developing manner in course of his long-time ***acquaintance*** with the language function as the generative factor to produce an ***infinite set***: the set of possible sentences which the individual can produce. In the general sense of the term linguistic competence is the entirely of language which the individual has mastered; in the specific sentence of the term, linguistic competence would mean only the two parallel finite sets: of the lexicon and of the generative rules, as one single ***formal system*** present in the individual speaker's cognitive structure.

As a formal (formalized) system linguistic competence has come to be equated to a ***theory***, the theory of the language which in the form of a set of formalised rules the child possesses. What the linguist as an investigator of human language endeavours is to explicate as an explanatory theory the 'formal system' which the speaker possesses in an implicit manner. Competence as a system of implicit rules does not present itself to the convert mind of the speaker, except in the case of the linguist as a speaker who explicates this system for explanatory purposes. In fact an explanatory explication of the implicit, formal system of linguistic competence by the linguist yields two kinds of accountings : (i) a theory of the ***particular grammar***, and (ii) the theory of the ***universal grammar***. The first paves way for the second; the first is a stepping-stone to the second; and the first implicitly contains the second. The ultimate aim of linguistic investigation is, thus, to reach an explanatory theory of the ***universals of language*** (see Ch. 7).

Linguistic competence of the speaker as an internalised, formal system constitutes the *Grammar* of the language (see Ch. 7). As such the linguistic competence comprises two intimate dimensions : (i) the ***universals***, and (ii) the ***differentials***. The various aspects of the (a) phonological, (b) grammatic and (c) semantic universals and the (a) phonological, (b) grammatic and (c) semantic differentials have already been looked into the in Ch. 7. We must only in this context keep in mind the distinction between the *Grammar* and the ***grammar*** of language as it is a concept central to the understanding of the system under consideration. Linguistic competence as the formal built-in system of language present in the cognitive structure of the speaker contains not only the grammar (syntax) of the language, but the Grammar which comprises the phonological, grammatical and semantic rules which go into the fundamental (core) structure of the language. While the ***phonological component*** as seen in detail (Ch. 8) governs the phonological behaviour and structure of language which includes the phonological universals and differentials, the syntactic component governs the grammatical structure and the syntactic behaviour of language, and the ***semantic component*** similarly governs the semantic structure and behaviour of the language.

Within the generative mechanism of language, again, competence as a formal system takes care of the grammar and the usage levels of language while it is linguistic performance which takes care of the use level of language as explicated in Ch. 7. Linguistic 'performance' and the level of 'use' as the word is technically used in the system are two different perspectives of the linguistic (idiolectic) behaviour of the individual speaker. While, again, competence as a formal system of rules (of the Grammar and usage of language) is posited as an ***abstracted system*** which penetrates in regard to its organization upto the level of the phonological representation of the sentence (which is a semi-abstract representation as seen in Ch. 8.), performance as the exercise of competence in speech or writing renders the formal system concrete in terms of the optional phonetic (graphic) representation. In this manner the intimate affiliation of the grammar and usage levels to competence, and of the level of use of performance can be established.

From what has been discussed so far we know that the syntactic component is the ***generative source*** where on the one hand the semantic organization (conceptual organization) and on the other the syntactic organization of abstract forms interpolate towards the production of what we know as the deep structure sentence. The formal ***deep structure***, in this process, as a system of ***phrase structure rules*** receives semantic representation by means of the semantic organization at the level of concepts. With the application of ***transformational rules*** which one central to the understanding of the syntactic component, the syntactic component provides a ***surface structure*** (***surface sentence***). As seen in Ch. 8, it is this surface sentence that is fed to the phonological component where it receives what we know as the 'phonological representation' and the 'phonetic representation'.

The syntactic component thus comprises a ***base element***, a ***transformational element*** and a ***surface element***. As seen above the base element is the deep structure where the meaning of the sentence is set in terms of the required conceptual organization. It is by and large a process of giving semantic representation to a system of syntactically organized phrase-structure slots which together yields the 'abstract deep structure sentence'. Thus the deep structure sentence or sentence can be finally regarded as an output consisting of syntactically organized set (sets) of 'abstract textical units.' Transformations are the rules which link deep and surface sentences. It consists of a process of reorganization oriented to yield the surface structure of the sentence.

3. Deep Level Syntax

The study of the generative features of syntax on the preceding pages have provided sufficient grounding for a detailed consideration of the syntactic elements which enter into the making of the syntactic component of language. Thus an explanatory account of the syntactic component of language will consist of three levels ; (i) *the deep level syntax* which is concerned about the base element or deep structure of syntax, (ii) *transformations* which accounts for the relations that link the deep structure to the surface structure, and (iii) *the surface level syntax* which is concerned about the surface structure of sentences.

We have seen that the creative, generative production of sentences springs from an interaction of two finite sets formal elements : (1) the formal system of rules, and (2) the lexicon of the language, which the speaker has internalised. The interplay of these two finite sets yield what we know as an infinite set of possible sentences which a speaker can produce. The two finite sets of rules thus are at once relevant to the deep level syntax. Deep level syntax thus consists of the lexicon of the language which of itself constitute a formal system in the deep level syntax, and two subuses of rules : (i) *phrase structure rules* and (ii) the *subcategorization rules.* The phrase structure rules are generally known also as *branching rules* or *constituent structure* rules or *Formation rules* or *generative rules of syntax.*

In the traditional explanation of the structure of a sentence we find a distinction between ***transitive*** and ***intransitive*** verbs. A transitive verb is one that occurs with an object as in ***The boy saw a picture.*** An intransitive verb is one that does not in the context occur with an object as in ***The boy slept well.*** We say the two forms transitive and intransitive are the ***subcategories*** of the category of 'verb'. Here we say that verbs in English are sub-categorized in regard to the function of taking or rejecting a 'direct object'. A detailed look into the structure of the English ***Verb Phrase*** shows that English verbs can be sub-categorized into a large variety of functions which enter into the structure of the Verb Phrase, such as 'place' (***The boy put the picture there***), 'manner' (***The boy*** slept well) 'duration' (The boy slept for a long time) and so on. Each of these functions is said to sub-categorize the category of verb. These sub-categorizations of verbs govern the construction of Verb Phrases in a language. The subcategories which are usually posited do not form water-tight compartments because it happens that there are overlaps or more technically what is known as an ***intersection*** of subcategories when for instance the same verb will function as transitive on one hand and intransitive on the other (He runs/He runs a shop).

In the same manner, the category of 'Noun' is considered to have a variety of subcategories with respect to the environment in which the Noun occurs or the functions the Noun enters into. A main subcategory is whether a Noun occurs with an article: ***common nouns*** and ***proper nouns*** (***The boy/***Rahim is clever). The two are not replaceable in an environment. The sub-categorization is based on certain ***constituents*** and we can thus sub-categorize verbs, nouns, adjectives and adverbs. The notion of sub-categorization functions as the chief principle of the underlying structure of a sentence. It is from the notion of sub-categorization that we enter into the notion of ***phrases*** as constituents which naturally go together in terms of their function. An article, thus, goes with its head, the noun, and not with the verb. This leads us to what is known as ***Immediate Constituent Analysis*** (Ch. 15) to find out the constituent elements of phrases. The principle of IC analysis is taken up in the transformational generative grammar and developed into what we know as phrase ***structure*** grammar. The content of these treatments is the structure of the basic phrases (Noun Phrase, and Verb Phrase (which enter into the construction of sentence. In phrase as ***a set of rules*** which govern the grouping of the Noun Phrase and the verb phrase in a sentence, we make use of ***labeled brackets*** (or ***phrase markers***) to express the grouping of the phrases: A past tense construction will receive will a labeled bracketing of the following kind:

The boy went to market.

$[_{S} [NP]^{1} [_{VP} [V\text{-past}]\ \text{prep.}\ [NP]^{2}\ ]_{VP}]_{S}$

The enclosed brackets indicate the structure of the NP and the VP which constitute the whole sentence. The same construction receives a 'tree diagram' in the following manner:

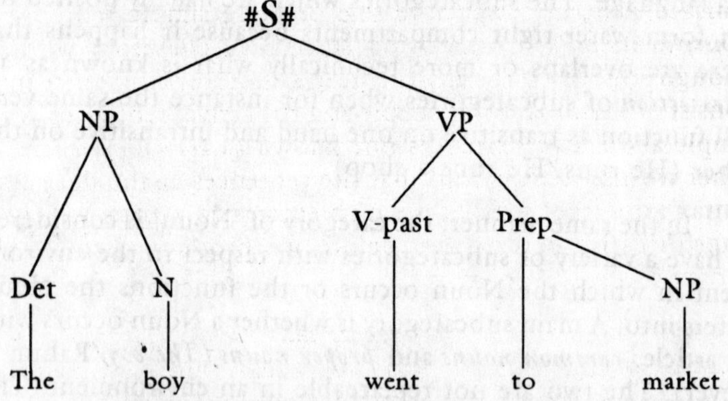

The phrase structure representation groups constituents which are subcategories of a particular head as well as groups together those constituents which together manifest a particular function. In other words the phrase structure as a sequence of slots oriented to yielding 'the abstract deep structure sentence' consists of an organization of ***syntactic rules*** which generate the deep level sentence. The ***string*** of *NP* and *VP* provides the *S* (the sentence) and the strings further take most elementary constituents are represented. In the generative grammar, these rules are known as 'expansion' or 'rewrite' rules. The tree above generate the following phrase structure rules:

1. S → NP + VP.
2. NP^1 → Det + N
3. VP → V-past + Prep. + NP^2
4. NP^2 → N.

The four rules above generate one tree or a labeled bracketting.

It is significant to understand that the deep level sentence has certain specific characteristic. The sentence of a language which is speaker produces and we receives after the phonetic representation (Phonation) can be a simple or complex sentence as the terms traditionally mean. In other words the sentence, we say, is ***embedded*** i.e. one enclosed in the other or one syntactically allied to the other in terms os ***subordination***. The constituent clauses of the sentence are subordinate to the main (or matrix) clause. In other words a surface sentence (surface structure) can have one or more simple sentence as ***constituents*** of the underlying structure. Therefore we have enough reasons to say that the deep structure of sentence must consist of ***one*** or ***more*** (a) simple and (b) active, sentences. Such simple and active sentences one known as ***kernel sentences***. In other words we may hold that the sentences at the deep level syntax are kernel sentences which enter into a large variety of transformational processes before we produce them at the surface level.

The sentence ***The boy knows that the girl has come*** is an embedded sentence with two constituent sentences: main and subordinate. At the deep structure level we posit two kernel sentences: (1) ***The boy knows it***, and (2) ***The girl has come.*** The underlying structures of the sentences will receive the following phrase-marker representations:

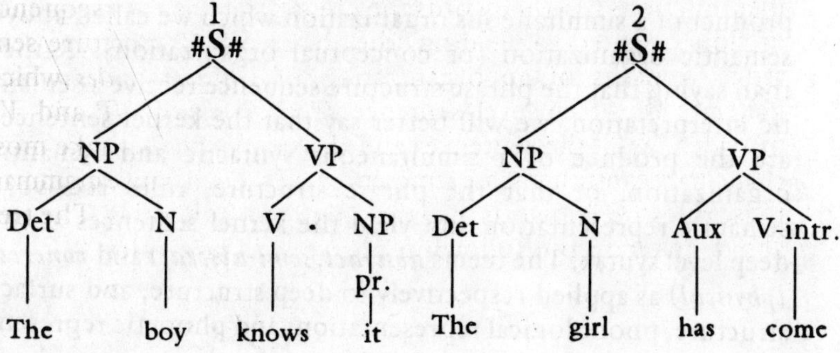

A generalized phrase marked which conjoins the two simple sentences in the transformation and yield the surface sentence will receive the following representation:

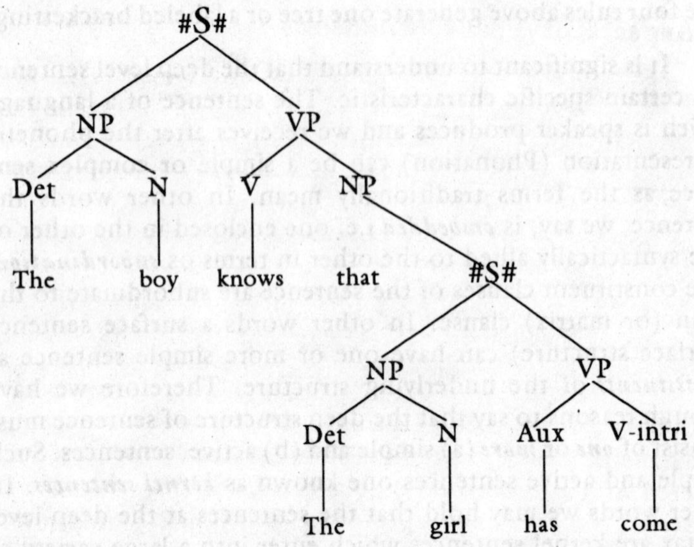

The concern here is not so much with the phrase structural analysis of sentences than the *role* the *phrase structure rules* play at the deep level syntax. The few instances examined above show how the phrase structure rules form the *slots* (the patterns required) in the form of simple constructions of basic sentence patterns. The kernel sentences should, thus the posited as consisting of syntactically organized sequences of abstract formal units of lexemes (each word bearing technical significance). These sequences (kernel sentences) of abstract lexemes are the product of a simultaneous organization which we called above semantic organization (or conceptual organization). Rather than saying that the phrase structure sequence receive a semantic interpretation, we will better say that the kernel sentences are the produce of a simultaneous syntactic and semantic organization, or that the phrase structure, rules receive a semantic representation and yield the kernel sentences at the deep level syntax. The teems *abstract, semi-abstract* and *concrete (physical)* as applied respectively to deep structure, and surface structure, phonological representation, and phonetic representation are significant in the context of the theory of language that we are concerned about. Deep level syntax is the base generative mechanism which produces the deep level sentence for transformation and surface representations.

4. Aspects of Transformations

The syntactic component as seen above comprises the three levels of (a) deep level syntax, (b) transformations, and (c) surface level syntax. The sub-categorizational features and the phrase structure rules of the deep level syntax are said to yield the deep structure sentence which receive the semantic representation. The generalized surface structure is the result of a set of transformational rules applied on the deep structure. We have seen that transformation is the process of yielding the surface structure from the deep structure, or that transformations are the rules that link deep structure to surface structure.

The transformational description of a sentence includes (i) a ***structural description*** of the phrase structure rules that have entered into the deep level construction of the sentence or sentence, (ii) a statement of the ***structural alternation*** which may (or must) take place in terms of (a) ***deletion*** (b) ***insertion*** and (c) ***permutation***, and (iii) a statement of the ***conditions for application***. The three aspects above constitute transformational description of a sentence. The operations which are employed in structural alternation are elimination (deletion), addition (insertion) and change (permutation) as above in the order of elements. The structural description as seen is a statement of the structure rules (or the phrase structure sequence) which constitute the branching rules of a tree as against the branching rules of another tree: the two forming parallel representations of the constituent clauses of a complex sentence. The structural descriptions of the two diagrams given above in section 3 would be the following:

1. Det N VP NP (Pr)
2. Det N NP (Aux vi-intr).

The two sentences when embedded would have the following structural description:

Det N V that #Det N VP(Aux V-intr).

It makes a difference whether the structural description relates to the higher nodes or lower nodes in the diagram. The higher the nodes mentioned are the more general the description will be and it will be inclusive of greater number of sentences; the lower the nodes are it receives greater specificity in regard to its application solely to one or other sentence. For instance the description *S→ NP+VP* is universal i.e. applicable to all possible sentences. These nodes (NP +VP) are supposed to be the highest in a diagram. The more specific the description becomes, the number of sentences which come under will correspondingly become limited to any specific pattern.

As mentioned above, the second aspect of a transformation as the ***structural change***. Structural change consists of deletion (eliminating) insertion (addition) and permutation (change in order). The transformational process of deletion may be thought of as the elimination of one constituent or other from the deep structure sentence. ***Deletion transformation*** occurs usually for instance with the English comparative. This happens with those constituent elements which are 'understood' in a sentence. Consider the following sentences:

1. The boy is smarter than the girl *is*
2. The boy is smarter than the girl.

In all transformations there are ***optional rules*** and ***obligatory rules***. There are certain rules in regard to which the speaker is free (optional) and there are certain others which must be followed (obligatory). The underlying (deep structure) sentences would be the following, covering the two sentences above:

3. The boy is more smart.
4. The girl is smart.

In the process of deletion transformation an elimination of ***smart*** which is repeated becomes obligatory while eliminating ***is*** is only optional as the sentences (1) and (2) show. Sentences (3) and (4) being the kernel sentences provide the following diagrams:

I.

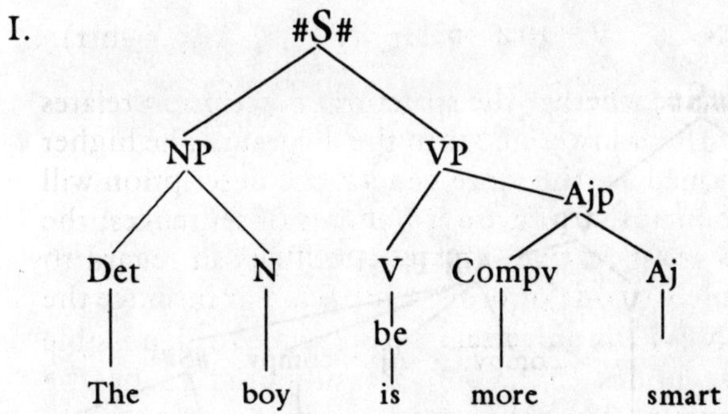

II.

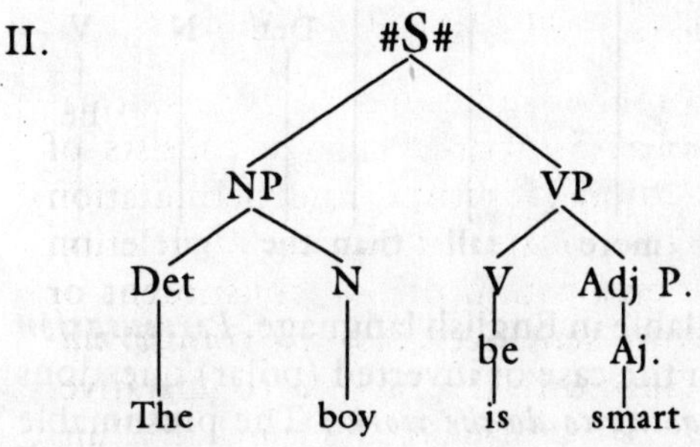

The structural description for the deletion transformation will be :

1. Det N be compv Aj.
2. Det N be Aj.

The deletion transformation would yield,

3. *Det N be compv Aj compv # Det N, be*

The structural description (3) gives the tree diagram (shown on p.186) pertaining to the surface sentence.

Insertion transformation occurs in the case of 'wh' questions where the addition of ***what, where, when, who*** etc. to an underlying sentence (posited as a proposition) in the form of ***you are doing something. What*** ? or ***you are going somewhere? Where*** ? etc. Not many isolated cases of deletion, insertion or permutation without any other transformation entering in the

III.

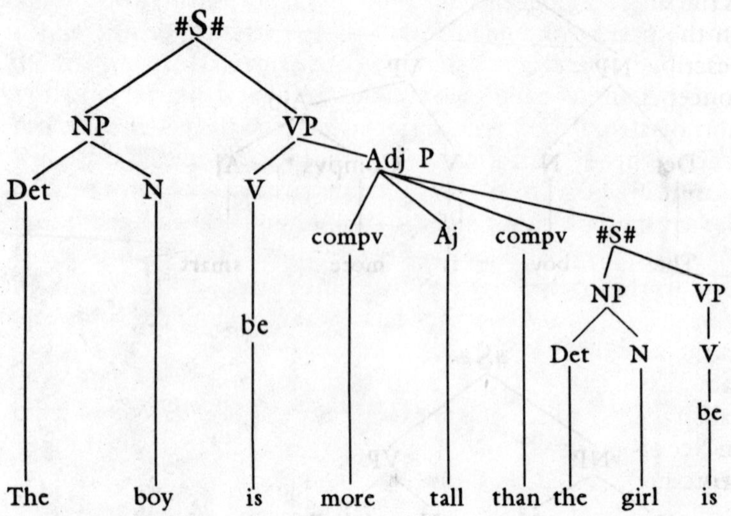

process will be easily available in English language. ***Permutation transformation*** occurs in the case of inverted (polar) questions in English. In ***Are you going to do the work***? The presumable underlying sentence will be the proposition ***You are going to do the work.*** In all these instances there is no doubt that were mostly fall back upon the traditional logical prepositions which are said to under surface sentences. The notion of deep level sentence and surface level sentence is nothings new to the transformationalist grammarians as it has been recognized by themselves. The intention here is only to bring home the aspect of transformation as a constituent of the syntactic component of language rather than get into the intricate and often unconvincing aspects of the processes involved in transformations as indicated by the transformational generative grammarians.

5. Surface Level Syntax

Of the three levels of the syntactic component of language, we have seen the intricacies of the deep level syntax and transformations. The generative transformational production of language is a coherent process with the kind of unification that can be broken down only for the precise purpose of theory-building. At the very depth of syntax there is what we have seen as the simultaneous organization of the deep structure sentence on the pattern provided by the phrase structure rules. This is described above as the simultaneous semantic organization of concepts and conceptual elements and the syntactic organization of abstract lexical forms to yield the deep structure sentence. The organization aspect of this generative process is significant because language production is a creative process. As a creative process and considering it in the right perspective, we must only posit an ***organization*** as occurring at the deepest level in the cognitive structure. This is an organization of the ***semantic*** and ***syntactic*** constituents described above as concepts (a mental reality) as against meanings (a linguistic reality) the same fact viewed from two perspectives, and lexical forms (abstract lexemes). The representation of the deep level syntax in Sec. 3 indicate how the syntactic organization of the deep structure takes place.

The transformational processes shown in Section 4 derive the surface sentences from the deep structure. This occurs as we have seen by means of the processes of insertion, deletion or permutation. What can be the precise nature of the surface structure as the most extrinsic level of the syntactic component? How does the surface structure of the syntactic component behave ? These are the two aspects of the present question with regard to the surface structure. The three levels we have postulated as constituting the entire spectrum of language are: the ***Grammar, usage*** and ***use*** (Ch. 7). The levels of the grammar and usage can be side to constitute the linguistic competence of the speaker (and of and the linguistic community as a whole), and the level of use constitute the linguistic performance of the speaker. The deep level syntax pertaining to (or in) the cognitive structure of the speaker with the associative and subsegment transformations together must have direct correspondence to what we know as the level (1) and level (2) of language : the grammar and usage. Similarly the surface levels syntax corresponds to the third level of language : use, while the deep level syntax transformations and surface structure pertain to the generative linguistic mechanism of the ***individual speaker*** (as representing the linguistic community), the levels of the grammar, usage and use pertain to the objective structure of human language and subsequently of a particular language. The two perspectives must be kept very distinct in the mind of the linguist.

The syntactic component of language must account for the two distinct dimensions of language as indicated above : (1) the *syntactic realization* of language in the cognitive structure of the speaker where linguistic competence remains present as a potential factor, and (2) the syntactic structure of the language, say, English as an structured, objective system. The distinction will at once lead us back in same way to the fundamental Sausscerian distinction between 'langue' and 'parole'. These two dichotomous aspects of syntax makes the syntactic component of language more complex. The only rationale that will penetrate the dichotomy is the distinction that we have drawn between (1) the *deep level syntax*, *transformation* and *surface level syntax* as constituting the subtactic component of language as a syntactic realization in the speaker's generative mechanism (or cognitive structure), and (2) the *Grammar, usage* and *use levels* of language as a structured, objective system which a linguistic community employs. No easy distinction of the 'langue-parole' type could take care of the complex dichotomy which we have been concerned about in the present context.

The surface level syntax as said above corresponds to the use level of language. What do we mean by this? The 'use' of language is the *idiolectic exercise* of language. Human language as an objective, structured system with a substantiality of its own receives concrete realization only in the idiolectic *use* of it. The use level of language is so significant because it is at this level i.e. in the individual speaker's exercise of it that the two linguistic dimensions converge: dimensions (1) and dimension (2) as indicated above. On the one hand the dimension of the objective system of language with the grammar, and usage, and on the other the dimension of the syntactic realization of language in the speaker with the three-level syntactic component in fact *converge* in the speaker's generative mechanism: at the level of use, on the one hand and the surface level syntax on the other. For this reasons identify as linguistic *performance* in the transformational generative sense receives the greatest and most detailed specification in terms of the three components: phonological, syntactic and semantic.

The surface level syntax receives, again, the most detailed structural description (N V NP Adv.) as the final product of the process of transformation. The base forms of the sentence under consideration, with the semantic and semantic organization lie at the deep level syntax. The transformations add to delete from or rearrange the constituent elements giving the structural description greater specificity. It is at the surface structure that we have finally organized set of constituent elements of the sentence available. The surface structure by virtue of it being identical with the level of use renders itself to a specification which takes care of all the idiolectic characteristics of grammar and meaning. Whether the sentence will receive the phonetic representation or graphic representation (Ch. 8) in the final resort the surface structure finalises all the necessary grammatical and semantic details (as part of the linguistic modifications done at the level of use).

The surface structure with its syntactically and semantically finalized sequence of forms first of all receives the phonological representation in the phonological component. While the surface structure is essentially a sequence of syntactically organized abstract texical forms, the phonological component as the more extrinsive level of language, assigns to this sequence of abstract lexical forms an added dimension of ***concreteness*** which somehow makes the it sequence of a ***semi-concrete*** lexical forms (for details see Ch. 8) The final concreteness and the physical characteristic which a phonated (or written) sentence possesses are assigned by the phonological component in the phonetic (or graphic) representation of the sentence i.e. when the sentence is finally spoken or written. Just as all work at the level of syntax is assigned to the syntactic component, every aspect of organization and representation that occurs in translating the surface structure to phonological and phonetic representations is assigned to the phonological component of language. The surface level syntax, in short, constitutes the final stage of a creative generative linguistic process which begins at the deep level syntax as the syntactic component penetrates the phonological and semantic components of language.

12
Semantics

1. The Semantic Component of Language

The phonological component (Ch. 8) governs the phonological structure and behaviour of language; the syntactic component (Ch. 11) governs the grammatical structure and syntactic behaviour of language while the semantic component which is the present concern, governs the semantic structure and behaviour of human language. In Ch. 11 we saw that at the deepest level of the human cognitive structure which is posited as the seat of all cogitative, sensitive and vegetative functions of man, we have a parallel linguistic organization: *syntactic organization* and *semantic organization*, where the sentence of a language initially takes shapes at the deepest level as a creative and generative product. In other words the semantic component is the *deepest organizational* (structural cum behavioural) *level of language* where, as seen in the preceding chapter, along with and simultaneous to the interpolational process of syntactic organization the *meanings* of language get organized. The parallel interpolational process of syntactic organization is examined in detail in the preceding chapter. Our present attention can be focussed on the deep level semantic organization of language and examine the intricate elements which constitute the semantic component.

Nowhere at any level of linguistic description is the linguist as an investigator called on to confront so much the intricacies of the human mind as at the semantic component of language. A description of the semantic component puts the linguist right on the realm of the mind, and as we noted at serval occasions in the preceding chapters, such a description is rendered impossible, illogical and groundless without taking the entirety of the mind into consideration as an existential, substantial factor. The present work takes for granted the entire psycholinguistic implications of bringing in the role of the mind in the description of language and all problems that would arise from such a description. No linguist, for that matter, can afford to neglect (as the structuralist linguistic once did) an accounting of the human mind so far as the sole foundation of human language, just because such an accounting would compel the linguist to confront problems which will take him directly into philosophy.

The semantic component is the level where, as said above, language and the mind meet in a most unified manner. The semantic component is that level of language where language becomes ***identified with*** mental realities. These mental realities we have described above as ***conceptual elements***, ***concepts*** and ***conceptual organization*** (or of concepts). It is the level where an interpolation of elements of language and elements of the mind takes place and becomes one and the same identical reality, ***meaning***. ***Semantics*** is the study of the meaning level of language and an enquiry into 'the meaning of meaning'. The semantic component thus is that level of language which comprises the meanings of human language. The structural and behavioural features of the units of meaning constitute the semantic component of a language. This makes it clear that the semantic component is a level where two distinct perspectives meet and become one identical reality: the perspective of language as the most complex human ***behaviour***, and the perspective of the mind which constitutes the substantial ***principle*** of all human behaviour. In other words the ***content*** of the semantic component we will be described as ***meaning units*** from perspective (i), and the same content is described here as ***concepts*** (more specifically as conceptual elements, concepts and conceptual organization) from perspective (ii). We have labeled perspective (i) as ***linguistic content*** (or content of language) and perspective (ii) as ***mental content*** (or content of the mind).

In the same manner the parallel perspectives of linguistic and mental content, again, lead us what we have seen earlier as a parallel organizational features. The semantic component comprises essentially a ***semantic organization*** at the sentence and discourse levels from perspective (i) the linguistic content; and the semantic component secondly comprises essentially a ***conceptual organization*** at the sentence and discourse levels from perspective (ii) the mental content. Thus one and the same reality, the semantic component as the deepest level of linguistic structure and behaviour is viewed on the one hand as semantic organization from two different perspectives: as a linguistic reality and as a mental reality. This is what we have thought as an interpolation of the two factors: the linguistic reality and the mental reality.

The semantic component puts human language at once closer to human experience. Language is ***double symbolic*** and is a representative mode. At the most surface level we have the ***phonetic representation*** of a sentence (see Ch. 8); further in the ***phonological representation*** maps the ***syntactic representation*** of the sentence into the phonetic representation. The ***graphic representation*** of a sentence is posited as the optional alternative for the phonetic representation which together with the interior phonological representation constitutes the phonological component (Ch. 8). The surface levels syntax, the transformation and the deep level syntax together constitute what we have called the syntactic representation of the sentence of a language. While at the surface level syntax the syntactic representation converges with the phonological representation, at the deep level syntax (see Ch. 11) the syntactic representation converges with and interpolates into the semantic representation of the sentence of a language. The semantic representation at the semantic component of language thus consists of what we have seen above as the semantic organization (or conceptual organization) that assigns to a sentence the semantic content it requires. The ***semantic component*** of language in other words assigns the ***semantic content*** of a deep level sentence in terms of ***semantic*** (or conceptual) ***organization*** which constitutes the ***semantic representation***. These aspects comprise the first level of human language as a representative mode as mentioned above.

The second level of language as a representative mode is contributed by the nature of the semantic component itself. The semantic component as we have seen is the level which places language right at the realm of the mind. As such as saw that the semantic component is identical with the mental content of language: an interpolation of linguistic content and mental content. In other words the semantic component is directly representative of human experience, while the more extrinsic representations, the syntactic, the phonological and the phonetic representations are representative of the semantic component. It is the semantic representation alone which places language at once closer to human experience so far as the relation between language and human experience are concerned.

The features of human experience such as the things, events and the relations forming part of the experience of man are represented (or symbolized or signified) by what we have called conceptual elements, concepts and conceptual streams which constitute the content of the mind. Thus the double symbolism of language consists in (i) the sounds and their organization representing the semantic content (or the mental content), and (ii) the semantic content in turn representing the features of human experience. Harein lies the double symbolism of language. The more extrinsic linguistic representations as seen above reach the reality outside the human mind only through the semantic component which directly represents the features of human experience with those reality outside of man. The semantic component of language is thus the liaison agent between the extrinsic linguistic elements and the features of human experience.

The sentence *The boy ate his meal* is a creative, generative linguistic product with multi-level representations. At the most extrinsic level we have the phonetic (spoken) or graphic (written) representation of the sentence. At further intrinsic level as seen in Ch. 8 we have the phonological representation of the sentence, the first being the concrete, physical representation in terms of the phonetic distinctive features of sounds and their organization and the second being the semi-abstract representation of the sentence as the link between the phonetic (graphic) level and the surface level sentence. The sentence receives representation at the phonological component as seen above only after the two level syntactic representations place: the deep level and the surface level sentence linked by transformation. Representation at the deep level syntax is a linguistic process simultaneous to the semantic representation of the sentence at the semantic component of language. The sentence *The boy ate his meal* assumes linguistic reality as a sentence primarily at the semantic component with the deep level syntax converging upon this process. Thus at the most intrinsic level of language what takes place is a semantic representation in terms of an organization of meaning units (organization of concepts) which assign to a sentence the semantic content in line with the requirements which the syntax of the language impose on the creative generation of the particular sentence.

2. Semantic Universals and Differentials

Semantic representation at the level of the semantic component of language retains quite characteristic features because of the dichotomy resulting from the association of language and mental contents at this level. Traditionally it is held that all concepts are universals because of the pervading nature of concepts over all the objects belonging to a particular specific or generic class. This aspect of the concept will be taken up for detailed discussion in the following sections. All concepts are held to be universals since a concept in the traditional sense represents all the particular objects belonging to the specific or generic class which the concept represents. Our present notion of a ***universal*** does not stand for the traditional notion and deviates from it considerably. A universal in the sense used in the present book as seen especially in chapter 7 consists of an element of language (phonological, grammatical or semantic), not necessarily semantic (conceptual), which is shared by and found in ***all languages*** spoken by man, not most or some. It calls for a much more rigorous restricted understanding of a universal as an element present in all human languages. What is significant to note is that such a notion of the universal belongs to the very ***nature of human language*** as such. Hereby we arrive at a set of linguistic features without which a language cannot exist or function. We apply the term universals only to such a sets of linguistic features whether they are phonological, grammatical or semantic.

We may examine some instance. Word-forms such as ***boy, meal, weapon, fruit*** represent their respective meaning units of 'boy', 'meal', 'weapon' and 'fruit'. As units of meaning these features of human experience are adequately represented in the cognitive structure of man and constitute the semantic representation at the semantic component. Upon closer examination we find that each unit of meaning give above is somehow ***simple*** and somehow ***complex*** at the sometime. Considering 'boy' as a conceptual content of the mind we find that the particular concept represents 'the young male human' (as against 'girl' which represents 'the young female human'). Traditionally this concept is universal because the concept stands for the essential features which constitute a boy as such (as against a girl).

Such an understanding of the term universal has considerable limitation as a closer examination will show. The word-form ***father*** as employed in English represents a given set of what has come to be known as semantic specificities which have received greater technical representation in the present book in terms of conceptual elements as seen earlier. The conceptual elements which enter into the structure of the concept of 'father' differ considerably from the set of conceptual elements which enter into the concept represented by the word-form ***pitha*** in Hindi or ***pithavu*** in Malayalam. Or again, the equivalents of ***boy, meal*** or ***weapon*** in Hindi and Malayalam represent respectively concepts whose conceptual elements differ in terms of ***more or less*** of features which the connected elements represent as part of the concept. In the case of some languages the equivalent of 'boy' (which the English word-form ***boy*** stands for) might include what in English we call ***child*** or ***young man***. This is what we have meant by more or less of conceptual elements going into the structure of a specific concept 'boy'.

What would this mean? This would primarily mean that a concept understood traditionally as a well defined, unitary, abstracted entity is not so well-defined and unitary and representation of the equivalent word-forms of all languages. This aspect of our understanding of a concept is very important. As we shall see in greater details in the sections that follow, a concept is not one simple entity; For every conceivable concept present in the human cognitive structure these are constituent conceptual elements that make a concept represented by the word-form of one language different at least in part (more or less) from the concept represented by the equivalent word-forms of other languages.

The fundamental reason for differences the concepts represented by the equivalent forms of different languages lies in the fact that the features of experience that the concepts represent further differ from community to community. The concept of marriage for instance is constituted as one unified concept only so far as the very basic features of the experience of marriage is concerned. As union of a man and a woman as husband and wife mediated by society, the equivalents word-forms of 'marriage' must be found in all languages. But these features constitute only the bare essentials of the concept 'marriage'. As we know well, marriage in terms of significance and its religious values including its ritualistic specifications etc. differ considerably from community to community. Marriage is in fact one instance where such socio—cultural features mark great difference from society to society. Therefore the traditional understanding of marriage as a feature of experience represented by one stable, universal and unitary concept which is represented by one word-form or other in all languages is certainly inconsistent with the present understanding of 'marriage' as a concept whose constituent conceptual elements vary (in terms of more or less) from community to community. Therefore the question now is how much of the concept of 'marriage' is universal? In fact we find that except for the very basic, essential skeletal conceptual features, 'marriage' does not constitute a universal concept applicable the same way to all human languages. Therefore we may conclude that a concept is universal only so far as it represents a class of features (e.g. food, fruit, knife and boy) in terms of its very essential conceptual elements that constituent the members of the class irrespective of the conceptual elements which make the members different within the given class.

This leads us to the very significant distinction we have

already drawn earlier between: the ***universals*** and the ***differentials*** of ***semantics*** (or the ***semantic universals*** and ***semantic differentials*** of language). We make distinction between those features of the semantic component of language which all human language share without exception (the semantic universals) and those features of the semantic component which are not shared by all languages but by most, some or unique to the particular language (semantic differentials), just as we have earlier drawn a distinction between the phonological universals and phonological differentials, and grammatical universals and the grammatical differentials. We have been consistently following these distinctions throughout the theory developed in the present book, and these distinctions must be seen as part of unified explanatory theory of human language.

The linguist is required to be on the look out for structural and behavioural dimensions of the semantic component, which are thus universal by nature. These dimension must be part of the human language as such however restricted the number of such linguistic features may be. Considering the examples shown above we find that word-forms in English such as ***father, boy, meal, weapon, fruit, food*** and ***marriage*** are said to represent respective concepts which are expressed one way or other in all languages. But we have seen that in several cases the apparently equivalent word-forms do not represent concepts with the same range of conceptual elements as constituent parts. ***Father*** or ***marriage***, for instance, has some very essential set of core conceptual elements which alone are central to all the concepts which the equivalent word-forms in other languages, represent. In other words, 'father' or 'marriage' constitutes a semantic universal so far as this set of conceptual elements which form the core of the concepts represented by word-forms of all languages is concerned. To say that all human languages share in one or other, in terms of one word-form or other, the concepts of 'father' and 'marriage' the linguist does not have to examine data from all possible languages. As mentioned several times earlier, concepts such as these do represent those features of experience which constitute part of the very life of man, in society.

With a view to developing an inventory of the semantic

universals of language the linguist therefore need only to look for those conceptual elements, concepts and conceptual organization (streams of concepts) which represents features of experience that constituent the very nature of man and human life. A concept is therefore regarded as a universal in the present theoretical context not by virtue of the fact that the specific concept represents a whole class of particular members (boy, father, marriage, meal) but by virtue of the fact that a specific concept in terms of its representative potential is ***shared by*** (realised in) ***all*** languages. This is principal distinction we make between the traditional understanding of concepts and the way considered in the present theoretical context. The reasons have been discussed already.

It is only because a concept ipso facto of its representative modality does to become a universal we have postulated the dimension of semantic differentials in contrast to the semantic universals as seen above. Once would probably make technical distinction between 'a universal' and 'universal' to account for the distinction which exists as above in our understanding of concepts. We may regard, in time with the traditional understanding, the concept as 'universal' because it represents a class of members with the same characteristics, while the concept as a universal because it is shared in the same way by ***all*** languages. A linguistic universal is thus concerned more about the realization of a particular features of language in all language rather than the class of members the universal represents.

The semantic differentials, we said, is a semantic features which is not realized in all human languages but may be realized in most, some or uniquely in one or other language. Just as there are the semantic universals of conceptual elements, concepts and conceptual organization, there area also the semantic differentials of conceptual organization. The conceptual element that adds to the concept 'father' the specification of 'priest' or 'God, the Father', is a differential conceptual element because it is not realized in the same way in all languages. In the same way, the conceptual element that adds to the concept 'marriage' the specification of 'exchange of rings' or 'signing before a magistrate' constitutes a semantic differential. The semantic differential just as the phonological or syntactic differentials may be realized in most languages, a few languages or it may be realized only in the particular language, depending on the uniqueness or generality of the particular feature of experience which the semantic unit represents. While the word-form *curry* has equivalents in other languages representing the concept 'highly-flavoured dish additional to the main dish' the Gujarati language has the word-form ***kadi*** (rooted in *curry*) which represents the concept 'a specific type of flavoured dish prepared, say, from butter-milk'. The word-form ***kadi*** means this particular dish in Gujarati while *curry* means any flavored dish as above in other languages. 'Kadi' therefore is a semantic differential unique to Gujarati. It is possible to discover upon examination semantic differentials unique to a particular language only if the investigator can arrive at those features things, events, relations etc.) which are part of the socio-cultural experience of only a particular community. Conceptual elements, concepts and conceptual organization as constituents of the universal and differential dimensions of the semantic component of language require further examination in relation to what we commonly understand by the term *meaning*.

3. Conceptual Elements as Meaning Units

A distinction is drawn between *conceptual elements, concepts* and *conceptual organization* the implications of which need to be looked into a detail. The semantic component is seen above as a level where we have a parallel perspective of function: the semantic organization on the one hand, and the conceptual organization on the other viewed from the *perspectives* of *language* and the *mind* and seen as one and the same representation at the semantic component. We are now faced with the task of co-ordinating these two apparently dichotomous perspectives and the elements inherent therein. How shall we exactly see the semantic organization at the semantic component as conceptual organization in the human mind? By finding answers to this problem were are arriving at the very point where language and the mind intimately intersect at the semantic component.

A conceptual element is postulated here to mean approximately the same as what is meant by a 'semantic specification'.

All the same semantic specifications are far too general and include too many aspects of meaning. Again, the term 'semantic specification' does not adequately represent the intimate role of the mind, and does not take us beyond the boundary of language to its very fundamental relation to the *reality* (features of human experience) which language is expected ultimately to represent. Human language holds any value whatsoever as a symbolic, representative system because of its presumed potential to adequately represent reality other than what language as such constitutes. Somehow or other language is believed to take us beyond the realm of the human cognitive structure, to the very features of human experience in relation to the reality outside.

It is therefore quite inadequate on the part of the linguist to overlook the mental reality (the mental content) that constitute essentially what we know as the *meaning* aspect of language. The present attempt is therefore to co-ordinate the two aspects and see whole thing in a unified perspective. The real significance of this co-ordination in our study of semantics is clear from what we have seen throughout. What the post-Bloomfieldians failed to see and what the earlier grammarians saw in part we are trying to see in its entirely: the real significance of human language lies in its semantic component which is a unification of (i) linguistic content and (ii) mental content which is expressed through the more extrinsic representations of language.

The meaning of language can be regarded as the meaning of a ***word*** (disregarding for the time being the morpheme-word distinction), a ***phrase*** (including any idiomatic expression), a ***sentence*** (which is posted as an organization of the above), and a ***discourse*** (any unit of language larger than a sentence regarded as an organization of sentences). The semantic component therefore consists of semantic representations at the levels of a word, a phrase, a sentence and a discourse. It is possible to conceive everyone of these as representing a unit of meaning (what is called earlier a ***meaning unit***). The constituent elements of such a meaning unit is usually known as a semantic specification which we looked into above. There is thus a meaning unit representing a word, a meaning unit representing a phrase, one representing a sentence and one representing a discourse. The structure of such meaning units in terms of their constituent elements gets more and more complex as we get higher up the order from word to discourse. The very abstract nature of meaning becomes evident as we try to regard these meaning units in terms of certain patterns. Even the simplest possible meaning unit in terms of its structure at once becomes a complex entity as we view it from a different perspective.

The word *meal* represents a meaning unit; the phrase *a good meal* represents another meaning unit; *The boy ate a good meal* represents still another, and lastly *The boy ate a good meal. That was his first food during the day. He also ate some fruit after the meal* as a discourse represents another meaning unit. As we examine these units right from the single word we find that what moves us in the complex structure of every unit rather than its simplicity. Even the meaning 'meal' posits a complex structure which if referred to a dictionary will be explained only in terms of *a set of* constituent elements which will in turn function further as separate meaning units. We find that the word *meal* represents the constituent elements of 'a main food of the day'. Again 'a main food of the day' applied to ten specific communities, for instance, will certainly yield ten different variety of 'main food' with 'move or less' and different constituent elements figuring in at all the ten instance of 'meal'. Thus not only that the meaning unit 'meal' consists of constituent meaning units of 'main and food' but much more the meaning unit in a particular community tends to be a complex of several constituent meaning units representing the items of the meal in that community.

As we move, now from the meaning units mentioned above as the linguistic content, to the mental content (posited as the two perspectives of the same reality) we find that the meaning unit represented by the word (*meal* is concept. We shall note that the word *meal* is regarded here as a separate lexical entry, which will enter into the making of the sentence *The boy ate a good meal*. As a concept 'meal' now represents a complex set of what we have called *conceptual elements* as we shall examine below. The phrase *a good meal* in turn does not represent a stream of concepts; it represents same concept 'meal' but with more conceptual elements entering into the concept 'meal' as constituent elements.

How do we then characterize the semantic component of the sentence *The boy ate a good meal*? Here the clustering of conceptual elements as above does not occur merely around the concept 'meal'. Instead we have an instance of what we have called *conceptual organization*. A set of concepts is organization at the semantic representation of the sentence *The boy ate a good meal.* The organization of the set of concepts (in the manner of a conceptual stream) represents in its totality a feature of experience so unified as to create the linearity and effect of a sentence in line with the simultaneous syntactic organization penetrating the semantic component. We will take up this point in the following sections.

It is important now to understand that any one lexical entry such as *fruit* or *meal* as either a conceptual element or a concept. The distinction becomes all the more important in our consideration of a conceptual element which is a meaning unit ('food' in 'main food') in contrast to a concept which is another meaning unit as seen above ('food' in *The boy ate food*). The same meaning unit assumes the stature a concept when represented toxical entry, for instance, *food* as found in *The boy ate food*, and the stature of a conceptual element when it figures in as a constituent of 'meal' in terms of a semantic specifications of the meaning 'meal'. One and the same meaning unit, therefore assumes the stature of a concept and conceptual element depending on the specificity it receives as part of the semantic representation of a given feature of experience.

The meaning unit represented by the word-form *meal* thus is a concept which is complex entity with more or less conceptual elements figuring in as the constituents. The differences in the nature of the constituent conceptual elements govern the differences of the concepts represented by apparently equivalent word-forms in different languages. What is regarded in traditional schoolatic philosophy (that stemming from the philosophy of the middle ages) as denotation (or extension) and connotation(or depth) of meaning are in fact only differences of meaning arising from the differences and number of conceptual elements entering into the structure of the concept which a given word-form represents. When we say that the denotation of the English word ***man*** in the specific 'sense is larger than that of ***man*** in the sense of gender what we mean is that the specific concept of 'man' has the constituent conceptual elements of 'human male and human female', as against the constituent conceptual elements of only 'an adult male human'. In terms of the features of experience represented by both 'man' and 'man' the first includes all humans or any human, while the second includes only adult human males. A specific description of the semantic component in terms of the ultimate conceptual elements entering into the structure of the concepts which receive semantic representation is indeed has greater linguistic explanatory adequacy than a description of the class of members which the concept further represents. The former is more adequately linguistic than the latter which is more at the realm of the discipline of philosophy if I may say so. The conceptual element takes us right into the depth of structure of the semantic component of language without leading us too far into the implications of philosophy.

4. Concepts as Meaning Units

Conceptual elements as seen above function as the meaning units which enter into the structure of a specific concept. Every conceptual element as representing a feature of experience related to the concept is a meaning unit which constitutes part of the lexical entry of the respective concept. Thus it is possible to visualize a specific feature of experience as represented respectively by a conceptual element which forms part of a concept representing a large feature of experience, and by concept itself without at once forming part of a larger representation. This aspect requires further elaboration.

We have also seen that the semantic component of language gets represented in terms of the meaning units of word, a phrase a sentence and a discourse. The same word-form figures in at all these levels as in ***meal***, a ***good meal***, ***The boy ate a good meal***, and ***The boy ate a good meal. That was his first food of the day*** .... Here the word-form ***meal*** has an ***extrinsic realization*** where a particular feature of experience ('meal' for instance) is extrinsically represented by means of the word-form *meal* in a word, phrase, sentence and a discourse. Such an extrinsic realization meaning unit occurs when the word-form in question represents a concept. The word *meal* as part of sentence as in *The boy ate a good meal* represents the concept 'meal' which directly forms part of the conceptual organization of the particular sentence. As against such an extrinsic realization, occurs an ***intrinsic realization*** of a meaning unit. By this we mean that the meaning unit functions as a conceptual element constituting part of a larger concept which in turn represents a neither specific meaning unit. But the specification of the particular conceptual element as part of the concept, is ***not*** apparently realized in the word-form. To put in another way that the realization of that particular meaning unit in the word-form is intrinsic, not extrinsic. The meaning unit 'food' has an intrinsic realization in the word-form 'meal' or the meaning unit 'boy' has an intrinsic realization in the word-form 'child' and so on. In other words we might very well say that a conceptual element as part of the concept has an intrinsic realization in the word-form representing that concept as in *Man is a thinking animal* where the word-form man has an intrinsic realization of the conceptual element 'man' which represents 'an adult male human'. On the other hand *That man is a coward* has 'man' as an extrinsic realization. In the former case 'man' as part of *man* (specific sense) is conceptual element as the constituent of the latter, while in the latter case.above 'man' is a concept with an independent lexical status of its own meaning 'an adult male human'. The distinction between intrinsic realization of a meaning unit and an extrinsic realization of the same meaning unit is significant to understand the distinction we have drawn between a conceptual element and a concept.

Meal as seen above is a word-form which represents the concept 'meal'. When the word *meal* becomes pat of an utterance as a words, phrase, sentence or a discourse, the word carries a semantic representation that is complex. The apparent equivalents of *meal* in other language constitute word-forms which represent in fact combinations of different sets of conceptual elements depending on the material that goes into the making of meal in particular community. The word-form meal, thus is an extrinsic realization of the meaning unit (concept) 'meal', and represents differently organized sets of conceptual elements as features intrinsically realized. In other words the linguist is able to isolate and explicate the inherent constituent conceptual elements of the concept 'meal' in terms of the features that enter into the experience of meal in respective communities. This is true apart from the dictionary meaning of the lexical entry *meal*. Thus the conceptual elements forming parts of 'a main food of the day' constitute only the most essential features designating a class which include the actual elements that go into a meal in every community.

A meal for the Gujarati community would consist of a dish containing a few chapatis (on any what preparation) a bit of rice, a particular vegetable preparation, dal or 'kadi' an papped fried on fire, and cup of milk. Asked to prepare a meal a Keralite woman would go for a very different sort of a dish. This would consist of plenty of rice, one or two highly dishes of vegetable preparation, a dish of meat, egg or fish and perhaps a pappad fried in oil. A meal similarly prepared by an English woman would consist of some soup, a side-dish of vegetable and meat, some bread, dissert and fruit. In other words we see that the concept of 'meal' for a Gujarati is complex of the constituent conceptual elements of, for instance, 'chappati or puri or any wheat preparation, rice, vegetable preparation, dal or 'kadi' pappad, fried on fire, and milk or curd. The concept of 'meal' for a Malayalam speaker has the conceptual elements of 'rice, curry, meat or fish dish and pappad fried in oil'. The concept of 'meal' for a native speaker of English has the conceptual elements of 'soup, vegetable, meat, bread, dissert and fruit'. The complexity of one combination out of several possible combinations of constituents in the meal of a community (combinations other than mentioned above) shows the possible number and variety of conceptual elements that go into the structure of one concept 'meal'. As we have noticed there are in fact very few elements which are common to the concepts represented by the apparently equivalent word-forms for meal in the communities we have examined.

'Meal' therefore becomes a semantic universal only so far as the essential conceptual elements: 'a main food of the day' are concerned. In some form or other, we hold that equivalents of the word-form *meal* must be part of all human languages but the universal semantic dimension of this particular feature of experience would only be the essential conceptual elements: 'a main food of the day'. The constituent conceptual elements we saw in detail as pertaining to specific communities constitute the differential semantic dimensions. We might therefore say that the word *meal* has a semantic representation consisting on the one hand of a set of semantic universals ('a main food of the day') and on the other a set of semantic differntials (the detailed conceptual elements seen above - 'wheat preparation' as contrasted to 'rice preparation' etc.).

It is again significant to see that every constituent conceptual element of 'meal' which has an intrinsic realization (see above) as part of word *meal* has an extrinsic realization as a word-form representing a concept of an independent status. In other words every such constituent conceptual element of 'meal' has an independent place in the lexicon of the language as representing a specific word-form. Thus 'chappati', 'rice', 'curry', 'dal', 'meat', 'fish', 'pappad', 'soup', 'bread', 'dissert', 'milk' and 'fruit' as conceptual elements entering, as part of the intrinsic realization, into the structure of the concept 'meal'. These conceptual elements on the other hand are assigned, in the semantic component of a language, the status of concept as representing the respective feature of experience and further represented in terms of independent extrinsically realized word-forms. The same conceptal elements thus assume the status of concepts and are represented in turn by the word-forms *chappati, rice, curry, meat, fish, pappad, soup, bread, dissert, milk* and *fruit.* These are such now have no intrinsic or extrinsic relation to the word-form *meal* at the semantic component unless the speaker of the language makes a conscious attempt to relate them in an explicit sentence like *The boy had rice for his meal.* Here what occurs is an explication in terms of extrinsic realization of the element 'rice' which otherwise forms a constituent conceptual element of 'meal'.

The instance that is examined above in detail shows how a concept is a complex of conceptual elements which function as the constituents of the particular concept. If the entire spectrum of the concept as a structured complex or the essential set of conceptual elements forming the core of the concept is found in all languages (or found to be part of the very nature of human life), the concept of such a set of conceptual elements will be called a semantic universal. The variety of conceptual elements representing the features of experience specific to a particular community can be called the semantic differentials.

Lastly we have seen that a conceptual element which forms a constituent of a concept in turn functions as an independent concept which would represent a lexical entry of the language. This concept which on the one hand forms part of another concept as a conceptual element of the concept now has in turn conceptual elements which constitute that concept. This conceptual element-concept chain as meaning units of one status or other goes on until we are able to reach a set of conceptual elements (a theoretical set) which are the simplest possible semantic units with no further conceptual elements entering into their structure. The meaning units of a word, phrase, sentence and discourse would thus be brought down in the last analysis to such a set of conceptual elements as the building blocks of the semantic component of language.

5. Conceptual Organization and Semantic Representation

Semantic representation at the semantic component of language is viewed above as consisting of three distinct levels : (i) conceptual elements as meaning units, (ii) concepts as meaning units, and lastly (iii) conceptual organization as meaning units. Conceptual elements are conceived as the intrinsically realized constituent units of a concept. Concepts on the other hand are conceived as the extrinsically realized meaning unit represented by a word-form. The detail of these are looked into the preceding sections. There is a third level where the meaning of language is represented, that is the level of conceptual organization.

Conceptual organization is viewed as a meaning unit from several perspectives as we shall see later. What is conceptual organization? If semantic specifications as meaning units are represented as a conceptual element and as a concept, then the representation also occurs in terms of the organization (or stream of concepts. It is possible for man to sit and think for a stretch of time without in any way giving expression to the thought in verbal utterances. Thought as the exercise of the mind in all its various forms is conceived as a stream or flow of concepts ('Psycholinguistic Foundations' Ch.5). We may rightly call it an organization of concepts (or conceptual organization. In the same manner we exercise continuous speech (just as we exercise continuous thinking), and we know that what constitutes the semantic component of our continuous speech as a discourse is the continuum of thought. All the parallelism we have drawn above makes this point evident.

The semantic representation of a sentence or a discourse is thus seen from the parallel perspectives of (1) ***semantic organization*** (language) and (2) ***Conceptual organization*** (mind). It is certainly not possible to demarcate the point where a concept ends and conceptual organization begins in the semantic representation of units of language larger than a word. As we are dealing with totally abstract units at the level of semantic representation such a demarcation is next to impossible as the conceptual representation of a word as a unit of language, and that of a phrase or sentence are bound to overlap in terms of the semantic structure of such units of language. Yet some point needs to be spotted where the two (concept Vs conceptual organization) can be distinguished.

The word-form ***meal*** designates a concept as examined in the sections preceding. There are problems, all the same, as we move over to a phrase as a unit of over to a phrase as a unit of language. The term phrase in the context is used to mean a ***sequence*** of more than one word-form other than a compound. We regard ***a good meal*** as a phrase while ***meal-time*** a compound subject to the rules of the language which govern compounding and phrase structure. Again in our consideration of the semantic representation of phrase and a compound there are bound to be further overlaps. From the grammatical perspective we agree that ***a good meal*** is phrase and ***meal-time*** is a compound, but both designate ***one*** meaning unit each from a certain viewpoint. The meaning unit of ***a good meal*** can well be considered as one concept just as that of ***meal-time*** is one concept if we regard ***a*** and ***good*** as extrinsically realized conceptual elements of the concept 'meal', just as we could regard 'meal' as a conceptual element entering into the structure of the concept 'time' (both extrinsically realized) as in ***breakfast-time, tea-time*** or ***leisure-time.*** Such considerations however are bound to make the issue of semantic representation unnecessarily complicated.

We therefore assign to the compound form the status of a concept as representing one feature of experience and presented by a sequence of more than one word forms. One the other hand we regard a phrase structure uniquely as a sequence or organization of more than one concept parallel to the syntactic organization that the phrase structure has received. Thus ***a good meal, the good meal that the boy had***, or ***the meal prepared by the young lady*** are all phrase structures which manifest an organization of concepts rather than the extension of one single concept. The feature of experience in such instance as expressed by a phrase may be just one but the organization of concepts which we have posited as representative of this feature of experience in fact represent ***aspects*** or shades of the feature of experience.

It is again significant to note that the conceptual organization at the semantic component, which represents the constituent aspect of a feature of experience functions like 'field structure'. The presence of such a field-type of organization is what gives us the impression that the semantic representation of a phrase structure is the constituent conceptual elements of one and the same concept rather than an organization of concepts. The phrase ***a beautiful black bird*** and ***an ugly black bird*** represent an organization of the concepts 'beautiful', 'black ', 'bird', and 'singular' (or 'specific') in phrase (ii), which in turn represent as seen above a set of aspects constituting part of the particular feature of experience (the speaker's perception of the bird as black and beautiful or as black and ugly). This conceptual organization at the semantic component is perceived as a ***field structure*** taking into consideration the fact that the specific aspects are as if built around the feature of experience (the bird in the present case).

The element of doubts so much attached to the semantic representation of the phrase structure with respect to the organization of concepts will not be such as we enter in to domain of sentences and discourses. The semantic representation of sentences and discourse clearly manifest a level of conceptual organization as constituting the ultimately structure of the semantic representation at these levels. *The boy ate a good meal* thus manifest an organization of concepts in the manner, again, of a field structure that comprises the semantic representation of that sentences. The sentence above represent an organization of a set of concepts: 'boy, 'singularity', 'particularity', 'eating', 'past', 'meal', 'good' and 'singularity'. This set of concepts which constitute the semantic representation of the sentence, in turn represent a set of *features* which constitute the experience that the the boy ate a good meal.

Just as the specific experience has no structural linearity in its occurrence with respect to its features, the conceptual organization is postulated as having no linearity at the semantic representation. This is an important consideration in the present understanding of the nature of the semantic component of language. The sentence at the deep level syntax assumes linearity only at the level of the syntactic organization of the abstract lexical forms. The semantic organization that takes place simultaneously at the semantic component does not possess a linearity of its own. Instead what is postulated is field structure as in the instances examination above. Thus the concepts of 'boy', 'singularity', 'particularity', 'eating' etc. that the sentence *The boy ate a good meal* represents do not have a lineal-type but a field-type organization just as the features of experience represented by the concepts above do not possess any linear structure. We might say therefore that the existential simplicity of an experience with its relevant spatial extension and temporal duration assumes a field structure at the semantic representation which in turn is assigned a linear structure at the syntactic component.

The conceptual organization at the semantic component of language assumes greater magnitude at the level of a discourse. At the level of discourse we have the greatest extension of a meaning unit postulated here as conceptual organization. *The boy ate a good meal. That was his first food during the day. He also ate some fruit after the meal............* is a discourse unit of language which has a semantic representation of a more complex nature. It is most adequate to see discourse as (i) an organization (sequence) of sentences (all extrinsically realized) representing (ii) a continuum of thought consisting of (iii) Layers of conceptual organization which in turn represent (iv) a set of detailed aspects of (v) a given feature of experience. Since a discourse consists of individually structured sentences, as we have seen, the whole discourse can be seen only as consisting of sequentially organized layers of field-structure in which each such field-structure of conceptual organization represents a given sentence in the discourse. Layers of field-structure conceptual representation at the semantic component represent in fact again *detailed aspects* of a given feature of experience just as in the above instance the discourse represents a few field-structure of conceptual organizations which in turn represents the aspects build around the experience of the boy eating his meal. In other words we could visualize the semantic representation of discourse unit of language as a stream of as many conceptual fields as there are sentences in the discourse, constituting what we have called earlier a 'stream of thought' occurring at the semantic component as the content of the mind which the discourse as a unit of language is structured to express. Such is the semantics of language with meaning units realized as component constituents as seen above at different levels of the semantic component.

Bibliography

Aboul–Fetouh, H.M., 1968, A Morphological study of Egyptian colloquial Arabic. Lingua. 28 : 180.

Adams, V., 1973, An Introduction to Modern English Word Formation. London : Orient Longman Ltd.

Ajmer, K., 1972, Some Aspects of Psychological Predicatives in English. Stockholm.

Allen, Harold B. ed., 1964, Readings in Applied English Linguistics. New York : Appleton-Century-Crofts.

Allen, RL., 1966, The Verb System of Present-day American English. The Hague.

Allen, W.F., 1948–'49, Ancient ideas on the origin and development of language. Transactions of the Philogical Society, pp. 35–60.

Andersen, James M., 1971, The Grammar of Case. Cambridge : M.I.T. Press.

_____________. The morphophonemics of gender in Spanish nouns. Lingua. 10 : 285.

Andersen, John M., and Charles Jones, 1974, Historical Linguistics, Vol. I. North-Holland : Amsterdam.

_____________., 1974, Historical Linguistics. Vol. II. Amsterdam : North-Holland.

Arnold, G.F. Stress in English words. Lingua. 7 : 221, 397.

Ayer, A.J., 1958, The Problem of Knowledge. London : Macmillan.

_____________., 1966, Language, Truth and Logic. Gollancz.

Bach and Harms, eds., 1969, Universals of Language. New York : Holt, Rinehart and Winston.

Ballard, DlLee, Jr., The Semantics of Inibaloi verbal suffxes. Lingua. 34 : 180.

Baron, N.S., A Reanalysis of English grammatical gender. Lingua. 27 : 113.

Barnes, M. and H. Esau., Germanic strong verbs : a case of morphological rule extension. Lingua 31 : 1.

Bauch, A.C., 1957, History of English Language. New York.

Bazell, C.E., 1949, On the problem of morpheme. *Archivum Linguisticum* 1, p. 209.

_____________., 1953, Linguistic Form. Istanbul Press.

Bendix, E.H., Componental analysis of general Vocabulary; the semantic structure of a set of verbs in English, Hindi and Japanese. Lingua 20 : 106.

Bever, Thomas, 1969, On Semantic Problems of Semantic Representation. Foundations of Language 5. New York : Elsevier.

_____________., 1970, On classifying semantic features. In Bierwisch and Heidolf, eds. *Progress in Lingusitics*. The Hague : Mouton.

_____________, et al., 1975, An Integrated Theory of Linguistic Ability. New York : Harper & Row.

Bidwell, C.E. : Outline of Bielorussian Morphology. *Lingua* 24 : 404.

__________ : Outline of Ukranian Morphology. *Lingua* 24 : 407.

Bloch, Bernard, 1947, English Verb Inflection. *Language* 23 : 399. Also in Joos (1958).

__________, and G.L. Tragger, 1942, Outline of Linguistic Analysis. Baltimore : Linguistic Co. of American.

Bloom, Luis, 1970, Language Development : Form and Function in Emerging Grammars. Cambridge : MIT Press.

Bloomfield, Leonard, 1924, Review of Saussure's 'Course in General Linguistics'. Modern Language Journal 8 : 317–19.

__________, 1926, A set of postulates for the science of language. Language 2 : 153.

__________, 1927, On recent works in general linguistics. Modern Philology 25 : 211. Also in Hockett (1970).

__________, 1933, Language. New York : Henry Holt & Co.

__________, 1935, Stressed vowels of American English. Language 11 : 97__________116.

__________, 1936, Language or Ideas. *Language* 12 : 89–95.

Bloomfield, Morton W. and Leonard NewMark, 1965, A Linguistic Introduction to the History of English. New York : Alfred A. Knopf.

Bolirger, Dwight L., 1965, The atomization of meaning. *Language* 41.

__________, 1968, Aspects of Language. New York : Harcourt, Brace & World.

__________, 1971, The Phrasal Verb in English. Cambridge : MIT Press.

Bulchvarov, Panayot, 1970, The Concept of Knowledge. Evanston : Northwestern Univ. Press.

Burt., 1971, From Deep to Surface Structure : An Introduction to Transformational Syntax. New York : Harper & Row.

Capell, A., : Some typological observations of Sudanese morphology. Lingua 15 : 435.

Cardenas, D., 1961, Applied Linguistics : Spanish, A Guide for Teachers, Boston : D.O. Heath & Co.

Carnap, Rudolf, 1965, Meaning and Necessity. Chicago : Chicago University Press.

Carroll, J.B., 1953, The Study of Language. Cambridge : Harward University Press.

Chafe, Wallace. 1970. Meaning and Structure of Language. Chicago : Chicago University Press.

Chomsky, Noam, 1957, Syntactic Structures. The Hague : Mouton.

____________, 1960, Explanatory models in linguistics, In Nagel et al., *Logic, Methodology and Philosophy of Science*. Sanford University Press.

____________, 1961a, On the notion 'Rule of Grammar'. In Roman Jackobson, *Structure of Language and Its Mathemattical Aspects*. Providence : American Mathematical Society.

____________, 1961 b, Some methodological remarks on generative grammar, *Word* 17 : 219–39.

____________, 1964 a, Current Issues in Linguistic Theory, The Hague : Mouton.

____________, 1964 b, The logical basis of linguistic theory. In Horace G. Lunt, ed., *Proceedings of the Ninth International Congress of Linguists*. The Hague : Mouton.

____________, 1965 a, Aspects of the Theory of Syntax. Cambridge : MIT Press.

____________, and Morris Halle, 1965 b, Some controvertial questions in phonological theory. Journal of Linguistics 1 : 97–138.

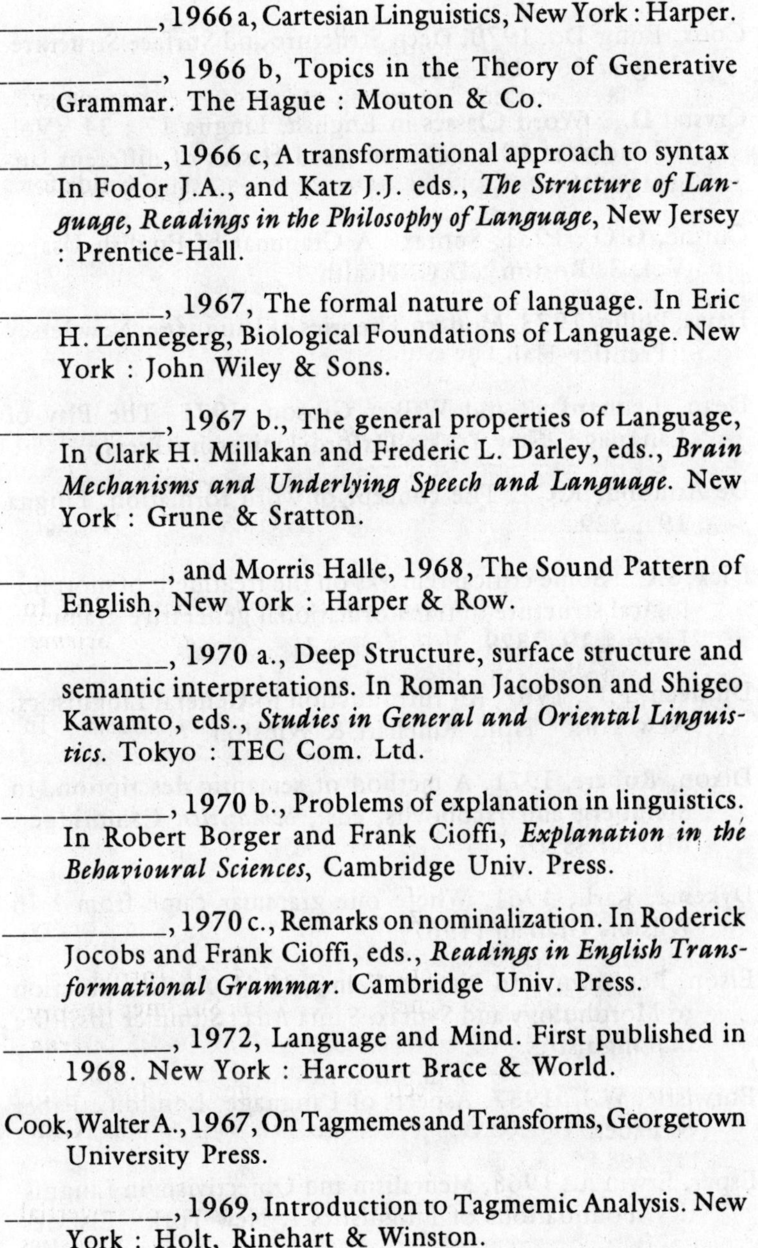

____________, 1966 a, Cartesian Linguistics, New York : Harper.

____________, 1966 b, Topics in the Theory of Generative Grammar. The Hague : Mouton & Co.

____________, 1966 c, A transformational approach to syntax In Fodor J.A., and Katz J.J. eds., *The Structure of Language, Readings in the Philosophy of Language*, New Jersey : Prentice-Hall.

____________, 1967, The formal nature of language. In Eric H. Lennegerg, Biological Foundations of Language. New York : John Wiley & Sons.

____________, 1967 b., The general properties of Language, In Clark H. Millakan and Frederic L. Darley, eds., *Brain Mechanisms and Underlying Speech and Language*. New York : Grune & Sratton.

____________, and Morris Halle, 1968, The Sound Pattern of English, New York : Harper & Row.

____________, 1970 a., Deep Structure, surface structure and semantic interpretations. In Roman Jacobson and Shigeo Kawamto, eds., *Studies in General and Oriental Linguistics*. Tokyo : TEC Com. Ltd.

____________, 1970 b., Problems of explanation in linguistics. In Robert Borger and Frank Cioffi, *Explanation in the Behavioural Sciences*, Cambridge Univ. Press.

____________, 1970 c., Remarks on nominalization. In Roderick Jocobs and Frank Cioffi, eds., *Readings in English Transformational Grammar*. Cambridge Univ. Press.

____________, 1972, Language and Mind. First published in 1968. New York : Harcourt Brace & World.

Cook, Walter A., 1967, On Tagmemes and Transforms, Georgetown University Press.

____________, 1969, Introduction to Tagmemic Analysis. New York : Holt, Rinehart & Winston.

Cook, Eung-Do, 1970, Deep Structure and Surface Structure. *Lingua* 25 : 101–14.

Crystal D., : Word Classes in English. Lingua 17 : 24. (Vol. 17 includes 10 articles on word classes of different languages).

Curme, G.O., 1931, Suntax : A Grammar of English Usage. Vol. 3. Boston : D.C. Health.

Davis, Philip, 1973, Modern Theories of Language. New Jersey : Prentice-Hall.

Dean, Leonard F. and Walker Gibson, 1971, The Play of Language, New York : Oxford University Press.

De Armond, R.C. : The concept of word formation, Lingua 19 : 329.

Dick, S.C. : Some critical remarks on the treatment of morphological structure in transformational generative grammar. Lingua 19 : 329.

Dinneen, F.P., 1967, An Introduction to General Linguistics. New York : Holt, Rinehart & Winston.

Dixon, Robert, 1971, A method of semantic description. In Steinberg and Jacobovits, eds., *Semantics*. Cambridge : MIT Press.

Dykema, Karl., 1961, Where our grammar came from ? In Wilson, Graham (1967).

Elson, Benjamin, and Pickett, Velma, 1964, An Introduction to Morphology and Syntax. Santa Ana : Summer Institute of Linguistics.

Entwistle, W.J., 1957, Aspects of Language. London : Faber & Faber.

Esper, Erwin A., 1968, Mentalism and Objectivism in Linguistics. Foundations of Linguistics I. New York : Elsevier.

Faust, George P., 1964, Something of morphemics. In Harold B. Allen (1964).

Fillmore, Charles, 1971, Types of lexical information. In Steinberg and Jacobvits, eds., Semantics. Cambridge : MIT Press.

Firth, J.R., 1951, Papers in Linguistics. Oxford Univeristy Press.

Fodor, J., and Jerrold Catz, eds., 1964, The Structure of Language. New Jersey : Prentice-Hall.

___________ and M. Garret, 1966, Some reflections on competence and performance. In Lyons J., and R.J. Wales, eds., Psycholinguistic Papers.

__________, 1975, The Language of Thought. New York : Harper & Row.

__________, 1977, Theories of Meaning in Generative Grammar, New York : Harper & Row.

Foster, B., 1968, The Changing English Language. London : Macmillan.

Fowler, Roger : Meaning and theory of the morpheme. Lingua 12 : 165.

Francis, Nelson W., 1931, The Structure of American English New York : Ronald Press.

__________, 1958, Revolution in Grammar. *Quarterly Journal of Speech* 40 : 299. Also in Harold B. Allen (1958).

Fries, Charles C., 1961, The Structure of English. London.

___________, 1954, Meaning and linguistic analysis. Language 30 : 57.

Gaeng, 1971, Introduction to the Principles of Language. New York : Harper & Row.

Gardiner, Alan, 1951, The Theory of Speech and Language, Oxford : Clarendon Press.

Garvin, P., 1964, On Linguistic Method. Selected Papers. The Hague : Mouton.

Gleason, H.A. Jr., 1955, An Introduction to Descriptive Linguistics. New York : Holt, Rinehart & Winston.

Godwin, W.W., 1894, A Greek Grammar. London : Macmillan.

Goodenough, Ward, 1956, Componental Analysis and the Study of meaning. *Language* 32.

Gross, Maurice, 1973, Mathematical Models in Linguistics. New Jersey : Prentice-Hall.

Guralnik, D.B., 1953, The Making of a New Dictionary. Cleveland : World Publishing Co.

Green R. : Linguistic Theory and Language Description. Lingua 15 : 386.

Greenberg, Joseph. ed., 1966, Language Universals. The Hague : Mouton.

Hall, Robert A., 1964, Introductory Linguistics. Philadelphia : Chilton.

Hall, Robert J., 1950, 'Analogy' from 'Leave your language alone'. Also In Dean, Leonard F. (1971).

____________, 1960, Linguistics and Your Language. New York : Double-day & Company.

Halle & Rayser, 1971, English Stress : Its Form, Its Growth and Its Role in Verse. New York : Harper & Row.

Halliday, M.A.K., 1968, Language and Experience. Educational Review (Birmingham) 20. 2 : 95.

____________, 1961, Categories of the theory of grammar. Word 17.

____________, 1969, Relevant models of language. Educational Review (Birmingham) 22.

____________, 1972, Explorations in the Functions of Language. London : Edward Arnold.

Harris, Zellig, S., 1942, Morpheme alternants in linguistic analysis. *Language* 18 : 169. In Martin Joos (1958).

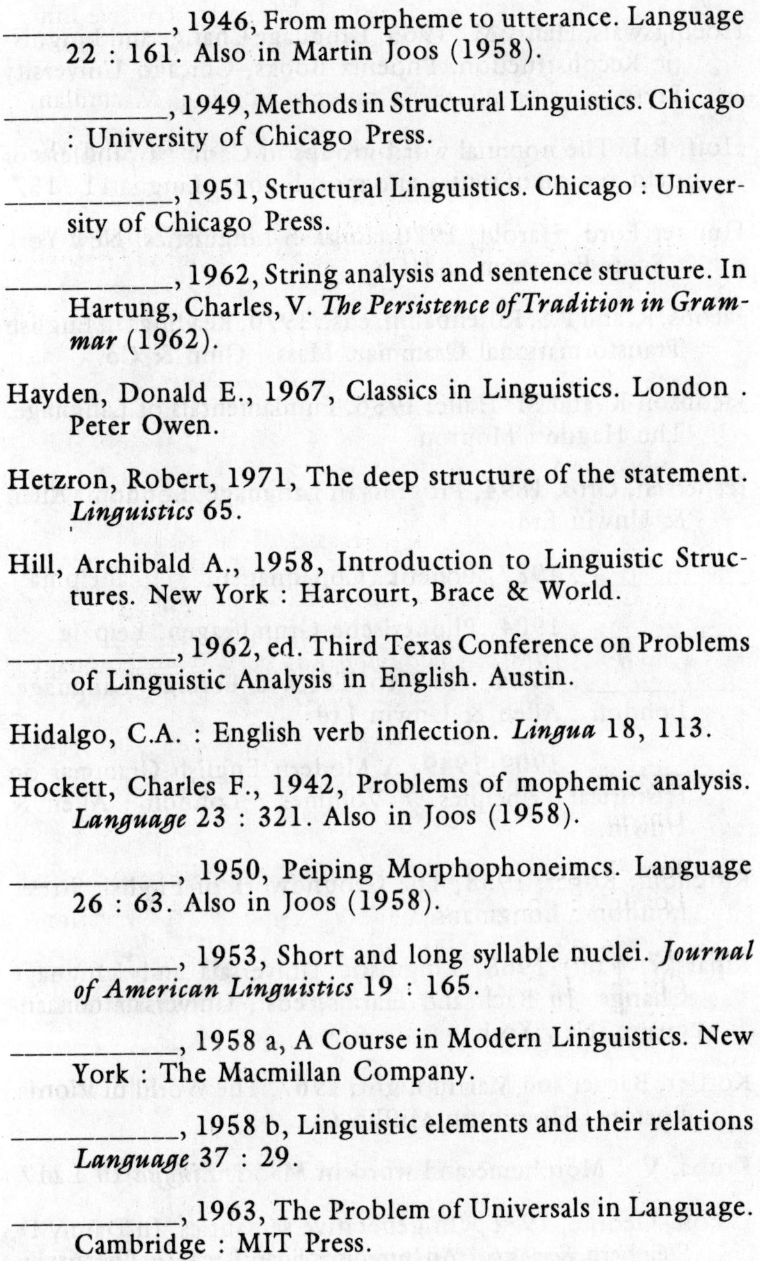

___________, 1946, From morpheme to utterance. Language 22 : 161. Also in Martin Joos (1958).

___________, 1949, Methods in Structural Linguistics. Chicago : University of Chicago Press.

___________, 1951, Structural Linguistics. Chicago : University of Chicago Press.

___________, 1962, String analysis and sentence structure. In Hartung, Charles, V. *The Persistence of Tradition in Grammar* (1962).

Hayden, Donald E., 1967, Classics in Linguistics. London . Peter Owen.

Hetzron, Robert, 1971, The deep structure of the statement. *Linguistics* 65.

Hill, Archibald A., 1958, Introduction to Linguistic Structures. New York : Harcourt, Brace & World.

___________, 1962, ed. Third Texas Conference on Problems of Linguistic Analysis in English. Austin.

Hidalgo, C.A. : English verb inflection. *Lingua* 18, 113.

Hockett, Charles F., 1942, Problems of mophemic analysis. *Language* 23 : 321. Also in Joos (1958).

___________, 1950, Peiping Morphophoneimcs. Language 26 : 63. Also in Joos (1958).

___________, 1953, Short and long syllable nuclei. *Journal of American Linguistics* 19 : 165.

___________, 1958 a, A Course in Modern Linguistics. New York : The Macmillan Company.

___________, 1958 b, Linguistic elements and their relations *Language* 37 : 29.

___________, 1963, The Problem of Universals in Language. Cambridge : MIT Press.

Hoenigswals, Henry M., 1965, Language Change and Linguistic Reconstruction. Phoenix Books, Chicago University Press.

Hoff, B.J. The nominal word-groups in Carib : a problem of delimitation of syntax and morphology. Lingua 11 : 157.

Hunger Ford, Harold, 1970, English Linguistics. New York : Scot, Foresman and Co.

Jacobs, R. and P.S. Rosenbaum. eds., 1970, Readings in English Transformational Grammar. Mass : Ginn & Co.

Jacobson R. and M. Halle, 1956, Fundamentals of Language. The Hague : Mouton.

Jespersen, Otto, 1894, Progress in Language. London : Allen & Unwin Ltd.

____________, 1987, Fonetik. Copehnagen.

____________, 1904, Phonetische Grundfragen. Leipzig.

____________, 1904, How to Teach a Foreign Language. London : Allen & Unwin Ltd.

____________, 1909–1949, A Modern English Grammar on Historical Principles. 7 Volumes : London : Allen & Unwin.

Kingdom, Roger, 1958, The Groundwork of English Stress. London : Longmans.

Kiparsky, Paul, 1968, Linguistic Universals and Language Change. In Bach and Harms, eds., Universals of Language, New York.

Kottler, Barnet and Martin Light, 1967, The World of Words. Boston : Houghton Mifflin Co.

Krupa, V. : Morpheme and word in Maori. *Lingua* 19 : 217.

Lakoff, George, 1971, On generative semantics. In Danny D. Steinberg, *Semantics*: An Interdisciplinary Reader in Philosophy, Linguistics and Psychology.

___________, 1970, Irregularity in Syntax. New York : Holt, Rinehart & Winston.

Lamberts, J.J., 1972, A Short Introduction to English Usage. New York : McGraw-Hill Publishing Co.

Lamb, Sydney, 1966, Outline of Stratificational Grammar. New York.

Langacker, Ronald W., 1972, Fundamentals of Linguistic Analysis. New York : Harcourt, Brace, Jovanovisch.

___________, 1967, The notion of a sentence. In E.L. Blansit. ed., *Monograph Series on Language and Linguistics*, 20.

Langendon, Terence, 1969, The Study of Syntax. Holt, Rinehart and Winston, New York.

Sebeck, Thomas A., 1966, Current Trends in Linguistics. Vol. III. Theoretical Foundations. The Hague : Mouton.

Lehrer, Adrienne, 1974, Semantics Fields and Lexical Structure. Amsterdam : North-Holland Pub. Co.

Lenneberg, E.H., 1967, Biological Foundations of Language. New York : Wiley.

Lepschy, Giulio C., 1970, A Survey of Structural Linguistics. New York : McGraw-Hill.

Leroy, Maurice, 1967, Ma in Trends in Modern Linguistics. Translated by Glanville Price. California : Univ. of California Press.

Lett, W. R., 1978, The Creative Artist at Work. Australia : McGraw-Hill.

Lewis, M.M., 1963, Language, Thought and Personality. New York : Basic Books.

Lyons, John, 1963, Structural Semantics, Oxford : Blackwells.

___________, 1968, Introduction to Theoretical Linguistics. Cambridge : Cambridge University Press.

____________, 1970, The meaning of meaning. Times Literary Supplement (London) July, 1970.

MaCawley, James, 1968, The role of semantics in a grammar. In Bach and Harms (1969).

Mahulkar, D.D., 1963, Literary criticism and linguistics. *Indian Linguistics* 24 (1963).

____________, 1979, Pathways in Linguistics. Baroda : M.S. University of Baroda Press.

Malkeil, Y. : Genetic Analysis of word formation. Lingua 24 : 398.

Malone, Joseph L. : Old Irish morphophonemics and ordered process rules. Lingua 16 : 238.

Markwardt, Albert H., 1964, The New Webster dictionary : a critical appraisal. (In Harold Allen. 1964).

Martinet, A., 1968, Elements in General Linguistics. London : Faber & Faber.

Mathews, P., 1966, The concept of rank in Neo-Firthian grammar. Journal of Linguistics 2, 101.

Mathews, P.H., 1972, Inflectional Morphology. London : Cambridge University Press.

____________, 1974, Morphology. London : Cambridge University Press.

Mathews, M.M. : A Survey of English Dictionaries. Oxford : Clarendon Press.

Miller, G.A., 1951, Language and Communication. New York : McGraw-Hill.

Morris, C.W., 1955, Signs, Language and Behaviour. New York : Prentice-Hall.

Negel, Ernest, 1961, The Structure of Science, New York : Harcourt, Brace & World. pp. 1–152.

Nelson, Francis, 1954, Revolution in grammar. Quarterly Journal of Speech, 40 : 299. Also in Allen (1958).

Nida, Eugene A., 1948, The identification of morphemes. Language 24 : 414. Also in Joos (1958).

__________, ·1949, Morphology : the Descriptive Analysis of Words. Ann Arbor : University of Michigan Press.

Norm, Abrams. : Word-base classes in Bilaan. Lingua 10 : 391.

Odenda 1, F.F. : Limitations of morphological processes. Lingua 12 : 220.

Ogden and Richards, I.A., 1946, The Meaning of Meaning. London : Routledge, Kegan Paul (8th ed.).

Palmer, F.R., 1965, A Linguistic Survey of English Verb. London : Longmans.

Palmer, Harold E. and V. Redman., 1968, This Language Learning Business. London : Oxford Univ. Press.

Palmer, L.R., 1972, Descriptive and Comparative Linguistics. London : Faber & Faber.

Pedersen, Holger, 1931, Linguistics Science in the Ninetheenth Century. Trans. by J.W. Spargo. Cambridge.

Pei, Mario., 1965, Invitation to Linguistics. London : Allen & Unwin Ltd.

__________, 1976, The Story of Latin and Romance Languages. New York : Harper & Row.

Pike, Kenneth, 1943, : Taxemes and Immediate constituents. Language 19 : 65.

__________, 1953, A note on allomorph classes and tonal technique. International Journal of American Linguists, 19 : 101.

__________, 149, A Problem of morphology—syntax division. Acta Linguistica 5 : 125–38.

____________, 158, Interpretation of Phonology, morphology, and syntax. ed., Proceedings of the 8th Int. Congress of Linguists, by Eva Sivertsen. Oslo University Press.

____________, 1964, Name fusions as high-level particles in matrix theory. Linguistics 6 : 83.

____________,Posner, R., 1970, An Introduction to Romance Linguistics. Original by Lordan-Orr Basil. Oxford : Blackwells.

Pyles, Thomas and John Algeo., 1970, English : An Introduction to Language. New York : Harcourt, Brace & World.

Quirk, Randolph, Sidney Greenbaum, Geoffrey Leech and Jan Svartvik, 1973, A Grammar of Contemporary English. London : Longman.

Roberts, Paul, 1967, Something about English. In Kottler, Barnet (1967).

Robins, R.H., 1967, A History of Linguistics. London : Longman.

____________, 1964, General Linguistics : An Introductory Survey. London : Longman.

Rosenbaum, Peter S., 1967, The Grammar of English Predicate Complement–Constructions. Cambridge : MIT Press.

Rosenfield, L.C., 1941, From Beast Machine to Man Machine. New York : Oxford University Press.

Sapir, Edward, 1970, Language. London : Rupert Hart–Davis.

Saporta, Sol., 1961, Psycholinguistics : A Book of Readings. New York : Holt, Rinehart and Winston.

Saumjan, S.K., 1971, Principles of Structural Linguistics. Translated by James Miller. The Hague.

Saussure, Ferdinand De., 1974, Course in General Linguistics. London : Peter Owen.

Sebeck, Thomas A., 1966, Current Trends in Linguistics. Vol. III. Theoretical Foundations. The Hague.

___________, 1967, Portraits of Linguistics (A Biographical Source Book). Indiana University Press.

Siro, P. : On the fundamentals of semantics structure. Lunt Proceedings. New York.

Spence, R.N. : Some notes on morpheme. Lingua 26 : 113.

Spitzbardt, Harry, 1977, The problem of universals in natural languages. CIEFL. Bulletin (Hyderabad) 13, 1.

Stall, J.F. : Word order in Sanskrit and universal grammar. Lingua 26 : 113.

Stam., 1976, Inquiries into the Origin of Language : The Fate of a question. New York : Harper & Row.

Strang, Barbera, 1970, A History of English. London : Mathuen & Co. Ltd.

Swadesh, Morris, 1972, The origin and diversification of language. ed., by Joel Sherzer. London : Routledge & Kegan Paul.

Sweet, Henry, 1860, New English Grammar. Originally published in 1891. Oxford : Clarendon Press.

Traugott, Elizabeth Closs, 1972, A History of English Syntax. New York : Holt, Rinehart, and Winston.

Trnka, B., 1964, Some thoughts on structrual morphology. In Josef Vachek, *A Prague School Reader in Linguistics. Bloomington* : Indiana Univ. Press.

___________, On the morphological classification of words. Lingua 11 : 422.

Uhlenbeck, E.M. : Limitations of morphological process. Lingua 11 : 422.

Vygotsky, L.S., 1962, Thought and Language. Cambridge : MIT.

Wardhaugh, Ronald, 1972, Introduction to Linguistics. New York : McGraw-Hill.

Waterman, J.T., 1963, Perspectives in Linguistics. Chicago.

Weinreich, Uriel, 1966, Explorations of a Semantic Theory. In Sebeck T.A., ed., (1966).

Wells, Rulon S., 1945, Immediate Constituents. Language 23 : 81.

Wilson, Graham, ed., 1967, A Linguistics Reader. New York : Harper & Row.

Wilson, Kenneth G., 1971, A History of English Language. In Leonard F., Dean (1971).

Whitehall, Harold, 1971, The development of English Dictionary. In Leonard F. Dean (1971).

Whorf, B.L., 1956, Language, Thought and Reality. J.B. Carrol, ed., Cambridge.

Wonder, J.P. : Ambiguity and the English Gerund. Lingua 25 : 254.

Zandvoort, R.W., 1957, A Handbook of English Grammar. London : Longmans.

Index